Toddlers: the Mumsnet Guide

mumsnet.com

Toddlers: the Mumsnet Guide

by Lucy Nicholls and the Mumsnet Mums

BLOOMSBURY

LONDON · BERLIN · NEW YORK

First published in Great Britain 2009

Copyright © 2009 by Mumsnet Limited

Illustrations © 2009 by Andy Ward

Edited by Carrie Longton and Justine Roberts

The moral right of the authors has been asserted

Bloomsbury Publishing, London, Berlin and New York

36 Soho Square, London W1D 3QY

A CIP catalogue record for this book is available
from the British Library

ISBN 978 0 7475 9588 5
10 9 8 7 6 5 4 3 2 1

Text design by Smith & Gilmour, London
Typeset by RefineCatch Ltd, Bungay, Suffolk
Printed in Great Britain by Clays Ltd, St Ives plc

The paper this book is printed on is certified by the
© 1996 Forest Stewardship Council A.C. (FSC). It is
ancient-forest friendly. The printer holds FSC chain of
custody SGS-COC-2061

FSC
Mixed Sources
Product group from well-managed
forests and other controlled sources
Cert no. SGS-COC-2061
www.fsc.org
© 1996 Forest Stewardship Council

www.bloomsbury.com/mumsnet

www.mumsnet.com

Thank you to the many, many Mumsnetters whose experience, wit and wisdom make Mumsnet what it is. This book relies upon the principle of the wisdom of crowds but, of course, the more intelligent the crowd, the better the wisdom.

Foreword

One afternoon back in 2000, a friend called me for some advice. She was six months pregnant and had been suffering from palpitations. Had I experienced them too? She asked anxiously. It shames me now to admit it, but I ruthlessly told her that I would only answer her question if she posted it on the bulletin board of the website I had started a few months earlier.

After all, we needed all the users we could get: until that point, the bulletin board had been populated almost exclusively by me and by Carrie – a friend from ante-natal class and co-founder of Mumsnet – and often by just one of us, switching between nicknames to maintain the appearance of a conversation. Me: 'What do you do if your child will only eat jelly?' Me Too: 'Have you tried carrot jelly?'

On this occasion, however, something different happened. By the time I had hurriedly logged on to reply to my friend's query, someone else – a real, actual person! – had beaten me to it. And in that instant I knew that Mumsnet was coming to life.

Since then it has blossomed into one of Britain's – perhaps the world's – most extraordinary online communities. A tad hyperbolic maybe but the *Sunday Telegraph* called Mumsnet 'an internet phenomenon', and *The Times* describes it as 'the country's most popular meeting point for parents'.

It's true that the sheer scale and energy of Mumsnet still strikes me almost every time I log on: the site now notches up a million visits a month and more than 20,000 postings every day on anything and everything from the advisability of using pull-up nappies to the acceptability of wearing socks with Crocs. As I write, Mumsnetters are discussing amongst many other things: the purpose of school; cantaloupe melons; how to remove mould from a wall; Jonathan Coe; petrol prices; hen party ideas that aren't rude; Gordon Brown's latest speech on social mobility; how to stop chickens coming through the cat flap; home births; Mooncups; ugly blokes who are strangely attractive; ugly women who are strangely beautiful; vasectomy reversals; fake tans; Citroen Xsara Picassos; boys' names to go with Jasper and things to do in Dorking.

But Mumsnet is about much more than sheer numbers. What makes it special is the intelligence, compassion and, perhaps most important, wit of its users. There was the time, for example, when we were facing legal action from a certain rather doctrinaire parenting guru and were forced to take the drastic step of banning all mention of her on our discussion boards. Within minutes of our announcement Mumsnetters had conceived a new Potter-inspired acronym – SWMNBN (She Who Must Not Be Named) – and that is how Gina Ford has been referred to ever since.

And this army of bolshy, brilliant parents (yes, there are quite a few dads, despite the name) can be powerful too. Just look at what happened to Waitrose Baby Bottom Butter once Mumsnetters discovered it worked wonders on their wrinkles (don't ask me how). Shortages were reported up and down the country and jars of the £2.49 cream were going on Ebay for £15 and more.

All of which may leave you wondering why you are reading this book, and are not sitting in front of a screen chewing the fat. And it's true that to feel the full Mumsnet experience you need to log on and plunge in. But a while ago it occurred to us that, without us ever planning it that way, Mumsnet Talk had turned into the most amazing archive of parenting wisdom. Whereas the child-rearing manuals offered you the wisdom of a single Leach or Stoppard, Mumsnet could bring you the collected wisdom of hundreds of thousands of parents. Just as Wikipedia has rendered almost obsolete the *Encyclopaedia Britannica*, so we wondered if there was a way to capture the wisdom of this remarkable crowd.

We thought a Mumsnet parenting manual might be different from its competition in another way too. Whisper it quietly, but if Mumsnet is such fun to read that some of its members begged us to ban them from it because they were spending too much of their lives on the boards, might it not be possible for a parenting book to be a good read too? Even with a thread on the grisliest of subjects, it is not unusual to find yourself chuckling over the keyboard. One member captured the wonderfully batty serendipity of the site recently: 'You know, you start a thread about vaginal discharge and within a few posts you find yourself recommending a reasonably priced shed or telling all about the little hotel you stayed at in the Cotswolds.'

At the same time we realised that long sequences of internet posts, however brilliant, can die when sandwiched between hard covers. So these books are not simply edited extracts from the Mumsnet's boards but instead they are lovingly crafted guides, distilled from the collected wisdom of our members.

And if traditional parenting manuals purport to reveal 'the right way' to bring up a child, our firm starting point is that there isn't one right way – most of the time – to do the parenting thing. If there were a Mumsnet philosophy it would be something along the lines of 'There's more than one way to skin a cat', so read this as a book of optimistic suggestions, rather than as a user's manual. What we provide is a range of options compiled from the hard-won know-how of what has worked for thousands of others: somewhere in here will be answers that work for you.

Fittingly, this first of our guides is written by a brilliant Mumsnetter best known for her dramatic cameo in a previous challenge to the unquestioned authority of the parenting gurus. She it was who, with tongue firmly in cheek, mischievously described a certain childcare expert as someone who 'straps babies to rockets and fires them into southern Lebanon'. The gag sparked a rather unseemly legal battle, but to SWMNBN we should offer fulsome thanks for bringing Lucy Nicholls to our attention, and, ultimately, for bringing you this book. A book, it has to be said, a few thought unlikely to materialise. As one Mumsnetter scoffed when we floated the idea of the guides, 'We could never write a book. We never agree on anything!'

Justine Roberts (Co-Founder, Mumsnet.com)

P.S. Mumsnetters, as you'll see, write under an array of weird and wonderful nicknames – VoluptuaGoodshag isn't really called VoluptuaGoodshag in real life. At least as far as we know he/she isn't.

Contents

Introduction

The talkboards on Mumsnet are full of posts from the parents of toddlers and they often contain the words 'wits' end'. Toddlers are both perfectly wonderful and incredibly infuriating, and it can be an exhausting experience looking after a little person who takes your emotions from adoration to abhorrence in a matter of minutes. 'Sometimes I want to run up a hill screaming "Get me out of here!" or lock myself in the shed where the children can't find me,' admits one mum. 'Other times, I just want to hold them and snuggle up to their warm little bodies while they sleep in our great big bed.'

For toddlers, discovering the world is a new and exciting adventure, but it can also be confusing and scary at times. For parents, whether you are tackling under-bed monsters or toilet terror, knowing that you are not alone can often help as you and your intrepid toddler progress in your journey of discovery. And it is good to be reminded that toddler terrors can sometimes be quashed with dialogue and understanding, as one Mumsnetter discovered when her two-year-old developed an aversion to the under-stairs cupboard, 'we finally realised why one day when I was doing some laundry, and he begged, "Mummy please don't get the lion out!" ... we keep the iron in there.'

On Mumsnet there are thousands of mums who can offer a sympathetic ear and sage advice when it comes to dealing with the tantrums and traumas of the toddler years, even if it is just the reassurance that 'this too shall pass.' And, as many can testify, although this might be one of the most exasperating times of your life, it will also give rise to many memorable and enjoyable moments: like the first time you find your bottom wedged halfway down a slide as you are scrutinised by a dozen more sensible parents; the morning you have to call a plumber to extract a plastic boat from the toilet u-bend and the occasion when you walk into your bedroom to find your guilty-looking three year old 'just trying on your boobies, mummy!'

'We all have times when we feel useless at parenting,' writes one mum, 'but you're not alone in how you feel, and you are certainly not a bad mother for feeling this way. If you were a bad mother, you wouldn't be seeking advice!'

Lucy Nicholls *aka* MORNINGPAPER

Behaviour

And When She Was Bad She Was Horrid (So We Put Her on the Naughty Step)

In this chapter ...

Introduction: Toddlers: What Are They Like?

When washed, brushed and freshly dressed, there is nothing more delicious than a toddler. In place of cradle cap and baldness there is soft, unruly hair; and where there used to be tiny feet and floppy legs there are now round toes, chubby calf-muscles and peachy bottoms, all ripe for kissing.

There are also times, of course, when there is nothing more disagreeable than a toddler. From food fights in the local café to screaming sit-ins on the supermarket floor, hardly a day passes without the suspicion that innocent passers-by are nervously racing for the condom aisle.

The Terrible Twos seem to strike many toddlers at around 18 months, and to last for about three years, so I'm afraid we are really talking about Terrible Toddlers. But there is plenty of good advice from the Mumsnet mums to help you when you are contemplating the whipping-and-starving parenting techniques of the Old Woman Who Lived in a Shoe. And in a couple of years you will be able to stuff this grim experience into a box in the back of your head marked 'fond memories' and raise a rueful eye at mothers of tantrumming toddlers while you tell them to enjoy it because it all passes in a flash.

Mumsnetiquette: Don't tell a toddler's parent that these are the best days of her life

If you are the parent of teenagers, do not smile wistfully at the mother of an out-of-control toddler and inform her that if she thinks it's bad now, just wait until he hits his teens. She will possibly explode with her need to inform you of your incredible good luck in being able to sleep for more than two hours at a time and to have a poo unaccompanied. You may only communicate with your teenager once a week, and that may be via text, but you have clearly forgotten that when your children are two this would seem to be the ideal parenting scenario.

Methods of Discipline:
One, Two, Three ...

Before you have children you have no doubt that the fruit of
your loins will be a well-behaved and attractive child who enjoys
playing quietly on a rug while you work on your PhD. The unruly
beasts that require the strong-arm tactics of Supernanny are
nothing like the charming creatures you will produce.

It comes as a bit of a surprise, then, when your own 12-month-
old suddenly discovers the joy of feeding biscuits into the DVD
player, scribbling on the cream wallpaper, whacking visitors
over the head with her train track and periodically screaming
hysterically from dawn till dusk.

You won't be long into the parenting lark before you realise
that everybody has boundaries they don't want their children to
cross, and children who want to cross boundaries before they have
even had a chance to wake up at 5 a.m. and smear the contents of
their nappy on their favourite toys. So what next?

'Pick your battles' is a mantra that is oft repeated on
Mumsnet. There is no point getting mad over every minor
indiscretion – if you are constantly reprimanding your children,
then your punishments will swiftly lose their impact. Make telling
off an unusual and rare (if possible!) response. Don't spend all day
battling with your child. Some things you just have to ignore. You
are managing a two-year-old, not a 20-year-old, and posting coins
into the CD player and emptying the contents of your handbag on
the front doorstep are part of what they do. Concentrate on the big
misdemeanours, the non-negotiable rights and wrongs.

Of course, what constitutes 'non-negotiable' behaviour varies
from parent to parent, and depends upon what is important to
you. For most parents, certain behaviour, such as hitting, is always
wrong. Likewise, pouring Ribena into sockets, charging into the
road and similar life-threatening actions require strict non-
negotiable boundaries. Other more minor discrepancies, such as
depositing milk over the cat, may or may not need the same level
of chastisement, depending on your disposition (and your cat's).

Once you have selected your battles, you need to decide on a
strategy to follow when your wayward toddler comes charging
over the top.

Outdated methods of disciplining children largely centred around pain and fear; smacking being a favourite. These days any response involving violence against children is considered extremely inappropriate. Smacking is generally a sign that the parent has lost control of the situation and is hitting out as a last resort. As one mum confesses, 'I have smacked before, but it has always been when I have lost my temper rather than because I thought that it was the right way to deal with a situation.'

There are times when all of us are pushed to our limits, when the noise and mess and frustration become too much. If you know you are at the end of your tether, it is often better just to step out of the room and return when you are calmer (after a minute or two composing yourself, as opposed to a couple of hours lying on your bed with a novel).

If you do lose the plot for whatever reason, most mums agree that it's best to apologise and admit that you were in the wrong.

'I haven't mastered the "never losing my temper" bit. And whilst it never justifies it, I do make a point of apologising to the children as soon as possible, so they understand that adults sometimes step over the line, too, and in the same way that they as children need to apologise, there are times when I do, too.' Ladymuck

Children can be remarkably understanding. As one mother admits, 'I shouted at my children today, horridly. I did apologise afterwards and my daughter said it was OK, that she understood I was crabby because I hadn't had my breakfast yet.'

Over the years you will probably employ a variety of the following methods. And of course, the method that works for one child might not work for another. Whichever method of discipline you choose, it is crucial to be consistent. You cannot allow certain behaviour on one day and forbid it the next. Your response needs to be the same each time. 'Be really, absolutely consistent and you will see results,' promises one old hand. 'If all else fails, you can always call Supernanny. Or send them to Grandma's.'

Ignoring

For young toddlers, particularly those prone to lashing out, putting them down and ignoring them can be an effective method of discipline. There is no fun in not being the centre of attention. Quite often, young toddlers learn that if they hit Mummy, she will make a fuss and need a cuddle. This can be a jolly good jape to a young toddler, but you need to nip it in the bud pronto.

'When he hits you, say no firmly and put him down for 60 seconds and ignore him. Do it consistently. It's a game to him. It's not violence, it's toddlerdom. He is just exploring and expressing his new-found independence.' Twiglett

It is odds on that putting a child down and ignoring him will result in wailing and tears. This is no bad thing, and means that the child does not like the consequences of his behaviour. Leave for a few seconds, then start a new activity: 'Right, do you want to come and help me with the washing now?' Your toddler should soon learn that the hitting game is not so much fun.

Three-strikes-and-you're-out

When bad behaviour occurs, give a simple warning and explanation: 'No, you do not touch the kettle because it might be hot.' If they re-offend, warn again and say that if they repeat the offence, there will be a consequence: 'I said no. If you touch it again you can sit on the floor.' And at the third offence, remove the child by placing them on the floor or out of reach. Ignore any shouting or protesting for a suitable period (not long, maybe half a minute or so, just enough for the results of their behaviour to sink in) and then, as above, resume a different activity: 'I'm going into the lounge now; do you want to come and play?'

Following through

It is crucial when disciplining children that you follow through whatever consequence (or punishment) that you threaten to carry out.

'After several embarrassing "Do that again and we won't go on holiday/have Christmas/ever watch telly again" moments, I try to keep the consequence realistic and logical.' Porpoise

It is also important not to threaten them with the removal of privilege that actually makes your life easier. If they watch television for half an hour before dinner, for instance, so that you can cook in peace and have a gin and tonic (perfectly reasonable, of course), then telling them that they can't watch television is going to be as much a punishment for you as for them. It is also likely that they will drive you to distraction and that you'll relent on the punishment (never good) so that you can sort out the fish fingers.

A suitable consequence might be: 'You can sit in the hall until you have calmed down.' Or if children are arguing over a toy, then confiscate it.

Counting to three

This is still a popular method of discipline for slightly older toddlers. If it is used rarely it can be effective for some children, as one mother remembers: 'My father used to count to three, although I don't know what would have happened at three – the thought of being naughty was so terrible to me that he never needed to get further than two.'

The Mumsnet pasta jar method for achieving toddler compliance (Patent Pending)

For older toddlers, 'the pasta jar' is a tool that a lot of mums use. The idea is that pasta is used as a sort of currency, which is earned for good behaviour and lost for bad behaviour.

'Take a glass jar and put five pieces of pasta in it at the start of the week (or day). When they are naughty, you give them a warning.

(continued)

If they persist then you take a piece of pasta out. For good or compliant behaviour, you put a piece of pasta into the jar. At the end of the week (or day), count up the pieces of pasta and when you have hit the "target" (say ten pieces), you swap the pasta for a small pressie/pocket money/praise. After a while, you will just need to hiss "pasta" and this should be a sufficient threat to ensure good behaviour.' *Twiglett*

The pasta jar works from any age where they understand the exchange for rewards.

A variation on this for younger toddlers can be edible currency.

'Use chocolate buttons instead of pasta, so she can see immediately that she's losing something worthwhile. If you have to take a chocolate button out because of a transgression, you get to eat it. Of course, you'll end up the size of a house but it's a small price to pay.' *SoupDragon*

For some children, the pasta jar method works incredibly well and pasta takes on a mythical value of its own. Collecting pasta can sometimes become enough of an incentive, without exchanging it for anything else. (Not our children, sadly – they always wanted cold hard cash.)

Star charts

A variation on the pasta jar theme, these tend to be useful for concentrating on a particular aspect of behaviour, rather than general naughtiness. The child is given a wall chart which is divided into days of the week. For 'good' days they are awarded a star or a sticker. At the end of the week, if the target is met (whatever you have decided is sufficient), then they are give a pre-agreed reward (perhaps a magazine, or a toy).

Some parents don't like pasta jars and reward systems, because they think it is important that children learn that you have to obey rules for their own sake, rather than to earn rewards, which smacks of bribery. As one mum explains, 'I stopped using reward systems because I felt that my daughter needed to learn there are a number of things you just have to do and rules that must be obeyed because you have to, not because of what you get out of it.'

Time Out

Another popular method of discipline is Time Out (see also page 18). A place is created in the house – a 'naughty step', for example (the bottom stair) – where the child must go (or be taken to) to calm down or contemplate his misdeeds. Generally, Time Out is used for serious misdemeanours where other methods have failed.

'We only use the step when our two-year-old does naughty things on purpose (like hitting or wilfully ignoring instructions). The idea is that it's supposed to teach her what's acceptable and what isn't, and it seems to work. We tend not to use it for the small stuff, only when she can understand that what she has done is really wrong.' Biza

Some children happily trot off to their bedrooms (if that is the designated place) and start playing, which is not the idea, of course. If they are that way inclined then choose a place where they are going to be suitably bored. As one Mumsnetter explains: 'With my sons, I use our entrance as a Time Out zone. It has two doors so they cannot go out, but no toys or anything interesting to do – it's a really boring place. The door is also a glass one so they can actually see what is happening in the living room and what they are missing out on.'

'We have a naughty mat but it's usually just referred to as "the mat": it's the front door mat. My son is three and a half and sits there after a few warnings. I put him there with a brief reason: "I'm putting you on the mat because you squashed your sister. I'll be back in three minutes." He sometimes just sits there, sometimes cries, and sometimes screams and shouts for me to come back. I just ignore everything.' Princessmel

Positive praise

Some children do seem to thrive on negative attention – so misbehaviour to wind up Mummy is rewarding in itself. For these children, you really need to concentrate on giving them your time and attention when they are being good and behaving well, and then ignoring bad behaviour.

'I know it is hard but ignore, ignore, ignore all the annoying things, and then when she is good, say in a bright, enthusiastic voice, "Good girl!" Praise the good and ignore the bad. My daughter is only two and I have found that really giving lots of positive attention is the only thing that works.' Oliveoil

It's important that you find something to be positive about in almost everything they do that's not naughty – wiping their feet, saying please and thank you, or just sitting nicely at the table. In addition, you need to go completely over the top with your effusive praise – 'Gosh, aren't you good at drinking from a cup!' The downside of this method is that you sound like a complete nutter, but reinforcing good behaviour really does work, and making a point of noticing it will remind you that your toddler is not all bad. You also get to go to bed feeling all smug for being a nice, non-shouty mum for once.

Tantrums: AKA Paddies, Wobblies, Hissy Fits, Meltdowns (We Could Go On)

'My son is two-and-a-half and is becoming impossible. I cannot go anywhere without him playing up. I'm so upset. I feel like such a bad mother. I met up with a friend today and he was being such a complete nightmare in front of her. I feel so embarrassed and useless. HELP!' Ameli

Before you have children, tantrums are what happen to rubbish parents. Then one day, out of the blue, you are the one in the middle of Marks & Spencer getting hot and bothered as your child screams for jelly pigs while other shoppers shoot you judgemental glances and shake their heads. Of course, the natural thing to do is to sink to the floor and cry, but don't despair: it is part of life with a toddler and this stage will pass (but probably not before you make it to the check-out).

Sadly, we cannot reassure you that tantrums are caused by one particular thing which we know JUST how to fix, thereby returning your beautiful toddler to his lovable self. But there *are* a few things that can help prevent tantrums from occurring so often.

Sidestepping tantrums

As with most of life's horrible traumas, prevention is better than cure. With small children, keeping them physically comfortable is essential to maintaining their good temper. Physical discomfort can trigger crabby behaviour in the best of us. So try to ensure that you are looking after their basic needs, which they might not realise they are lacking (many small children don't recognise hunger pangs, the need for the loo, or cold, for example). Make sure they eat regular, nutritious meals or snacks, and get plenty of sleep and exercise.

'In my opinion, toddlers are just Labradors with less fur. Both need daily walks. We have a Labrador, too – and some days you'd be hard pressed to tell them apart.' Welliemum

Toddler tantrums are largely about frustration. He is developing a sense of self and has a vague idea that his emotions and experiences are not shared by everybody. He is also unsure about his feelings and often has no way of communicating this to other people. As a result, he can become easily frustrated when he does not get what he wants, and cannot understand, for example, why the whole world is not pulling together to assist him in his quest for more mango juice. This confusion is often too much for a frustrated little ego, and can quickly turn into screaming hysteria.

'Children tend to have tantrums for the same reason grown-ups do – they feel they are not being heard.' Barking

The most important thing to remember is to listen to your child. They may be too young to express their needs coherently, but you might be able to resolve the matter and avert a crisis.

It's also worth keeping your child in the loop, and making sure you explain things in simple terms that they can understand.

'I was once advised that you should treat a toddler like a confused elderly aunt – just keep talking to them kindly, gently but firmly (without any judgement in your voice), explaining everything slowly.' Barking

Children often cope better if they feel they have some control over what is happening during the day, and a rough idea of the timetable of events helps. They don't like surprises because it makes them feel out of control. Some toddlers benefit from having a 'visual timetable' so that they are more mentally prepared. You can use photographs or simple drawings to put together a poster of the day's events, such as waking up, having breakfast, getting dressed, brushing teeth and hair, going to nursery. Equally, as you progress through the day, talk about what you are doing so that they can prepare themselves for what will happen next.

'Count down or give notice of the next event. For example, say, "In five minutes we are going to put on our coats" (ideally point to the picture on your schedule poster). It doesn't matter if he doesn't know how long five minutes is – it's just important that he can anticipate a change is coming.' Raggydoll

Another way of giving some control to your child is to present them with choices, so that they feel they are making the important decisions. You don't really care if she wears the pink top or the yellow top, but if you give her the choice, she is less likely to object and you are less likely to be confronted by: 'I-don't-want-to-get-dreeesssed!'

If you're managing a toddler who's liable to tip over the edge at any minute, you need to slow things down to avoid becoming stressed yourself. Getting out of the house for an urgent appointment is a recipe for tears and frustration all round, so build in as much preparation time as possible. That way you can give them more freedom to do things for themselves.

If you are going out, make sure he knows what is happening and what behaviour is expected of him. For example: 'We are going to the supermarket to buy some groceries this morning. We are going to go there in the car and you can listen to some music on the way if you like. When we get there you can sit in the trolley and help me by holding my shopping list, and when we get home you can help by unpacking all your yoghurts into the fridge.'

You might sound like a complete idiot but on balance that's preferable to public humiliation in Tesco.

Dealing with tantrums

Of course, there will be times (probably a good deal of them) when, despite your best attempts at avoiding tantrums, your child quite simply goes off on one. What should you do? Well if there's one thing any veteran toddler-handler will tell you it's this: YOU MUST NOT GIVE IN!

If a child gets their own way by having a tantrum, then as sure as eggs is eggs you will end up with a child who throws a wobbly every time he passes the shelf with the Noddy magazines. Although your little darling may not yet be familiar with the works of the philosopher David Hume, he will nevertheless have a sufficient understanding of cause and effect to know that if a no becomes a yes after a bit of screaming and wailing, then screaming and wailing is the way to go.

So if you're resolved not to give in, what should you do?

Children crave our attention. Even if that attention is negative (i.e. a red-faced and angry parent), the child's desire for it is so great that a tantrum can be a fast route to meeting this need.

One common approach to a child in the heat of a tantrum, therefore, is to ignore, ignore, ignore. The last thing you want to do is encourage a child to have regular tantrums. Let them know that they will have your attention only when they have calmed down again and stopped flapping.

'My husband's technique, which I never manage to perform as well as him, is to say, "Ooh – you're having a tantrum? Wait a minute: let's find a nice soft bit of floor for you so you're comfortable. And I'll just go and get your blankie so you have something with which to flail. Let me know when you've finished your tantrum and we can do a bit more playing."' Wulfricsmummy

Of course, it's not always easy to ignore a tantrum 'especially if they are hanging on to you, or if you are on the phone', as one Mumsnetter points out. But if you can, many parents have found that it is the fastest route to resolving the situation, even in public, which can be more of a challenge.

'I find that any interaction just prolongs the paddy. When she's calmed down I then start playing with her toys and invite her to join in and carry on as normal.' Cktwo

Another weapon in your anti-tantrum armoury is distraction. Stick on a favourite video, rattle the biscuit tin, or suggest a walk to the park. If this is going to work, it will do so pretty quickly. Distraction works best in the early stages of a tantrum before the heaving sobs set in.

'My daughter came to the supermarket with me and I wouldn't let her go into the café so she moaned a bit then lay face down on the floor. Then I asked her if she wanted to smell the flowers. She came over and all was forgiven.' Hayls

Distraction is really about changing the subject, and toddlers are generally quite open to this approach. It's worth, as one mum advises, having 'a supply of placatory snacks/drinks/toys/books/other-tricks-up-your-sleeve to distract from imminent tantrums when out and about.'

Even when a child is in the throes of an emotional meltdown, the sight of a bus outside or the flash of a crisp packet can be enough for him to forget the hysteria-inducing crisis.

Although it's difficult, try to focus on your child, rather than worrying about your neighbours' twitching curtains. If you give your child your full attention you are more likely to get an idea of exactly what is upsetting him, and hopefully be more likely to respond in a way that calms him down.

'The last thing you should worry about is the tutting and glaring of onlookers. Anyone with children or who has had children just feels immense sympathy for you and is probably bloody grateful that it's not their child screaming his or her head off! We've all been there, and if you can avoid losing your temper then you deserve a big pat on the back.' Satine

Tantrums in shops

'I scoop him up under my arm and hold him so I cannot see his face and carry on with what I am doing. People just have to get out of the way of the kicking legs.' *Mung*

'I just put him in the trolley and continue with the shopping.' *Moosh*

'I abandon the trolley and take the toddler home.' *Doormat*

'I say, "OK, you stay there, see you later!" and then disappear round the corner (always keeping an eye on them). They always come running. Well, almost always.' *Misdee*

'I let her sit in the trolley and feed her chocolate buttons.' *Knat*

'I shop online.' *Handlemecarefully*

Time Out for tantrums

As toddlers get older, tantrums may need to be tackled with discipline. Although confusion and frustration still play a part in tantrums, there comes a point when the child needs to learn that her behaviour is not acceptable. At this point, Time Out is often a preferred response.

'Basically, I remove her from the room so she is on her own with no stimulation from others until the tantrum has subsided. I then ask her if she is going to play nicely. If she answers yes she comes in; if she answers no she stays in the hallway longer, until eventually the answer is yes. The tantrums are abating!' Tori32

If all else fails, you can take one mum-of-three's novel approach: 'I put myself in Time Out if I get too worked up. I lock myself in the bathroom to calm down.'

Tackling tantrums

What doesn't work

- Smacking. Hitting children is always a bad response and will only add to your child's fear and confusion.
- Rushing. Life is bewildering for young children. Don't give them 10 seconds to get dressed and out of the door. Take it easy.
- Don't give in. If you give in when they are two, they will still behave this way when they are 14.

What does work

- Keep your toddler in tip-top condition with regular, healthy snacks and meals, and lots of exercise and fresh air.
- *At all times*: brief him about where you are going, what you will be doing, and what is expected of him.
- *When the tantrum begins*: be firm and explain in simple terms why something can't happen/must happen.
- *As the tantrum progresses*: ignore him.
- *As the tantrum continues* (for older toddlers): put him in Time Out for two to three minutes to calm down. If you are out and about

(continued)

and you can't do this easily, just get on with whatever needs doing and try to ignore the tutting. If it all gets too much, go home. (Drive carefully through blur of tears and shattered shopping plans.)
- *When he is calm*: cuddle and resume talks.
- Be consistent. Always respond the same way.

Aggressive Behaviour

As well as the joys of tantrums, some mums find that their lovely children also develop an aggressive streak. This seems particularly common in boys during late-toddlerdom. As with most challenging behaviour, this tends to get worse with changes of routine, or if they are under the weather.

Many of the tactics for dealing with aggression are similar to those for dealing with tantrums (for example, regular snacks, exercise, advance warning about plans). However, it is quite hard to ignore a small child who is knee-capping you when you are signing for a recorded delivery parcel or chatting to a client on the phone. Nevertheless, if you can manage it, it is important to try to keep your cool.

'If my son makes a swipe at me I just tell him firmly that we don't hit other people, then perhaps try to distract him. If he is really kicking off, I usually ask him to go and sit somewhere to calm down.' FrayedKnot

Some children use aggression as a way of attracting attention. They may hit out for the first time for some other reason, but once they see the fantastically colourful reaction from the adult looking after them, they decide that it might be fun to repeat it.

The difficulty for adults is that these episodes of aggression often happen in social situations – playgroups or playdates – and no one wants to be seen to be condoning violence, especially when your little ruffian is beating the angelic daughter of some random stranger over the head with a toy brick.

The trick in trying to stamp out violent behaviour (no pun intended) is to give the other child – the one that's been injured – lots of attention. Then, having asked your child in a low, firm voice to say sorry and told them not to do it again, distract them with something else. This works even for young toddlers, who get the message early on that hitting isn't going to get them attention.

Biting is another common problem and can start from babydom, although a small baby testing out his single tooth is not the same as a two-year-old with a full set of gnashers taking a chunk out of your arm. If the recipient of the bite is another child, then the technique of making a huge fuss of the injured party and a low-key response to the biter is the one to follow. If, however, you are the one being bitten it's sometimes harder to conceal the agony, but try to keep the reaction as minimal as possible, and under no circumstances retaliate.

'My mother-in-law insisted that the best way to stop my three-year-old biting was to bite him back. Great plan, Grandma. The next time he did it and I remonstrated with him, he came out with, "Well, Grandma bites." To my mind, biting back's a bit like saying to a swearing child, "Don't bl**dy swear at me." ' Muncher

One thing worth trying when biters, pinchers or hitters ambush you is to give them an alternative action. Tell them not to bite/hit/pinch but to kiss, stroke your face or cuddle you instead – show them what you mean and then give them heaps and heaps of praise and attention when they do it. It might not work straight away, but at least you'll get a cuddle.

Klingons: Easing the Pain of Separation Anxiety

'My daughter is two-and-a-half and has terrible separation anxiety. I can't even leave the room without her howling. I feel suffocated. What can I do?' Mummy2aaron

Toddlers can become incredibly clingy, and it can be maddening. There is nothing you want more than to sit down with a coffee and magazine while your toddler skips away to play at the other side of toddler group, or gaily joins his friends at pre-school, but instead he is howling like a dog and clinging with white knuckles to your shins. What to do?

If you need to leave your child in a playgroup or similar pre-school, don't worry too much about traumatic exits – they are often par for the course. Usually, the child who is crying as you walk back up the path will be chortling happily and whacking his friend over the head with a dinosaur by the time you are back at home or work. However, some children are more resistant to separation and refuse to settle for the entire morning or session. This can be very distressing.

In order to be independent, your child needs to be secure in their dependence. In other words, your child is clingy because she is panicking that you are going to bugger off and leave her (which you want to) and she isn't confident enough yet (note the yet) to survive for an hour or so without you.

One remedy is to continue providing a secure environment for your child, so that she learns to feel secure – and from that sense of security will feel confident enough to be able to relinquish your shins and explore the world. It is very tedious, but this stage will pass. In the meantime, if you can bear to pander to it, keep her close, take her everywhere, smother her with love and she'll start to feel more secure. As one Mumsnetter puts it: 'Not being good at mixing and being clingy are totally normal ways to be at two. And my belief is that there is no point in trying to "get her used" to being left. I think, if she has what she needs NOW, which is to be with you, then she will be better equipped to be left later.'

'I think the baby psychology goes something like: "I want you, I need you, now, now, now, now!" If you can say back (a million times or so): "I want you, I need you, now, now, now, now, TOO!" then on the million-and-oneth time your child will say: "Oh good grief, give me some space, you're crowding me ..."' Swampster

It can be very stressful if you want your child to settle into playgroup or pre-school but she becomes very distressed when you leave. If it is at all possible to wait a while longer, you may find that she will settle much more easily when she is a little older.

'I tried for a term and a half to get my son settled into a playgroup when he was two. Eventually, I plucked up the courage to say, "No More!" and stopped trying to take him. Six months later the critter went off to nursery and I had to be evicted from the classroom in floods of tears. He ignored me and jumped into his new life.' Vikkin

Of course, not everyone has the luxury of being able to choose when to put their clingy toddler into some kind of daycare. If you and your toddler have to be parted, there are various tricks to make it less painful.

Toddlers fear the unknown. Before you start nursery or playgroup, and during the early days, you should teach your child all about her new environment and what to expect. There are lots of books about starting playgroup which can help to explain what happens during the day (your local children's library should be able to help you find some). You can also talk about starting playgroup and what it will be like. Make it sound as exciting as possible and don't mention anything negative. Find out if your child has any particular worries (for example, eating, or going to the toilet) and explain exactly what will happen in those situations. Make everything seem fun, as well as simple to understand.

Most playgroups will phase in time when your child is left alone. For the first session, you and your child stay together for an hour or so, for the second session, you might leave for half an hour, and then, in time, a couple of hours. This tried-and-tested method seems to work very well for a lot of children, and is certainly worth trying before you do anything else.

If your child already knows a child at playgroup, one mum advises 'arranging playdates so he can build on his friendships'. Then you can keep reminding him that he will be able to play with Jonny at playgroup and what a marvellous time they will have!

Ask the carer or nursery nurse for advice. She will have plenty of ideas for clingy creatures. But have these conversations out of earshot of your toddler, if possible – hearing Mummy talking about her worries is not reassuring.

Cleaving yourself from your wailing child is horrid for you, but try not to show it. It is important to avoid giving your child messages about your own anxiety. Say bye-bye and leave. The more anxious you are, the harder it is on BOTH of you. Try to be cheery and optimistic – even if you are going to burst into tears as soon as you get back in the car. One mum advises, 'Be cheerful, give him a kiss and hug, and then leave. Don't prolong it.'

Some children worry that Mummy is going to be doing exciting things that they will miss out on, so reassure them that you are going to do something dull, like spending the morning ironing. If you are going to work then make it sound rather dull, even though you may be leaping with glee at the thought of sitting down and drinking a whole cup of tea undisturbed (except by grown-ups). One mum told her son that she was going to the sweetshop to buy him some sweets.

If your child will settle better with a favourite toy, then you can take Bear along to comfort her. If the nursery doesn't normally allow toys, but you think it would help, ask for a dispensation until your toddler is more settled.

Some children find it easier to leave Mummy if they are the one doing the leaving. So instead of going into the hall or classroom and then walking out yourself, your toddler can be called by his carer and might then be happy to walk away from you into the room with her. This avoids the pain of watching Mummy's back disappearing through the door as she skips off to her glamorous, child-free life.

'I'd recommend trying to get your toddler to adore one of the staff there, someone who looks like a long-term prospect. If they have a key-worker, they may be the ideal candidate. My son bounds into playschool because his teacher is there, and he loves her, and she is the prettiest, and he is going to marry her, and she is gorgeous, and he likes to cuddle her, etc.' Colditz

After a period, most children will learn to settle at playgroup and will hopefully look forward to their time there. If your child does not settle after several weeks, or if you think the playgroup isn't meeting his needs, it is worth considering a different one. The dynamics of each playgroup vary, and one might suit your child better than others. Eventually your child should start to feel at home in the playgroup environment and it is unlikely that the fears of this mum will be realised: 'I am envisaging having to sit in the corner while my son has his GCSE English lessons.'

Absence makes the heart grow fonder: Tips for starting playgroup

- Read books and talk about it.
- Phase in your toddler's sessions.
- Arrange playdates to build on existing friendships.
- Don't fret about traumatic exits – toddlers can be remarkably happy once you are out of earshot.
- Take advice from the playgroup staff.
- Say goodbye cheerfully – no blubbing.
- Tell your toddler that Mummy is doing something very boring e.g. ironing, washing up, sitting at work staring at the computer.
- Take a favourite toy or comforter.
- Encourage attachment to a key-worker or particular staff member.
- Postpone starting nursery if your toddler is very clingy or anxious.

Thumb-Sucking: Can You Stop It and Does It Matter?

Babies are born with the reflex to suck. It is both a necessity for feeding and, for many babies, a source of comfort. Some babies are simply 'suckier' than others, and many mums, after a few weeks of hoovering and shopping with a baby attached to a nipple, decide to offer a dummy as a substitute, which can work very successfully and provide relief to the most determined sucker. Other babies manage to find a soothing thumb themselves, which works just as well for oral gratification purposes.

This is all very well for babies but once they start toddling around, the issue of sucking becomes a tad controversial. Some people think that toddlers with a dummy or their thumbs in their mouths don't look *nice*, and others worry about the potential detrimental effects that constant sucking might have on developing teeth and jaws.

The British Dental Association advises that sucking a dummy is preferable to sucking a thumb, partly because it is less likely to affect teeth, but also because it is easier to remove a dummy than a thumb. (NB thumb removal is not the recommended weaning technique from this particular habit). However, its favoured option is to allow neither thumb nor dummy sucking, because both can potentially cause problems.

Many Mumsnet mums think that teeth worries, which may or may not be a problem in later years, are not a sufficient reason to deprive a young child of his source of comfort.

'Leave him to it. He'll stop eventually. (However, I will admit that I go around the bedrooms at night unplugging three little thumbs.)' Frogs

If you do decide to stop it – or if your child wants to stop and you want to help him – there are a few tried-and-tested methods. For example, one common approach is to use the nasty-tasting nail paint that is sold for nail-biters.

'I told my son that his thumb was looking poorly, because it had a hard knobble on it where he sucks, and that I had got some medicine. The medicine was a vicious-tasting substance for persistent nail-biters that I painted on the nail. I initially used it at night. He realised straight away it was nasty, and would try to suck, but would then lie in bed just looking at his thumb! I did this for a couple of nights, and then at odd times in the day. After a while he was in fear of tasting it, so just never bothered trying to suck again.' Tigi

Another mum persuaded her son to wear some highly desirable Batman plasters on his thumb, to remind him not to suck on it during the day. And a more extreme solution was discovered by this Mumsnetter: 'I found a thumb-guard on the internet, which seemed rather drastic but I was desperate. It really worked! He only wore it at night and within a month he didn't need or want to suck his thumb any more. Now if only there was something I could buy to get rid of his other annoying habits ...'

If all else fails, reassure yourself that most people will grow out of thumb-sucking eventually. And even if they don't, maybe it isn't the end of the world. As one mum protests: 'I am 34 and still sucking my thumb. I am a perfectly normal, well-adjusted professional. Obviously I don't do it at work, although on the night shift there is always the temptation ...'

Another mum announces that her 16-year-old daughter has finally stopped sucking her thumb 'because she's had her lip pierced and it hurts too much to suck.' So perhaps next time you witness that little thumb drifting to his mouth you can breathe a sigh of relief that at least you are only worrying about thumb-sucking, rather than facial piercing, which of course comes later.

Giving Up Dummy

Many hours have been spent on Mumsnet agonising about when and how to get a child to give up the dummy, and indeed whether a child should have to forgo his comfort just because you've decided it's time. Arguments for giving up range from anxieties about teeth to worries that they might inhibit speech, though the latter was ruled out by one Mumsnetter's husband:

'I understand from my in-laws that my wife had a dummy until she was four and she never stops talking. If it's true that dummies can slow speech development then I shudder to think what she might have been like if she hadn't had one.' Dada2

How much you worry about what others think when your four-year-old is still insisting on taking a dummy to school is up to you, but once you've decided, for whatever reason, to lose the facial adornment, how do you do it?

Cold turkey with incentive

Cold turkey can be helped by various ploys including the Dummy Tree or the Dummy Fairy. Pick a day when you decide there will be no more dummies and ceremonially plant them all in the garden under a tree (or for those without a garden, leave them out at night, wrapped up for the Dummy Fairy). Next morning make sure there's a present from the Dummy Fairy waiting under the tree/in the house for the child who has survived a whole night without a dummy. This works best for older dummy-suckers.

Cold turkey with no incentive

This (and indeed the method above) may well involve controlled crying, which, if you've had a dream sleeper, may not appeal to you. But if for some reason you're desperate for your little one to stop sucking, this can work. Just be prepared for a few disturbed nights (and warn the neighbours).

Softly, softly

If your child is an all-day sucker, start by limiting the dummy to rest and nap times and then gradually cut down until it's just night-time use.Then you can either stick with this until she's old enough to use the Dummy Tree/Fairy, or go for the straight cold turkey.

Star charts

For older toddlers star charts with an incentive for every day or week they manage without a dummy can work.

Or you can take the easy road and leave them to their dummy pleasure until they are old enough to be shamed or bribed into giving up. It is, after all, rare to see a ten-year-old with a dummy.

Sensible dummy use

- Restrict 'dummy time' to sleep times and long journeys.
- Buy 'orthodontically friendly' dummies, which are shaped to minimise damage to teeth.
- Don't tie a dummy around a child's neck. It doesn't look nice. And they might strangle themselves.
- Never fill dummies with drinks, especially sugary ones. Or brandy, whatever your grandmother might say about it improving his sleeping.
- Get rid of the dummy before adult teeth come through (from the age of five).

Manners Maketh the Toddler

'One of the joys of parenthood is looking upon your offspring as little angels. An adjacent pleasure is having others share that view. The interface between the two will depend on their manners.' Joan Bakewell

The sight of a toddler saying, 'Excuse me' while squeezing past the family cat is a joy to behold. Whereas the sight of a small child charging out of your abode without so much as a ThankYouFor HavingMe, particularly when she has left your house in a state of near-devastation, is not. And no, it does not count if the parent of the said child squeaks 'thank you' in a high falsetto. Children aren't puppets and can and should be taught basic manners.

'I can't bear it when kids who know me just look blankly at me,' complains one mother. 'Motherhood might render one suddenly invisible to attractive young men in the street but to be snubbed by the noisy spawn that have robbed us of our figures and second-glances is a double whammy.'

In order to teach your child manners, you must, of course, model polite behaviour yourself. There is no point berating your child if you are unable to be civil. As one frustrated mum says, 'My partner eats with his knife and fork in the wrong hands and shovels food in his mouth like someone is about to pinch it; it makes me so angry when I see the children picking up these habits.' So, rule number one is to be polite to your children and to treat them with respect. Say please and thank you and sorry when you accidentally break their Lego with your best stilettos.

If your or your partner's manners leave something to be desired, then there are other things that can help your children learn theirs. For babies and very small children, playing the 'please and thank you' game is a good start to the basic rules. This just involves passing a toy to the child and back to you again, and encouraging them to say thank you and please as it goes back and forth. Of course, you will need to ham it up and say, 'Please?' in your best Good Girl voice and give exuberant thanks when the toy is handed back.

Other than that, you just need to brace yourself for a lifetime of nagging and teaching that when X is desired one must say please, and when X is received one says thank you. This is very tedious and will of course drive you to distraction, but they will thank you for it one day (hopefully).

'All my children always say thank you, even my second son who has very limited language and severe autistic spectrum disorder. I always find it amusing when waiters serve him and he interrupts his humming/rocking/muttering to look up and say a very clear "FANK YOU". It is usually very loud as he is always extremely grateful for his chicken and it is as a consequence a little scary. But sincere and polite none the less.' Pagwatch

How far you choose to extend your basic manners lesson is of course your choice. There are mothers for whom 'Can I ...' grates like fingernails along a blackboard; the same blackboard no doubt from which they learnt the difference between 'Can I' and 'May I' many moons previously. As one mum sighs, 'I turn into my third-form geography teacher, Mr Vimes, and say, "I am sure you are able to have that but whether you may is a different matter altogether."'

Thank you letters are also still *de rigueur* for many. For smaller children, a scrawled picture will suffice, or you can print photographs of the children and get older toddlers to add a few kisses or even their names, if they have mastered that sort of thing. Producing basic cards with 'Thank you' outlined in glitter or some rudimentary drawing or painting can be a creative way to spend a post-birthday afternoon, if you can brace yourself for the cleaning-up required afterwards.

'Thank you letters are non-negotiable in our house, however naff or useless the gift. I cast my beady eye over the letters and if they are lazy, I make them draw a picture as well – over the years this has ensured very full and newsy thank you letters. When my son was eight he received a boomerang in the post from someone in Australia. He thanked her for the "half a boomerang" which he "doubted could ever be used".' Caroline1852

Of course, the constant drilling of children to be polite is a long and arduous chore, and even the most well-mannered parents can produce offspring who get carried away in the excitement of the moment and let their lovely manners slip. One mother asks that we reserve judgement for those with children who are not so compliant to their parents' wishes: 'Please spare a thought for those of us with less malleable children – who, despite regular exhortations and reminders, fail to remember their manners unbidden. I always have a slight frisson of trepidation when my daughter goes for a playdate that the host's parents will think she has been raised by wolves.'

Mumsnet guide to modern manners for toddlers

Essential

please
thank you
sorry
excuse me when passing
greeting familiar faces
hand in front of mouth for sneezing/coughing
thanking adults for hospitality
bums on seats at table

Desirable

not interrupting (saying 'excuse me' and waiting)
excuse me for farting/burping
closing mouth when eating
not picking nose or playing with bits in public
giving an adult a seat and happily sitting on the floor if there are
    not enough chairs
giving up seats on buses/trains
thank you letters/pictures
holding doors open for grown-ups
asking to get down from table
thanking adults for meals
'Please may I' rather than 'Please can I'

And don't forget table manners. Before parenthood, there was nothing more revolting than the sight of a small child slurping food off his plate, examining and testing biscuits from the tin and then replacing them, and talking and chewing with his dribbling mouth full. After parenthood and months of shovelling mush in one end and scraping it off the other, one becomes rather de-sensitised to how unsavoury one's own children can appear. However, if your children – and you – would like any sort of social life, it is essential that you try to tame their more revolting table habits and turn them into civilised people who are able to eat a meal with the minimum of disgust being aroused in other diners.

Mumsnetiquette: Always have a table-plan when eating with a toddler

When sharing a meal at a table with child-free or sensitive adults, remember to place your children out of their direct eyeline. Definitely do not place your two-year-old and her bowl of spaghetti opposite your easily repulsed child-free sister-in-law. She will not want to repeat the experience and your social life will rapidly dwindle to nothing. Ideally, place yourself in between the sensitive person and your offspring, and head off any offence by quick swipes with a napkin or babywipe, which you should discreetly hide in your lap. (Do not place it on the table.) Under no circumstances allow trails of snot to trickle on to a spoon that your child is using. I know you've forgotten, but it's really repulsive.

Tangles and Wrangles: Grooming Your Toddler

Getting your child dressed

Everyone wants their child to look as lovely as possible, but from a very early age some toddlers show a flair for fashion that's decidedly avant-garde. For every girl who wants to be Barbie, there's a three-year-old boy tugging on a tutu ready to be Barbie's prettier younger sister. Likewise you may have a house full of pink frills and a girl toddler who insists on wearing Spiderman pyjamas (and not just at bedtime). Then there are the coat-phobics, and those who will wear only swimwear even in the depths of winter. The outrageous get-up that can seem quite amusing at home is sometimes less so when they insist on wearing it to pre-school, playgroup or, heaven forbid, the in-laws'.

Mumsnetters' advice on this, as on so many toddler traumas, is to relax and, most importantly, don't listen to anyone who tells you (or, more likely, implies with *that* look) that your child is strange in any way. Flamboyant dressers, cross-dressers and unseasonal dressers are just experimenting and enjoying dressing up. It's one of the few times in their lives when they can. Before long they'll be in uniforms (even if their school doesn't have one, jeans become a uniform for most after a while) so let them have fun. It really is just a phase, and if you get enough photos you can blackmail them later in life.

'My little boy has been through every dressing-up phase going. At the age of two-and-a-half he would only wear tutus and ballet gear, then he moved on to sportswear, then a brief phase of wearing a three-piece suit and tie (aged three-and-a-half). He recently went to school wearing his Harry Potter glasses and was immortalised as Harry Potter in the pre-school photo. The photographer thought they were real.' Bon

More troublesome is the toddler who refuses to get dressed at all. Daily dressing battles can be exhausting, time-consuming and extremely depressing. Strategies for coping with these tussles include:

- Invest in some easy-to-pull-on gear. Toddler attention spans are short at the best of times, and if you have to faff around with buttons and bows it's just not going to work. With easy-to-pull-on clothes you can let them try to dress themselves. And if you have to use the pin-'em-down-and-dress-'em technique, at least it should be less painful for all concerned. Either way, once dressed, immediately give them lots of praise, tell them how wonderful they look and distract them with something they really like. This strategy works until they learn how to undress themselves. After that it's relatively pointless.
- Give the toddler a choice between two outfits. This can help them feel more in control of the situation.
- If you're feeling braver, and have the time, let them choose part of their own outfit – for example, any dress or pair of trousers

– and you choose the rest. Be warned – this can have interesting consequences.
- Distraction. Undress and dress them while they are playing with toys or watching television. With a bit of luck they'll hardly notice what you're doing.

If all else fails, you could try one Mumsnetter's patented solution to the runaway naked toddler reluctant to cover up: 'I put his undies on first, but leave them round his ankles. If he tries to run away, he falls down pretty quickly. It only took a few falls before he realised that it made more sense to stand still.'

Hair-brushing traumas

Children with long flowing locks can look angelic, but it usually involves tussles in the seventh circle of hell to make them look that way. Twice-daily fights with the hairbrush are infuriating for all concerned, and easily disintegrate into a physical battle that is none too pleasant. Lots of mums conclude that it's 'just not worth the constant aggro – get it cut.' Threats of chopping off her locks can work wonders in convincing a girl with princess aspirations that she needs to stand still for five minutes while you sort out the bird's nest. Or it can just add to the trauma, as one exhausted mum explains: 'My daughter is three and has tantrums when I brush her hair. Detangler didn't help. ("NO! NO! Not the detangler!! Noooooooo!") I've suggested she has it cut off, but she has tantrums about that idea, too, as she has a big old mermaid/princess/fairy complex. Sometimes if I sing, "What a beautiful fairy with her long fairy hair" she will let me brush it without too much fuss. Or if I manage to tell her an impromptu story (probably about mermaids/princesses/fairies) then she may stop crying so that she can hear what happens. Sometimes I just yell and scream at her. It doesn't help get her hair brushed, but it helps me to vent. That is crap advice, obviously.'

If your child's hair is long enough, keeping it in plaits can help keep very big snarls at bay – and also prevent hair from swishing around, which can reduce the chances of collecting the dreaded nits from their mates.

Tips from Rapunzel

- Use conditioner/spray-on detangler/hair serums.
- Play 'hairdressers' – let her brush your hair and then tell her it's your turn to brush hers.
- Invest in a natural bristle brush – it's easier to comb out tangles.
- Work with her fantasies: tell her that princesses have to brush their hair 100 times a night.
- Sing to her or tell her stories as you brush.
- Keep long hair in plaits as much as possible – particularly at night.
- Brush her hair while she is watching television.
- Start at the bottom to comb out tangles.
- Make her comb her own hair and take over when she has had enough.
- As a last resort, cut it short – even just below shoulder level is much easier to keep knot-free than longer hair.

Open Wide, Mr Crocodile: Teeth-Cleaning for Resistant Toddlers

'Every morning and evening it is a battle to get my little boy to brush his teeth. He is generally well-behaved and easy-going, but when it comes to brushing his teeth he clamps his mouth shut and flatly refuses.' JoshuasYummyMummy

Dentists recommend that you brush your child's teeth and don't let them have total control over their own toothbrushing until at least school age. Most toddlers will decide at some point that they do not want their teeth brushed, and it is rather tricky when they clamp their mouth shut and refuse to open up to Mr Brush. The thought of horrible toddler tooth decay can make this resistance very stressful.

Before you go in with the half-nelson, beware that your child might be teething and that this could cause brushing to be quite painful. Have a look in her mouth and see if you can see anything, or ask her if she is hurting. If this is the case, go very gently or use a flannel over a finger for a few days, until the teething pain goes away.

Take them shopping to choose their own brush – there are lots of different ones available and they might open up to a pretty princess toothbrush, or one that flashes like a police car. There are also a variety of flavoured toothpastes which your child might prefer to taste rather than your adult toothpaste – strawberry and mild mint, for example, or fennel if your child is of the hippy variety.

Explain to your child that they need to brush their teeth. It can be hard to convey the importance of this to a toddler, and you need to make sure you use language that they understand.

'I have told him that we need to brush away the "sugarbugs" and he seems quite taken with this idea.' ENTP

Sometimes simple distraction can help, such as playing in the sink or with another toothbrush, or looking in the mirror. A monologue about food-stuck-in-teeth is another simple technique that might appeal: 'Ooh, I can see a Cornflake from breakfast! Let me get rid of that ... Ooh, did you have ham sandwiches for lunch? I can see one! Let me just scrub it away ...that's better ...' Some resort to comedy routines – singing seems popular with others. One mum confesses, 'We have now progressed to singing in operatic style (LAAAAA, LAAAAA ad infinitum) which allows brushing without screaming. We have also found baaaing like intoxicated sheep to work quite well.'

Giving them something to 'do' while you brush can be effective as a method of distraction, as can role play. You can ask your child to brush your teeth while you brush theirs – try not to gag or scream when they jam the toothbrush into the back of your throat. You can also use their toothbrush to brush dolly's teeth, and then move on to your child's: 'Now it's your turn!' One mother took role play to an extreme: 'My daughter used to like the cat to brush her teeth, so I'd have to hold a struggling cat under one arm while trying to brush her teeth, but making it look like the cat was doing it.'

For some parents, all these techniques fail and they decide that they have to resort to pinning the child down. This doesn't tend to last for ever – they quickly learn that resistance is futile. Once they start complying, make it fun and rewarding by using some of the suggestions above.

'In the end I pinned my son down, on the grounds that being pinned down by someone who loves you is better than having to undergo potentially very frightening dental treatment.' FrannyandZooey

The Baby and the Bath Water: How to Tackle Bath Phobia

At some stage, most toddlers will develop bath phobia. Occasionally, this is precipitated by some sort of crisis such as being unexpectedly showered with cold water, slipping in the bath, or suddenly becoming quite convinced that that they might disappear down the plughole and end up in Australia. Unlike dogs, who will generally just cower sadly under the shower head, bath-phobic toddlers are more of a challenge, due to their ability to 'pole vault over the side to get out' as one mum discovered.

There are a variety of techniques that you can employ to persuade your toddler that Bathtime Is Fun. A step-by-step approach can work – for example, getting them used to being in the bath without being chest-deep in water. One little girl slipped in the bath but was cured of her subsequent worries, as her mother explains, 'by putting her in the bath before the water was in, then running the water (while I sat with my hand under the tap to make sure it was the right temperature).' You can try putting a tiny amount of water in the bath until they get used to it, and then add a bit more each day.

If your toddler is not jumping in mud every day, you might want to resort to a quick flannel-down as a short-term solution. One mum advises avoiding big bathtime sessions for a while:

'Give it a break for a day or so ... longer if you can bear it. After a break, he might feel more inclined to enjoy his bath again.'

New toys might act as sufficient bribery and/or distraction. There are many obvious bath toys – the old-fashioned classics such as stacking cups and rubber ducks. Crayons that you can use to 'draw' on the side of the bath are popular – although it is worth briefing them beforehand that this practice cannot be extended to other areas of the house.

You can also sprinkle the bath with very fine holographic glitter, available from craft shops. One mum suggests, 'Say that you went to the bathroom and there were fairies in the bath! Look at the mess they made. Does she want to get in and play with the fairy dust?' However, this technique comes with a warning to 'reduce glitter quantities over time or you will end up with a £60 a week habit.'

Another creative mum's solution was to create 'tropical rainforest showers'. For this you 'collect every plant from around the house to put around the bath sides, create lots of steam and put all the plastic animals you've got into the bath with her!' (Avoid cacti.) Another idea is to turn off the lights and play with cheap waterproof torches in a very bubbly bath, which even worked for one 'hyper-sophisticated ten-year-old'.

A bath with Mummy or Daddy can sometimes help – especially if they are worried about falling and need reassuring cuddles. Instead of making it their bathtime, you can always get in the bath and suggest that they join you ('Do you want to get in Mummy's bath?').

If hair-washing in the bath is a problem, try giving them a pair of swimming goggles to wear. These stop the soap getting in their eyes and the novelty takes their minds off the job in hand. Some children are scared of having their hair rinsed under the shower, which, given the fact that showers often throw out water that's scalding or icy, is not surprising. Try using stacking cups or a watering can instead – they're less threatening and do the job just as well, if not quite so speedily.

If it's summer and it's hot, you can use a paddling pool substitute – throw in some bubblebath and a bucket of warm water and it's just a bath in the garden – as long as your toddler doesn't race straight out into your flowerbeds, of course. You can also try using the hosepipe (and possibly a sprinkler) although you might want to check for hosepipe bans first.

If all else fails, you could resort to one mum's solution of washing them in the kitchen sink instead. Just remember to remove last night's dishes beforehand.

Mumsnetiquette: Don't go hysterical when they poo in the bath

This is very common and the inevitable fishing-out-poo-with-your-bare-hands experience is one that we have all shared. But screaming – although a perfectly understandable reaction – does not really reassure your toddler. So sort it out without too much fuss, and pour yourself a large glass of wine when he is in bed.

Swearers, Flashers and Thieves: What to Do About Inappropriate Behaviour

Although the days are long gone when swearing had the capacity to shock tender women into a state of swooning, there is still something rather horrifying about the F-word on the rosebud lips of a three-year-old. And Grandma won't be impressed, either. Swearing is so prevalent now that your child probably hears swear words every time you go shopping, put the radio on, or have some bastard cut you up on a roundabout. Of course, there are lots of toddlers who swear inadvertently. If yours does this, try not to worry. She won't be the only little girl begging to watch her *Wan King* DVD.

It is best to avoid using swear words at home in front of your children, although this is understandably very difficult if you have used them for most of your adult life and are now in an environment where there are tiny pieces of Lego liberally scattered over your laminate floor. But children learn by example, and if you are swearing around the house then your children will learn to do this, too.

'We were out near the river with some friends and their well-behaved kids, and my two-year-old son started bellowing, "F*** off, ducks! F*** off!" I was mortified.' Bimblin

The best place to start is replacing swear words in your own vocabulary with something more tame. Now is the time to make like the Secret Seven and pepper your talk with 'Golly!' and 'Gosh!' and, perhaps, 'Sugar!' There are times when you need to vent with some vocal obscenity, particularly when you are three and can barely make it up a small flight of stairs without smacking yourself on the head or wetting yourself. Giving your child these acceptable alternatives to swear words allows them to swear in their own way.

Not in public, dear

'A colleague of mine brought her two-year-old into the office. He walked up to the one person in the room we all disliked and said, "Are you Bloody Sheila?" ' *Sobernow*

'My daughter gets a bit upset if you try to force her to go in a particular direction when out for a walk. She shouts, "Don't hurt me, Mummy," REALLY loudly if I try to take her hand, as if I was beating her at home. I'm just waiting to be accosted by a social worker in the street.' *Susanmt*

'When having difficulty either getting his toy car to go round corners or doing a jigsaw, my son has been known to utter, "Oh for f***'s sake." My only consolation for being a terrible mother is that at least he is swearing in the right context.' *Willow2*

'We were in the changing rooms after swimming and an older naked lady was standing at her locker fumbling around for something. My son went up to her, put his hands on her buttocks and tried to part them. He wanted to see what was in there. I just stood there, rooted to the spot, and mouthed, "Sorry." Fortunately she was really sweet about it. She just turned round slowly and patted him on the head.' *MrsMills*

Some parents deviously suggest polite alternatives when their children have picked up 'real' swear words. One mum uses 'the replacement trick': 'If my son comes out with a swear word I give him an alternative and say, 'If you must use that word say it properly: fudge. Can you say fudge?'

Others manage to bluff their way out of their own obscenities with some quick-thinking. 'We were driving along,' recalls one Mumsnetter, 'and a van came flying round the corner on the wrong side of the road and I shouted, "Oh f*ck!" This was repeated gleefully by my son until his aunty had the presence of mind to say, "A fox, a fox! Mummy saw a fox!"'

Swearing for (people with) dummies

FOR F***'S SAKE!

- for frog's sake
- fluffy sheep
- fishcakes
- fishhooks
- for crying out loud
- for chuff's sake

SHIT

- sugar
- poo
- poop
- shoot
- poxy

BOLLOCKS

- bollards
- dollops

F***

- fish
- fiddle
- chuff
- fiddlesticks

GOD

- gosh
- golly
- Man Almighty
- Gordon Bennett

FOR GENERAL USAGE

- pants
- blimey
- darn
- bother
- blast

When your child swears, your gut reaction might be to laugh (largely through shock) or to scream. Both are obviously not very helpful responses and will probably encourage more of the same behaviour. As one mother points out, 'To small children the word "f***" has about the same resonance as "poo-poo head" and will be used in pretty much the same sort of way.'

If your child becomes a persistent swearer, you might need to develop an action plan to tackle the problem. Generally, mums advise one of two approaches: either ignoring the child (if they are swearing to get attention); or disciplining them (Time Out or whatever is your preferred method). The approach you take will depend on the child and what you think will be most effective, and of course how offensive you find the cursing.

Playing With Bits

Playing with bits starts at a very young age, as soon as a child has enough coordination to reach the right place, and for most of us is the start of a lifelong hobby.

Children play with their bits because it is another part of their body to explore and when they do so, it feels nice. Some children are more interested in their bits than others. As one mum succinctly puts it, 'Just as some kids twizzle their hair more than others, or play with labels more than others, some little children constantly have a hand down their pants.'

Enjoying and exploring the parts between their legs can take several forms. Some children just like to fiddle with their hands, others like rocking astride the arm of a convenient chair, and some even like stuffing their cuddly toys between their legs and humping them with a surprising amount of enthusiasm. Some boys enjoy testing the limits of their anatomies. 'My son used to pull his penis because he was convinced it would go over his head,' remembers one mum, 'and my husband would cry every time.'

'Once I found my son naked, sitting cross-legged and playing with his cars. He had his penis stretched out and was holding it down on his ankle, using it as a bridge.' Gigglinggoblin

All this touching and experimenting is entirely natural and not something to be unduly concerned about.

'I was worrying because my daughter plays with herself a lot and is starting school next week, but a teacher friend of mine said, "Don't worry, they will all be fiddling with themselves, especially during storytime!"' Hovely

Nevertheless, it is probably necessary to have some basic rules in place both to meet health and safety legislation and not to horrify nice old ladies from church that might be calling in for tea and biscuits. Some children can be easily distracted from such pursuits in public, but it is usually necessary to teach them that this is a private rather than a spectator sport.

Most gently steer their children towards reserving this sort of play for the privacy of their own bedrooms. 'My daughter was a major fiddler,' explains one mum. 'I told her that she should wait until bedtime or pop off to her room. She would regularly pop off to her room and it took her a long time to outgrow it.' (It is worth remembering that if you use your child's bedroom for Time Out, they might associate being asked to do something in their room as a telling-off – so try to make it clear that it is something that is quite OK, but just reserved for private moments.)

'As soon as my son "discovered" his penis I made sure that he had time after his bath each night to just run around naked and look at/explore his whole body if that's what he wanted to do. I wish people would be more laid back about it because that's really all it is, just curiosity and exploration that also happens to feel nice.' Jabberwocky

For persistent fiddlers, it is probably a good idea to have a 'no playing with your bits at the table' rule (the modern day equivalent of 'no elbows on the table'), and perhaps also a 'you must wear pants at the table' rule. But try not to convey the message that their bits are 'dirty' – you don't want to make them feel negative about any part of their body.

It is worth mentioning at this point that little boys get erections from a very early age – many from birth. This is quite normal and not 'sexual' in the adult understanding of the word, but just a natural function of their bodies, and something that will slowly become more and more associated with enjoyable physical stimulation as they get older.

Again, this is another aspect of their bodies that you might wish to emphasise is private and not for sharing with visitors, as one aunty discovered: 'When my nephew was about two-and-a-half he was staying at my mum's house and walked into the kitchen where she was sitting with friends, and announced, "Look, Granny! My willy is doing the rocket thing again!" and exposed himself proudly to them all.'

Most children grow out of the constant fiddling phase, or at least learn to do it in private. Trying to keep the message positive-but-private can be a challenge, but is a message that they need to hear if they are to grow up enjoying and respecting their bodies. In the meantime, you will just have to try to control your embarrassment when visitors are confronted by the sight of a row of small children watching television with legs akimbo and little hands down their tights.

'I have decided to ignore their behaviour at home, and if they play with themselves when we are out, I am letting them know that they should wait until they get home. This was fine until two days ago on a shopping trip and my son piped up, "Mummy, can we please go home soon? I really want to play with my penis."' EmilyF

What to Name Bits

'My daughter once asked her father, "What's that on your fanny?" to which his most affronted answer was that it was his willy, thank you very much.' Motherinferior

The question about what to call your genitals is a hot potato amongst mums. Thousands of contributions to Mumsnet have been about whether 'fanny' or 'willy' are acceptable terms and which bit you can really call a vagina. Most commonly parents refer to anything inside the pants department as 'your bits' which covers a broad spectrum of possibilities.

Mothers of boys are generally content with 'penis' or 'willy', but naming girls' genitals is trickier. As one frustrated mother moans, 'Bloody hell, we pee from them, we have sex with them, we give birth from them and we *still* haven't got a totally acceptable word for our genitals!'

The word 'vulva' is generally approved of for being the most anatomically accurate and least twee of all. 'Fanjo' has been adopted as the nouveau euphemism of choice among Mumsnetters. 'Fanny' is still popular but smacks of the playground and sounds rather crude to many ears.

Euphemisms all have their downsides, however. 'My friend used to call hers a tuppence,' notes one mother. 'She says she remembers laughing a great deal at Mary Poppins feeding the birds.' Another laments, 'We've hummed and hawed for too long about this issue, and now it's become "twinkle". It brings a whole new meaning to "Twinkle Twinkle Little Star".'

Whatever term you plump for, it is worth making them familiar with a few others before they start school, where they will no doubt hear a variety of colourful terms bandied about the playground. And as one sex-education teacher notes, 'It is useful if they know the right words, because it makes my life much easier in Year Seven!'

The Gina Monologues: What to call the genitals?

(in approximate order of popularity on Mumsnet)

Girls'	Boys'
bits	bits
vagina or 'gina	penis
fanjo	willy
vulva	winkie
fanny	twinkle
minnie	peanuts
foo-foo	
fairy	
flower	
tootie	

And So to Bed ...

'Have just been up to check on my three-year-old daughter. She is sprawled across her bed with covers kicked off, and clutching her beloved doggy toy like she will never let him go. She looks so blissful and innocent. I feel like all is right with the world.' Amysoph

You know it's going to be a tough day when you look at the clock at 9 a.m. and find yourself calculating how many more hours until their bedtime. Sometimes every day with a toddler can feel like an exhaustingly slow slog to the finishing line when they are finally asleep. And when they are asleep you can be overwhelmed by how perfect and wonderful they are.

It's easy to feel tortured and guilty for all the times when you didn't quite live up to your ideal of a patient, forgiving, fun, lively, empathetic and not-very-shouty mother. Toddlers can be a real challenge. Don't forget to tell yourself that you are doing your best and also that you are doing a fantastic job. Pour yourself a glass of wine and get some sleep before they wake you up again. And give yourself a pat on the back.

Food

All We Are Saying, Is Give Peas a Chance

In this chapter ...

Introduction

'I always feel such a prat standing in my well-stocked kitchen in a country with horrible rates of obesity cajoling my children to eat.' Issymum

Toddlers are notoriously fussy eaters. A delicious platter of the finest cod mornay with a side order of steamed, organic vegetables procured from the local farmers' market can be pushed across the table in the time it takes to declare, 'Don't want that.'

It may be true that no toddler has ever starved themselves to death, but that doesn't stop you worrying about rickets when your toddler has raced about from dawn until dusk fuelled by nothing more than three mini-cheese biscuits and a lollypop. Height and weight charts, merrily provided by your local health visitor, only serve to deepen your food neurosis. But Mumsnetters are full of good advice to beat the dinnertime blues and make eating a fun activity – or at least to stop torturing yourself and obsessing over those centiles.

When tested by your toddler, ask yourself this important question (which also applies to almost all your toddler troubles): 'Is this a battle worth fighting?' As far as food is concerned, the answer is usually no. Rule number one is to avoid mealtimes becoming a battleground.

Hunger Strikers and Fussy Eaters

Of course, food is not just about fulfilling our needs for fuel. Eating is very much a social activity and most Mumsnetters agree that the place to start learning good eating habits is around the family table. You don't have to have the best china and napkin rings three times a day, but sitting the poor child in a highchair in the middle of the kitchen surrounded by a heavily sterilised moat of linoleum is not going to teach her that eating is a lovely and enjoyable thing.

Shared mealtimes are great for chatting – even though the witty repartee of your pre-children years has undoubtedly been replaced with, 'Oooh, what yummy pasta. Isn't Daddy a good boy and eating nicely!'

As well as learning about the social aspects of eating, dining together teaches your child about the enjoyment of good food.

'Make sure you tell him how nice your food is. Do lots of oooh-ing and look like you are really enjoying it. Offer a little spoonful from your plate now and then. If he asks for more, let him have some.' Clumsymum

Often food on Mummy's plate might seem more interesting than food on your child's plate – and if you are struggling with a fussy eater, you might be able to get a mouthful or two into your child this way. 'My two-year-old will push her plate to one side and shout, "Want yours!" – even though we are all eating the same meal,' sighs one mum. 'Sometimes I just swap plates and find myself tucking into a nicely-cut-up plate of spaghetti bolognaise on a Teletubbies plastic tray while she flicks long spaghetti over herself with a great deal of concentration.'

A crucial aspect of eating together is teaching by example – and it is obviously beneficial if your child sees you eating your veg and enjoying the whole dinner experience.

Of course, this is all very well if you are all home and ready for food at 5.30 p.m. If that's just not possible, make a special effort to have some family meals at weekends, even if you'd all rather be in front of the telly with a tray on lap. Try also to make sure that someone sits down and engages with the child as they eat. Or invite other children round so that they can eat together. This can work particularly well if the invitee is a healthy eater. There's nothing like a bit of peer pressure – 'Look how well Anna's eating her fish' or 'Show Anna how you use your Barbie fork' – to encourage food into a reluctant eater's mouth.

Reassuring food facts

It is depressing to read that your child can make up his iron and calcium quota for the day by consuming his body-weight in kale and sardines. But do not fear, there are other sources of these important nutrients that he is more likely to eat.

Protein
Your toddler needs about 16g of protein per day.

8oz milk = 8g
1 small pot yoghurt = 4g
1 large egg = 6g
1 oz cheddar cheese = 7g
1 oz chicken = 7g
3 oz tofu = 7g
½ cup baked beans = 7g
tablespoon of peanut butter = 7g
small bag of chocolate buttons = 2.5g (shhh!)

Iron
Your toddler needs about 7mg of iron per day.

1 slice of roast beef = 1mg
3 tablespoons of baked beans = 1.7mg
2 dried figs = 1.7mg
1 slice wholemeal bread = 1mg
1 boiled egg = 1mg

The iron in red meat is most easily absorbed by the body. Serve iron-rich foods with a source of vitamin C, such as fruit or veg or fruit juice, because the body needs vitamin C to absorb iron.

Calcium
Your toddler needs 500mg of calcium per day.

8oz milk = 300mg
1 small pot yoghurt = 200mg
1 oz cheese (matchbox size) = 200mg
1 small pot cottage cheese = 150mg

(continued)

1 oz mozzarella (matchbox size) = 150 mg
1 sweet potato = 70mg
$^1/_2$ can baked beans = 90mg

And don't forget ...

- Toddlers have small stomachs – about the size of a small fist. So don't be surprised if they prefer snacking on smaller, frequent meals rather than two or three big meals over the course of a day. (*Source:* Food Standards Agency)
- Don't worry too much about wholegrains. Young children's stomachs can't cope with too much wholemeal pasta and brown rice, and too much fibre can sometimes affect their bodies' absorption of nutrients. So don't feel guilty about offering white pasta and white bread. (*Source:* Food Standards Agency)
- Toddlers often prefer to have the same thing to eat day after day. They do not have the adult desire for a wide variety of foods. So don't feel bad if they are living on a 'boring' diet. Most children grow out of this by school age. (Only to lose it again when they become students.)
- A cold meal can be just as nutritious as a hot meal – whatever Grandma might think. Bread, cheese, fruit and veg make a good cold meal.
- There is not much nutritional difference between a homemade pizza and a cheese and tomato sandwich.
- An egg is packed with a range of vitamins and minerals including protein, essential vitamins A, D, E, and B group as well as iron, phosphorus, zinc, iodine, selenium and choline. (*Source:* The British Egg Information Service)
- From the age of two, you can start giving your toddler semi-skimmed milk instead of full-fat milk. (But fully skimmed milk isn't suitable as a main drink until they are five years old – they still need the calories contained in semi-skimmed milk.) (*Source:* Food Standards Agency)

What not to eat: Put down the salt cellar, Granny

There are plenty of Mumsnetters who have entered the kitchen to discover Granny adding salt to their baby's purées on the grounds that 'It tastes disgusting!' but there is no need to add salt to a child's food. Staples such as bread, cheese and cereals come packed with salt already, and it's pretty easy to reach the recommended maximum even before your child has finished his toast and cereal. Make a habit of checking the nutritional contents of the food you buy, even items marketed as suitable for children.

Toddlers should be having no more than 2g of salt a day.

Other foods to avoid:

- Don't add sugar or honey to your toddler's food. Your mum might have poured sugar on your Cornflakes in the seventies, but we know better now. It's bad for their teeth and they don't need it.
- Don't give fizzy drinks and fruit squash – they cause tooth decay. Between meals, it's even best to avoid fruit juices; give water or milk to drink instead. (Serve fruit juices at meals if you like; the vitamin C will help absorb the iron in their food.)
- Don't give toddlers tea or coffee; it reduces the amount of iron they can absorb and contains caffeine. Toddlers don't need any more encouragement to bounce off the walls. Stick to cooled herbal teas if you want to give them hot drinks, or apple juice and warm water, or maybe hot chocolate made with milk for a treat.
- Avoid raw eggs and food that contains raw eggs because of the risk of salmonella, which causes food poisoning. Regurgitated eggy sheets are not pleasant to wash.
- Avoid choking hazards until you are sure that your child is old enough to chew things up and swallow properly; avoid whole nuts, boiled sweets, or whole grapes.
- Avoid giving your toddler shark, swordfish and marlin because these fish contain relatively high levels of mercury, which might affect a child's developing nervous system. And let's face it, it's a bit poncy.

(Source: Food Standards Agency)

Here Comes the Choo-choo!

If your child is not easily persuaded of the joy of food, you might want to try getting creative and transform their plate of dinner into faces, birds' nests, stars, life-size model of Greendale etc., depending upon your other commitments, of course. Hopefully the distraction of a monster hand, constructed entirely from fish fingers, or a *Close Encounters*-style volcano of mashed potatoes will divert your child's attention sufficiently for them to eat a few mouthfuls.

'Try smiley faces with halved cherry tomatoes, small pancakes, cubes of cheese and strips of cucumber. My son loved the red eyes so much he forgot he didn't want to eat.' Mum2FunkyDude

You won't get any Michelin stars but some children do respond well to the comedy food routine. With a bit of imagination any dish can be transformed into something vaguely recognisable. Spaghetti can be passed off as worms and you can be mummy bird feeding her chicks. Another distraction technique is imaginative story-telling. One Mumsnetter says, 'My son will eat his porridge if I tell him the bears will eat it if he doesn't!' And don't forget the old cliché of the spoon being an aeroplane or a train going into a tunnel. It works for some children ...

Can Eat, Won't Eat

When you are regularly exceeding your own daily recommended calorie intake before elevenses, it's a real worry when your child doesn't seem to have any interest in his quota at all.

'Yesterday all he ate was a boiled egg and half a slice of buttered bread. Is that normal for a three-year-old?' WishYouACrappyChristmas

One wise mother advises, 'Don't forget: some kids survive fine on white bread and chips!' It's easy to forget that our varied and bountiful diets were not available to our grandparents' generation, who made it through the winter on a few turnips. Children's needs vary a great deal, even between siblings, and they often thrive on less food than we might expect.

'This country is suffering from a growing obesity crisis so the last thing we should be doing is forcing our kids to eat more! We should be encouraging kids to have a healthy relationship with food and decide themselves when they've had enough. There's nothing wrong with a child who is eating bits of fruit and a few peas, especially if you can get them to drink some lovely, calorie-rich milk.' Spiderfan

If you really are worried about your child's eating habits, it's a good idea to write it all down. 'Try to keep a weekly diary of what your child eats,' suggests one mum. 'Chances are he does eat some healthy things and it's possible he eats lots some days and not so much on others.' Aside from giving you a more balanced view it's very useful if you want to seek advice from your health visitor or GP.

Some children seem to prefer having small plates of food in front of them – and of course this helps reduce food waste. 'We don't give a huge amount to start,' explains one mum, 'and we give him a star for his star chart if he clears his plate or tries something new.'

Most mums avoid offering snacks in the hour or two leading up to a meal, but if the hunger pangs strike early, try offering something from their main meal that they are not too keen on, such as the vegetables. For some, imposing a rule of three-meals-a-day and no snacks in between can work.

'My eldest daughter started to eat well when she went to school: no-choice hot dinner, no snacks, peer pressure and if you're not finished by the time the bell rings, your plate gets cleared away. Observing how well that worked for her, we've instituted the same approach for her younger sister. Nothing to eat between meals apart from a piece of fruit mid-morning, no pressure to eat, no fuss. She ate virtually nothing for two days, we held our nerve and by the third day she was eating well.' Issymum

However, some children will need to eat little and often, so if they start whining or throwing themselves on the floor at the supermarket at 3 p.m., they might be the sort that needs more regular sustenance. Choose healthy options such as cheese and fruit and veg – snacks that have lots of nutrients – rather than just taking the edge off their hunger with nutritionally empty food.

It is also a good idea to build up a good appetite just before a meal. 'Some fresh air and a quick run around in the garden can work wonders,' suggests one mum. 'And I always find that if we've been swimming, my kids eat so much better. I also have a much better success rate with "new" foods when they are really hungry.'

Just make sure you have some food ready for when they roll in through the front door (or stick some reasonably healthy snacks in the swimming bag). It's no fun peeling potatoes with a starving toddler clinging to your leg and begging for food.

If you have a very fussy eater, you may have to take the decision at some point that getting them to eat needs to take precedence over where that food is eaten. If your top priority is table manners, these tips won't be for you. But if survival's your main objective, try a few of the following:

• Change the location. If it's been a particularly bad food day, try feeding them in the bath. It's easy enough to wash the inevitable mess away and while they are distracted with bubbles you can push in a few mouthfuls.

- Or – purists, please look away now – have a picnic in front of the TV. Not something you'd like to encourage on a daily basis, but if you think sharing their meal with PC Plum will help, it's worth a try.
- Bribery. Have their favourite book at the table. For every mouthful, read one page. Don't read the next page until that mouthful is finished and the next one is in. Works best for older toddlers.
- Take tasty and healthy snacks when you go to feed the ducks. Fussy toddlers seem only too happy to tuck into stale and mouldy bread when feeding ducks, so give the ducks a treat and mix up a fresh picnic – fruit, nuts, even sandwiches – in a bag she can then share with her feathered friends.

Milk Monsters

If your child seems genuinely not to have any appetite, it's worth checking his milk intake. For many toddlers a bottle or beaker of milk is the ultimate comfort food, and because it's so nutritious it's easy to give in and let it become a food substitute. As one mum admits, 'It was a vicious circle. I was so worried about how little he ate that I just kept giving him milk because I knew he'd take that. But of course when it came to mealtimes he was so full of milk he wouldn't eat a thing.'

If you suspect this might be a problem, try cutting back on how much milk they consume during the day (and the night), and make it a rule that there's definitely no milk before meals. Save the big milk drinks for after breakfast, lunch and dinner and if necessary bring mealtimes forward to prevent them getting too hungry and therefore too fractious to eat.

Eat Your Greens: How to Handle Veggie Rejection

'I serve veg every day, we eat them every day, but my son will not put them in his mouth!' Colditz

When you started weaning your lovely baby, you probably proudly spoon-fed him all sorts of liquidised steamed vegetables and your heart warmed at the thought of the great start you were giving him by educating his palate to love all things green. And yet for some reason, when he hits the age of about two, his widely educated palate becomes a vegetable-filter, and the tiniest slip of carrot will be spat out and rejected.

It seems frustratingly common for toddlers suddenly to develop an aversion for vegetables. It is so common that there have even been studies that propose various evolutionary theories to explain why your lovely son can suddenly detect broccoli at 50 paces. However, none of this is particularly helpful to you, when you just want him to eat his five-a-day and grow into a big strong boy.

A common toddler response to vegetable-hating is to try to put the vegetables as far away from his acceptable food as possible – perhaps by flicking them across the table or placing them on Mummy's plate. But Mumsnetters agree that continuing to provide vegetables with each and every meal is very important, even if your child doesn't like them.

'Keep putting the vegetables on his plate. If he pushes them off the plate, simply point out that this is not what we should do when eating at the table. One of my children hated some veg until he was about ten. I always added them to his plate, and tried not to talk about it.' Williamsmummy

It's worth remembering that although toddlers can be cunning and manipulative, you have had possibly 30 years of practice at these skills, so you should use this to your advantage when trying to persuade your toddler to eat his greens. Gobble up your carrots with enthusiasm, tell him that you hope he isn't going to eat those green beans, because you *really, really* want to eat them yourself, challenge him to a fast-eating vegetable contest, see how many peas you can get on a fork before eating them, get him to close his eyes and make a floret of broccoli disappear in your mouth – all of these are worth trying. Some toddlers are easily fooled.

'One thing I used to do with my charges was to ask them to close their eyes and guess what I was putting in their mouth! It worked every time.' Starlover

One mum suggests 'taking him shopping and asking him to pick something from the shelves which he wants to eat, to make it "his special choice".' Some toddlers might be persuaded to eat something that they have chosen for themselves. Perhaps a stroll around the vegetable aisle holding their own basket might encourage them to eat something green and wholesome – or they might recognise something that they have eaten and enjoyed at nursery or at a friend's house – baby sweetcorn or tiny plum tomatoes, perhaps.

Dinner-table negotiation is a popular technique for persuading children to eat more. Although there is the old favourite of 'one more spoonful', this can also be extended to 'four more peas', which could be presented as a challenge to the über-competitive child: 'I bet you can't count out FOUR peas and eat them! Can you count to four?' (Don't forget the wide-eyed amazement when he does.)

'I negotiate: "Please eat five peas and you can have another squirt of tomato ketchup." My reasoning is that I am actually teaching him to count and also to negotiate: "Just three peas for half a squirt of ketchup, please, Mummy!"' Bobbybob

If all these approaches fail, try your hand at a few culinary magic tricks, and sneak the veggies into food so that they can't detect them. 'From about 12 months my son started to reject vegetables, so I hid them in his food by mashing and blending,' confides one mum. This is a very popular technique for secretly getting small children to eat their veggies.

'I hid puréed veg and fruit in everything. He had puréed fruit in his porridge for breakfast, and all of his meals had several different types of puréed veg in them. If you batch-cook it's easy.' Laura032004

Grated carrots can easily be sneaked into all sorts of homemade meals, including burgers, bolognaise sauce and shepherd's pie. And who can resist a slab of carrot cake? Whizzing up vegetables in a blender and transforming them into pasta sauce is another popular way of serving them to toddlers.

'My daughter is a nightmare to cater for but she will eat pasta with everything. So now I make all Annabel Karmel's recipes, liquidise them and then serve them with pasta which she loves to eat!' ReindeerNosebagAddiction

It is also worth offering the vegetables you are preparing for dinner as titbits or snacks if they are starving before dinnertime – carrot sticks are ideal. When vegetables are the only option, they are more likely to gobble them up. If you object, saying, 'You're stealing my vegetables! They're really for dinner!' then let them help themselves to a few bits from your saucepan, it might even give the veg fresh appeal as a prized victory.

Invisible vegetable tomato sauce

'I made some of this yesterday and used it for pizzas on wholemeal pitta bread. My son wolfed them down!' *Monkeytrousers*

Ingredients
aubergine
peppers
courgettes
mushrooms
onions
celery
etc.

Heat oven to around 180 degrees (gas mark 4).

Roast aubergine, peppers, courgettes, mushrooms, onions and celery in a covered oven dish until they're soft and easily mushed up – this takes about an hour. Then blitz them with a blender.

Mix together with either a jar of shop-bought tomato-based pasta sauce or your own (fry a bit of garlic and onion, toss in a can or two of tomatoes and cook on the hob on a low heat for up to an hour or more).

Use this as the base for homemade pizzas, shepherd's pie, pasta sauce, or spaghetti bolognaise.

(NB For super-fussy toddlers you might need to peel the courgettes, as they leave green flecks, and/or miss out the mushrooms, which might be detected owing to their texture.)

Vegetables by stealth: how to sneak veggies into food

- Spaghetti bolognaise is fab for hiding vegetables – grated carrot, diced swede, sweet potato, puréed peppers.
- Mashed potato can act as a Trojan horse for butternut squash, sweet potato or well-cooked carrots and swede.
- Hide vegetables by smothering in ketchup or gravy.
- Serve carrots in honey or cauliflower cheese.
- Make homemade soup and provide bread for dipping. Whiz it up so that it's smooth with no lumps. Make it from sweet-tasting veg, like butternut squash.
- If they like sweet potatoes you might get away with roasting pumpkin or butternut squash together with the sweet potatoes – they look and taste similar.
- Juicing vegetables. Juiced leeks might be pushing your luck, but some children will drink carrot juice, especially if it's mixed with apple or orange.

Tactics: What Do You Do When They Won't Eat Their Dinner?

You've spent half the afternoon tripping over toys and picking up stray items of clothing, yet you've still managed to cook something delicious and nutritious. But as soon as you strap your lovely child into her highchair she shrieks, 'Don't liiiike it!' and pushes away her plate. What should you do?

Remember, food rejection is not a battle worth fighting. However, that does not mean going back to the kitchen to rustle up another cooked meal. It just means not showing your child that you are so full of rage that you want to scream, 'EAT IT OR WEAR IT!' and rub it into her hair. Let her know that her rejection of your food is just *boring* and you will be well on your way to dinner victory.

'My children (aged two and four) eat what's put in front of them, and there is nothing else. However, I do try to make allowances for what they might be in the mood for that day. If possible I ask them what they might want for dinner (I do actually get fairly reasonable and varied responses) and I also try to check with them as to how much they want of each item before serving them ... it makes it easier to expect them to eat what's on their plate.' SofiaAmes

Lots of parents feel anguished at the thought of their little one going to bed hungry, and unlike previous generations we have cupboards and fridges stuffed full of good food, so it is tempting to want to provide an alternative dinner for your child. However, if you set this precedent now, you will find yourself cooking two or three meals every night for the next 20 years, which will leave you with less time for the enjoyable things in life, like not cooking dinner.

'As far as dinner is concerned, I put it in front of them, and if they don't like it, they don't eat it. I have fulfilled my Good Mother bit by cooking it. If you worry about them going to bed hungry you can always allow them a bit of fruit, but no treats and definitely no rustling up anything different.' MarsLady

Of course, if you are eating something that your child is going to dislike, such as a hot chilli or a spicy curry, then you can cook something similar for her – such as the mince or chicken from your meal served with rice. But not something that requires a separate trip to the fishmonger's and five different pans. The main thing is that there is something on her plate that you know she likes (or has liked in the past).

'In this house you get the same as everyone else and if you don't eat it there are no alternatives. The End.' Nailpolish

Obviously, there will be times when you suspect that your little one might be feeling under the weather (as toddlers often do) or has had a difficult day, in which case you could offer something lighter or more snacky. And there are always times when it is more appropriate to put on your pyjamas and cuddle up on the sofa with some toast and television whether you're a toddler or not.

Roll up, roll up for the worst eater competition

'Whose child has eaten the worst today? My three-year-old has eaten the same today as yesterday: two bowls of cornflakes without milk, one piece of toast, one sesame snap, one mouthful of chicken and a glass of grape juice. I've noticed that she has fallen off the bottom of the height charts again. Ah well, at least she will never have to worry about towering over her boyfriends.' *Morningpaper*

'A bowl of Cheerios, one ham sandwich, one bottle of yoghurt, one banana, one tube of smarties. Refused dinner.' *Waterfalls*

'One-eighth of a banana, the tiniest bit of kiwi you could imagine, one currant bun, one bag of chocolate buttons (courtesy of my mother-in-law), one potato, one-eighth of a tin of spaghetti. I don't worry about charts any more; she is what she is!' *Staceym11*

'One spoonful of cornflakes, one packet of chocolate buttons, half a cheese roll, one Smiley Face, one mouthful of baked beans, one mouthful of chicken, one piece of swiss roll. Today was a good day!' *Marne*

'Half a piece of toast, a slice of ham, two Maltesers, a mouthful of spag bol, a small pot of yoghurt.' *Nemo1977*

'One packet of Mini-Cheddars, one packet plain Hula Hoops, one custard cream biscuit. That's it.' *Pfer*

'Well, I have two vegetarians who don't eat veg!' *Somanykiddies*

'Shreddies with milk and sugar, some cornflakes, one banana, soup, half a baguette, two biscuits. Refused dinner.' *Joanie*

'One mouthful of porridge, two bites of fruit bread, a few bites of apple, raisins, one head of a gingerbread man.' *Harpsichordcarrier*

'Dry ice-cream cones for breakfast.' *Suzywong*

'Bowl of dried cereal, stick of cheese, top of French bread, two bites of sausage, one chocolate mousse. Refused tea.' *MummyJules*

'Well, this is good to see. I keep reassuring myself that it's highly unlikely that there will be a whole generation of people in 20 years' time who won't go to restaurants for dinner because they only eat Hula Hoops and dry toast followed by yoghurts without "bits" in.' *Chocolatequeen*

Dessert Dilemma: Pudding Rules

'No way, José! If your tummy is too full for food it is too full for treats!' LGJ

There is a divide amongst Mumsnetters about whether or not to allow pudding if you don't eat your dinner. On one hand, you have those who think that the dessert is an integral part of the whole meal, so the availability of pudding should not be determined by the consumption of the main course. And on the other, there is the school of thought that believes pudding is only for good girls and boys who have eaten all their tea. Most Mumsnetters forge a *via media* between the two extremes.

'My twins don't get pudding (not even fruit) unless they have eaten at least two-thirds of their main course. I'm a decent cook and don't serve them rubbish, so I don't expect it to be rejected.' Milge

You need to be quite specific about your instructions to a two-year-old, of course. One mother says, 'My rule used to be, "You can't have pudding unless more than half your food has gone", but my son tried putting the food down the side of his chair to make it "gone" so we had to change it to "unless more than half is eaten".'

The 'one more mouthful' request works for many as the negotiating finale before dessert.

'If my daughter eats "enough" of her meal then she will get a pudding. I usually follow the "one more mouthful for me" routine, though.' Helsi

Those who feel that pudding is an integral part of the meal avoid all of this negotiating. They just dish out desserts once everyone has decided that they have eaten enough of the main course. Providing a balanced and nutritional pudding is part of this plan, however – not just a bowlful of Haribos with custard.

'I always give my girls their pudding. I strongly feel that it is an integral part of the meal, and would not deprive them of part of it because they hadn't eaten their main course, in the same way I wouldn't deprive them of a drink. However, the pudding offered varies depending on how much (and what) they have eaten.

For example, if they've not eaten their veg I'll offer a fruit salad for pud; if they've cleared their plates they're more likely to get ice-cream.' Orinoco

Lots of families have a pudding which comprises wholesome options – yoghurt and fruit is a very popular combination. Some parents just offer fruit for pudding. One mum only provides puddings as a weekend treat to avoid arguing during the week. Some don't have puddings at all.

'I rarely give my son "pudding", anyway, so it hasn't become set up as the Holy Grail that is badly wanted. I am uncomfortable with setting one form of food up as more important/desirable.' Blu

One mum confesses that she and her partner curl up on the sofa to have secret desserts (with a glass of wine) after their children are in bed. Just don't let them know, or they'll never go to sleep.

After-Dinner High Jinks

It is rather irksome to hear the cry of 'Huuungry! Want food!' ten minutes after you have scraped a large plate of shepherd's pie into the food bin and finished washing up 27 pans. It is nigh-on impossible to stop the words, 'Well, you should have eaten your dinner then!' from tripping off your bitter and twisted tongue, as though you have morphed into your own mother. This is an inevitable part of living with a fussy toddler and there are various approaches to dealing with it.

You can keep their dinner to one side, covered with clingfilm or a plate cover. You can then answer their cries of hunger with, 'Well, aren't you lucky? I've kept your dinner for you!' and present them with their previously spurned meal. If it's something that would be more appetising warm, heat it up in the microwave if you have one. Cold congealed cauliflower cheese is a harsh offering, even for an annoying child who played up at dinnertime.

If you cooked something that was pretty vile and you think they really didn't like it, you could be more sensitive and offer an alternative snack, perhaps some fruit or cheese.

'Tonight my son didn't eat his pasta and came to me crying half an hour later saying he was hungry. I caved in and let him have cheese and crackers, because he seemed to genuinely dislike my homemade tuna pasta. Sniff.' Gobbledigook

Some children will sleep badly if they go to bed hungry, and obviously this is a cost that is too high for everyone, so providing a suitable pre-bedtime snack is a good idea. Just try not to make it a regular reward for rejecting dinner or you will be forever scraping mince into the food bin while your child wolfs down bread and butter every night.

'I wouldn't make anyone eat food they really don't like. I couldn't send him to bed hungry, though, so I would find a way of filling him up (otherwise he'd just wake up too early and ratty in the morning).' Mistletoe

Fruit Camp

Some mums make fruit available at all times, so anyone who is hungry after dinner can simply avail themselves of the fruit bowl.

'My children eat a lot of fruit and this could be because I never have biscuits or crisps in the house, so fruit is all that is available for a snack.' Elasticwoman

As a rule toddlers seem to favour fruit over vegetables, because it is naturally sweeter and children normally prefer sweet things. But some children refuse fruit as well as vegetables, which is rather annoying because they need their vitamins.

When even one-a-day is a challenge, you need to get imaginative. Try tinned fruit, or fruit in jelly. Dried fruit like apricots and raisins are often popular with small children (and full of goodness, too). Be aware, though, that all dried fruit is seen as the devil's work by dentists – the same or worse than sweets – so ideally it should only be eaten with a meal and a drink (of water, not fruit juice), and you need to be meticulous about teeth-cleaning.

When children are bored or peckish they will often nibble on fruit if there is nothing else to do/eat.

'I get loads of fruit into my son by offering it as snacks when we are in the car. He often just chomps away at an apple out of boredom, though I make sure I keep an eye on him to check he doesn't choke. I also tend to offer it on the way home from a playground, when he's really hungry.' Gingernut

Another mum describes an innovative solution for getting more fruit into her children:

'My two used to like to collect as many different sticky labels off apples, bananas, and satsumas from the supermarket, and stick them in a book. The rules were that the fruit had to be eaten and they weren't allowed to just pinch stickers from the fruit aisle! This worked wonders for increasing fruit consumption.' Mandylifeboats

Milkshakes can be a good way of hiding fruit, especially in the summer when they can be a nice treat after running around in the hot sun. Bananas are easily whizzed into a nice thick shake, and strawberries are popular, too. Add a scoop of vanilla ice-cream and you will have a thick shake that is hard to resist. Likewise smoothies.

Don't forget that fruit juice is also full of vitamins, and although it lacks the fibre of fresh fruit or a smoothie, a glass of fresh juice is better than no fruit at all. Don't overdo the juice, because it's full of sugar and not great for teeth, but a glass or a fruit juice lolly a day is a good start for children who refuse any other fruit, and thankfully counts as one of the five portions of fruit and veg we're all striving for.

If you have tried every technique that you can think of and your toddler still turns their nose up at fruit, you might want to consider supplementing their diet with children's vitamins in various forms – liquid and in 'sweetie' shapes. But have a chat with your GP or health visitor first.

'My son loves vitamin syrup and thinks it is a real treat. I give him some in the mornings so at least I know he's got some vitamins in him.' Casmie

Make do and blend

Summer fruits smoothie
1 peach
1 nectarine
2 apricots
handful of berries

'I buy melons, purée them in the blender and then freeze in ice-cube trays. I then use this instead of ice and blend it all together with different fruits.' *SoupDragon*

Raspberry yoghurt smoothie
1 handful of raspberries
small tub of low-fat yoghurt

Mango and strawberry smoothie
2 mangos (or 1 tin)
punnet of strawberries

Tropical fruit smoothie
1 mango
1 orange
$^{1}/_{2}$ pineapple

'Don't forget to use drinking straws. It makes it more fun, even for me and I'm 44!' *Cakeshoplady*

Chocolate and banana milkshake
1 banana
glass of milk
spoonful of chocolate milkshake powder or cocoa powder
(Sprinkle a pinch of chocolate powder on top if you are feeling
   posh.)

Bananaberry thickshake
sliced-up banana, frozen
handful of frozen berries from a freezer bag
milk

'If your children won't drink smoothies, then put the smoothie mix into ice lolly moulds and freeze. Maybe they'll eat them instead!' *Fussymummy*

Eating in Public with a Toddler

'The same kind of people that moan about children being fed McHappy crap then go on to complain if children are in "their" restaurants ...' Lennygirl

The sight of a toddler in a highchair at the table adjoining yours is apparently enough to strike fear into the heart of many Brits who want their Chicken Cacciatore.and glass of Frascati undisturbed by toddler chatter. Condemning parents who bring children to restaurants comes just as naturally to British diners as condemning parents who take their children to burger bars. And therein lies the problem. How do you teach a child good restaurant behaviour when you are cowering in terror that nice, child-free diners are going to boil over with rage at the first peep from your offspring?

As you may recall from the days before you had children, eating out is an enjoyable and relaxing experience, and one of life's pleasures. Eating out with children does not always meet these expectations, but it is not something that should be abandoned once the little ones arrive. Families eating together in public is an important part of learning about the joy of sharing food together and how you're meant to behave in a public place.

Of course, if you empathise with the Mumsnetter who 'gets easily stressed out by people tutting or staring and usually end up starting an argument,' then it is best to stick to family-friendly places in order to avoid too many scenes. Generally, if you are not 100 per cent certain that your lovely child is going to be an angel with his appetisers then it is best to avoid anywhere with a Michelin Star and customers in silk eveningwear.

If you are lucky enough to have the pleasure of dining out on the Continent you may observe a procession of chortling waiters bringing baskets of crisps and sweets to delight your child, although in the UK the best you can realistically expect is a packet of primary coloured crayons and an A4 sheet to colour in.

'My 18-month-old is generally an angel when we go to restaurants. I put it down to the following things: he MUST sit in a highchair or a comfortable and safe seat; service must be quick or at least he must have something to eat within five minutes, such as bread; I also get him a drink (not the house red obviously); I bring books and a car to keep him occupied; he mustn't be tired, so I get him to nap before we eat.' Pupuce

Back at home, though, our expectations are rather lower. 'I actually don't expect restaurants to go to any particular effort for children but I do expect a friendly welcome and sensible accommodation of their needs,' writes one mother. And restaurateurs take note. 'It's lovely when restaurants have "child packs" on offer, with toys and colouring. That's a really nice way of being friendly and saying, "You're welcome here, and so are your children."' Restaurants that provide a child-friendly service include most pizza chains, family-oriented pubs, eateries in shopping malls and anywhere that prominently displays large red and yellow plastic items.

'It's a good idea, if possible, to have a minimum one-adult-per-child ratio, so that your child can enjoy your full attention without first having to empty the salt cellar on to your lap. As one mum says, 'I think that the more adult the place, the higher the adult-to-child ratio should be.' With one adult per child, it is easier to manage if one child kicks off – you can work in shifts eating and jiggling the noisy child out of earshot, so that at least you can consume the food you have paid for, even if the experience is not quite the candlelit bliss of yesteryear. It is also difficult to coordinate toilet breaks if you have more than one child to manage; many people have returned to the table after a loo visit only to find that their food has been cleared away.

It's worth taking along some things that will distract your child while he is waiting for his food. 'I have a handbag to rival Mary

Poppins,' boasts one Mumsnetter. 'It contains about a hundred small toys and cars, small notebooks and pencils, spare trousers and babywipes.'

'We live in Italy and it's lovely that there are never any disapproving stares (except from English holiday-makers).' Ven95

To avoid crabbiness which might lead to noisy scenes, it is wise to ensure that your child is comfortable before you sit down to eat – not over-tired or starving hungry (give a banana or similar beforehand if necessary) and knows what is going to happen and how she is expected to behave.

Occasionally, despite your best plans, your little one might kick off in a restaurant. A bit of moaning is all very well but no one wants to hear a screaming child while they are nibbling their calamari. 'Placate with treats and take for a walk to cool off and calm down,' advises one dad, and others agree that restaurants are not the place for screaming children. 'If our son has a meltdown we take him outside, and we wait there until he has calmed down, brief him about how he is expected to behave or we will have to go outside again, then go back in. This works pretty well.'

Eventually, you should be able to enjoy eating out with your child. Admittedly, it might not be the leisurely brunch languishing over the Sunday papers that you enjoyed in your pre-children days, but it should be pleasant enough and, of course, a chance for someone else to have their carefully crafted dinner rejected by your fussy offspring. And to cook and wash up afterwards. 'It's so nice when you have a lovely meal out,' sighs one satisfied mum. 'It's like seeing light at the end of the tunnel.'

Mumsnetiquette

Although you might concur with the Mumsnetter who claims, 'Having worked in restaurants I can say without a doubt that old ladies with scones are *far* messier than babies,' it is good manners to clear up some of the detritus that your lovely toddler has left at the feet of her highchair. You don't need to go as far as your mother and scrape and stack the plates, but your waiter will appreciate it if you tidy up the worst of the slimy chewed pasta with your napkin. Cleaning has its own rewards – it is highly possible that the discarded Yorkshire pudding is hiding your house keys. If you have reached the end of your tether and need to make a quick exit, then at least leave a decent tip (of a fiscal nature) on the table, to compensate for the large tip under the table.

Chicken nuggets and smiley faces: how to enjoy eating out with a toddler

- Take them to 'safe' child-friendly places until you are confident about taking them somewhere nicer. Supermarket cafés, child-friendly pubs, most pizza chains, and shopping malls are usually suitable. They tend to be less busy (with fewer people to offend) mid-week.
- Places with buffets are good for hungry children as they mean less waiting. And adults can, with practice, develop an expertise for fitting three courses on one plate to keep eating time short.
- Window seats are a good choice for providing ample distraction in the way of passers-by or pigeons.
- Take reins for highchairs if your child needs serious restraint (and for extra safety).
- Ask to plate up children's food on cold plates (so it's not piping hot when it arrives).

(continued)

- Lots of places will offer half-portions if you want to avoid ordering 'chicken maggots'.
- Take some distractions. Acceptable toys in restaurants include crayons and notepads, small cars and figures. Unacceptable toys include anything noisy, particularly toy phones.
- Eat very quickly.

Wham-Bam, Thank You, Mum: Quick Meals

After a long, hard day at the office or marshalling a two-year-old, often the last thing you fancy doing is cooking a meal. But do it you must and there's no doubt that quick and simple recipes are the way to go. As one mum says, 'I'm struggling with cooking on work nights – I want to get a decent dinner on the table that I can pull together in 10–15 minutes with a toddler fussing round my ankles.'

Another Mumsnetter suggests cooking in bulk and utilising your freezer to reduce the time you spend preparing food: 'Cook double on days you are not working and then defrost it for work nights. Then it's just a question of warming up said meal and maybe doing some accompaniments.' Popular meals to make and freeze include shepherd's pie, cottage pie, pasta sauces such as bolognaise, lasagne, meat stews, curry sauce, chilli and home-made soups.

Lots of Mumsnetters recommend that you go to work (or come home from work) on an egg. A favourite quick meal is frittata. 'I throw in some tomatoes, mushrooms or courgettes softened in a little butter, with parsley and cheese and serve with salad or veg,' says one mother. Omelettes can also be prepared with similar ingredients.

Pasta is a perennial fall-back item for a quick dinner with very little preparation. Mix with pesto from the fridge for a super-simple supper. Pasta and tomato sauce is easy (if you make your own tomato sauce and freeze it in small batches you can just heat some through on the hob). You can add pretty much anything to pasta: a can of tuna, a tin of chickpeas or kidney beans, chopped-up ham, a sprinkling of cheese – or fry some veggies in a pan and mix it all together. Macaroni cheese is easy to make once you have mastered a quick cheese sauce, and a carbonara sauce is a good staple to add to your repertoire – it's nothing more complicated than egg, bacon and cheese. Green pasta, otherwise known as Alien Pasta, is another family favourite.

Alien pasta

Ingredients
olive oil
onion and garlic, chopped
any veg, including fresh or frozen peas and spinach
milk
flour or cornflour
grated cheese
pasta

Fry the onion and garlic. Add any veg you have lying about, plus some frozen peas and frozen spinach (if not fresh), add a little flour or cornflour, slowly add milk to cover, stirring all the time until sauce is thick and veg are cooked. Then whiz in the blender and serve with the pasta and some grated cheese.

Stirfry is a popular suggestion for a quick fresh meal. One Mumsnetter says, 'I stirfry veggies that my sons will eat (thin slices of carrots, baby sweetcorn, beansprouts) in a sauce made from soy, orange juice, honey and sesame seeds, and serve with rice or noodles.' You can grill a bit of fish (such as tuna) or a chop to serve on top.

If you can bear it, meal-planning, where you plan and shop for your week's meals in advance, is the best way to reduce kitchen stress and have easily prepared food on the table. If you have all the ingredients ready then you can rustle up a vast array of delectable dishes in no time at all. Meal-planning might be boring, but it really is far better than sobbing over a large block of cheese at 6 p.m. to the accompaniment of a toddler screaming, 'Eat now, Mum!'

Spaghetti carbonara

Ingredients
olive oil
4 slices of bacon, chopped
2 eggs, beaten
spaghetti

Fry the bacon in a big splash of olive oil until it is crispy. Throw the drained, cooked spaghetti into the pan. Swish it all around. Toss in the eggs and swish for a minute or two until the egg is set slightly (it should set from the heat of the freshly cooked spaghetti, but you can keep the heat on low to make sure it is all cooked as you like it). Serve with black pepper for the grown-ups. You can add a small pot of single cream or crème fraiche to this recipe, and some like frying some chopped onion and garlic with the bacon. But the original recipe is simple.

How to Distract Toddlers While You Cook

Pre-children you probably envisaged yourself merrily perusing farmers' markets and spending afternoons in a floral pinny perfecting wholesome family meals. This soon gives way to the difficult reality of trying not to set the slinged-up baby alight during late-night bacon-frying sessions. Once they become mobile, even a simple task such as draining a saucepan of pasta becomes a health-and-safety nightmare.

There are various techniques to distract a toddler while you get on with the business of preparing food. 'Let your daughter "help" chop the veggies with a blunt knife. She might even eat a few bits while she's at it,' advises one mum. 'Sit her on a chair next to you and give her some of the food to "cook", too.' One mum does all her food preparation at the kitchen table, with her son in his highchair 'helping out' by chopping vegetables. ('We eat a lot of casseroles.')

Playdough and colouring can easily be done by a toddler working next to you on the kitchen worksurface – although keep an eye out for playdough meatballs in your beef stew. Playing with water while standing at the sink will distract a toddler for some time, although cleaning up the resulting flood is often not worth the time it will buy you.

One mum recommends banishing small children from the kitchen from an early age, although this depends on whether you have the sort of child who will happily play by himself, rather than the sort who will scream and throw cars at you until you pick him up. 'We had a stairgate across our kitchen from the moment they became mobile. I used to put their toys on the floor outside the door so they could still see me. Our kitchen is quite small and it would be an accident waiting to happen if one of them was around my feet.'

Allowing your child access to all areas of the kitchen cupboards is a popular distraction technique, and banging on saucepans is of course a traditional toddler pursuit.

'Keep one or two cupboards full of unbreakable things and when he starts whinging, just open the door. I guarantee it will distract him for at least five minutes. For the rest of the time, you need to learn the toddler-hop. It takes some skill, but once you've got the hang of it you can dance over your toddler while he twirls around in search of a leg to cling to. It works best to country music.' SenoraPostrophe

For lots of mothers, this is the perfect time to encourage a spot of television watching. If you have some favourite DVDs then the cooking hour is a great time to put them on. Your child is probably tired from nursery or playing all day, and flopping on the sofa is one way for her to relax and wind down while you get busy. You can always counteract the evil influence of television by giving her a bowl of carrot sticks to nibble while she's chilling out.

Six O'Clock is Wine O'Clock

It's easy to say, of course, but do try not to stress too much about feeding your toddler. From the moment your baby is born, feeding it is such an important responsibility, and when it's not going as planned it is natural to worry and feel that you are somehow failing as a parent. Rest assured that most of the toddler-containing households in the country are sharing your food worries, and don't forget that toddlers were eating and growing long before height and weight charts were invented and when there was not much more to eat than a hunk of bread and some cheese if you were especially good.

Once it's past six o'clock, remember that a glass of red wine contains antioxidants which are reputed to offer many health benefits and seem to be an essential part of many Mumsnetters' diets. Cheers!

Sleep

The No-Sleep Cry Solution

In this chapter ...

Introduction

When it comes to the night shift, the first rule of parenting is to keep quiet and not discuss it with anyone. Particularly health visitors. Or other parents. Or your own parents. They will all tell you that their child slept through from six weeks because they are all better parents than you. They are also likely to mutter the phrase 'a rod for your own back' regardless of what course of action you are or are not taking.

'I have made one of those rod things for my back.' Cappuccino

So let's start by reassuring you that, as one mum rightly says, 'If your child is not a good sleeper, this is not a reflection on your parenting.' Of course we all like to think that if our child is 'good' at something, this is because we are better at this parenting lark than our peers whose children don't sleep, don't eat, have tantrums or smear poo on the dining room walls, but as with so many things pertaining to toddlerhood, there is a wide spectrum of experience and someone always has to draw the short straw.

And if you have read this far, then it's probably you. (And isn't that your child waking up again? Bookmark the page now and come back in 40 minutes.)

As your baby gets older it is frustrating if they don't sleep for longer periods. As they hit other milestones it is natural to feel that they should be 'improving' on the sleep front, too.

'I'm sure that non-sleeping toddlers are much more common than we are led to believe by all these bloody parenting guides.' LoveAngelGabriel

It can be depressing when all your friends' children seem to settle down like good girls and boys and leave their parents with the unspeakable blessing of 12 hours 'off'. 'How come I never meet sleep-deprived mums in real life?' rants one exhausted mum. 'All the ones I meet seem to have it sussed!'

Rest assured (not literally, obviously), we feel your pain. 'I completely relate to the sheer hell of extended sleep deprivation,' sympathises one mum. 'If only my daughter would sleep through – if bloody only – I would feel on top of the world!' weeps another. 'I look like crap with black bags under my eyes, I cannot be bothered to do anything, I feel like I am struggling to be a mum.' And another ended up distraught after taking her health visitor's advice and keeping a sleep diary: 'For the first three nights I was up 17 times. I stopped the diary after that as I wanted to drive off a cliff.'

Toddlers have different sleep issues to those of babies; for a start, they are more physically independent, able to get out of bed and wander around the house, perhaps appearing at your bedside making demands at regular intervals. Moving from a cot is a big change, as is the appearance of new siblings on the scene. And toddlers have their own night-time worries to contend with and articulate, from bad dreams to phobias about everything, including monsters, spiders and the 'scary duvet cover'!

There are two common bugbears that parents generally would like to 'fix': 1. Getting them to actually go to sleep without screaming and thrashing around, and 2. Getting them to sleep through the night. Read on for suggestions about things you could try. And, of course, we'll offer lots of sympathy along the way.

How sleep deprivation affects Mumsnetters

'I'm finding myself filled with irrational rage about tiny things. I'm apparently quite irritable (my partner said this in a shaky whisper from his refuge in the linen cupboard), and I want to cry all the time. I'm also eating quite a lot of chocolate.' *Iaterosemaryconleyforbreakfast*

'I have zero memory and I want everyone to leave me alone. It's been nearly three years now since I've had more than three hours' continuous sleep.' *TrinityTheProgressingRhino*

'I can't do maths. Yesterday I went to buy a newspaper, and pulled out a handful of change. I stared at it blankly, then just held it out so the newsagent could take the right money, like I was abroad.' *Beautiful*

'All molehills seem like mountains. I cry more easily.' *Egg*

'I cope very badly, I have no concentration, I am snappy – basically a bitch to all around me!' *Davidtennantsmistress*

'I go to bed every night at half seven because this is the only time my little one sleeps for three hours.' *Cosima*

'Sometimes I fall asleep on the loo at 3 a.m. and wake up freezing cold 20 minutes later.' *Gingeme*

'I couldn't find my mobile phone earlier and when I checked my bag I found a packet of cheese ... Yes, my phone was in the fridge.' *TrinityTheProgressingRhino*

Does My Toddler Have a Sleep Problem?

The definition of a sleep problem depends on your own expectations, ability to cope with interrupted sleep, family dynamics and ideas about what is acceptable in terms of night-time parenting. Some parents are happy to spend 12 hours lolling together with their children in a giant bed. Others can function quite happily playing musical beds and dispensing cuddles throughout the night. And some parents require 12 hours of children being neither seen nor heard. Whether you have a sleep problem will depend to a large part on where you fit on the spectrum.

Likewise, as far as going-to-sleep is concerned, some parents are happy to sit up on the sofa with their little ones until they drop off; others want the children in bed at 7 p.m. so they can catch up on *Dr Who* and enjoy a curry without being pestered.

So what may be a sleep problem for one is perfectly acceptable to another. If you are OK with the way things are, don't feel obliged to discuss your child's sleep with another parent. Or feel free to just smile and nod and declare, 'Oh yes, they sleep just fine all night!' even if you are secretly spending the night on the sofa while your husband deals with six children in a giant nest of duvets and teddy bears.

Mumsnet sleep statistics

Where does your toddler sleep for most of the night?

- in their own room on their own: 69 per cent
- in a shared room with siblings: 17 per cent
- in the parental bed: 8 per cent
- in a separate bed in parents' room: 5 per cent

The Path of Least Resistance: Taking No Action

Some parents think that crap sleeping is quite normal in a toddler, and comforting them in the night is just a part of the parenting job. 'It is fine to give her whatever comfort she needs during the night,' writes one mum. 'She is small, and night-times are scary without another person there. She isn't doing anything naughty or wrong.'

Others think that if 'sleep training' (encouraging a child to sleep by themselves through the night – more on this later) involves the child getting distressed or crying a lot, then this is best avoided. They choose instead to go with the flow and do whatever the child is happiest with, feeling that eventually, when the child is ready, he will sleep through the night (and, if you are co-sleeping, move into his own room).

'I have sleep conversations with all and sundry and have met several people who had kids who took a good while to sleep through – but I've not met anyone who has said it went on for ever.' Tipex

This approach might mean being physically near the child who is waking during the night, either by co-sleeping in the same bed or room, or having a bed or mattress on the floor of the child's bedroom. If you take this approach, over time (the theory goes) your toddler can eventually be encouraged to move into his own sleeping space, thus avoiding the need for 'training'.

'If I was upset and scared and someone tried to "shhhh!" me without making eye contact I think I would get hysterical myself to be honest.' FrannyandZooey

The main advantage of this approach is that you avoid the need for putting your child through the stress of sleep training, which may involve them getting distressed, i.e. screaming their head off. The disadvantage is that some parents go completely loopy if they have to parent 24 hours a day, and would rather eat their own pillow than have a wriggling toddler's legs kicking them in the stomach at regular intervals throughout the night. But, none the less, if you are the sort who absolutely cannot bear to hear your child cry, and think you can take the pace of night-time parenting, then the 'let it pass' school of thought may be the right one for you.

'My son is nearly three and has never slept well. My husband and I start the night in the same bed but in the morning one of us (usually my husband) is in the spare room with our son. We do moan about it but we actually quite like sleeping with our son. We know he'll grow out of it one day.' StressTeddy

The Big Sleep Issue One: Getting Your Toddler to Sleep

Some parents like to put their children to bed, kiss them on the head, and leave them to fall asleep by themselves. In reality, lots of children want their parents in the room with them, cuddling them or sitting them with, while they fall asleep. Whether you are happy to keep doing that probably depends on how long they take to fall asleep, and how many other things you have to do before you fall asleep yourself.

If you are quite happy sitting with your toddler while he drops off, and if you can get away with reading a book with a small bookmark-light while he is doing so, then you can effectively multi-task (it's good to look busy, especially if your partner is washing up downstairs).

Getting them to fall asleep by themselves method one: Appealing to their better natures

As has been noted before, toddlers often respond well to simple bribery, and it is worth giving this a go when it comes to bedtime shenanigans. Sometimes employing a star chart or a sticker chart, with the promise of treats when a certain target is reached, can have some success. A typical example might be to give one star for going to bed nicely, and one star for staying in their own bed all night.

Some toddlers are more open to bribery than others. 'I can't believe how well bribery has worked!' declares one ecstatic mum. 'We had a look through the Argos book, she chose some Dora rollerskates which she absolutely loves and she is working towards them. She woke last night but I reminded her about it all and she settled with very few tears.'

But others are not particularly interested in the promise of a dinosaur sticker in the morning. So if bribery fails, you might need to think of another strategy.

'When I put him to bed tonight, I said in desperation, "If you stay in your room all night you can have a Milky Way!" but he said, "No, Mummy, me cuddle you MORE than Milky Way."' Popsycal

The old trick of 'I'll come and check on you in X minutes' can work for some toddlers. Say something along the lines of, 'I'll just be in my bedroom and I'll come and check on you in two minutes if you are quiet, otherwise I'll go downstairs.' Some toddlers can be persuaded by this, but do remember to check on them, otherwise they will get very annoyed and won't believe you next time.

You can also try giving them a tool to measure a specified period of time such as a kitchen- or egg-timer, and tell them that you will come back in when the timer goes off.

'Our son has a frog-shaped timer that often helps him get back to sleep. We put it on and say he can call for us again if he's still awake when it goes off. He goes to sleep and we sneak in and switch it off.' Snowleopard

Getting them to fall sleep by themselves method two: Gradual withdrawal

The method called 'gradual withdrawal' or 'gradual retreat' does what it says on the tin, and involves you moving further and further away from your toddler each night, without causing them distress, until you are eventually so far away that you are skipping downstairs where your glass of Rioja and the telly awaits. 'Gradual withdrawal is a good technique for more anxious and tearful children, who are bleating, "Don't leave me, Mummy,"' suggests one mum.

If you are already cuddling your child to sleep, then try one night just holding his hand, perhaps the next night sitting on his bed, and so on. The idea is that your child is still comforted but you move further away each night. Some parents even use this as a method for dealing with middle-of-the-night wakings, by moving the mattress that they sleep on in their child's bedroom further away each night. You must combine this with being as boring as possible, perhaps saying 'shhh' but no entertainment or chat. Eventually (theoretically) you should just be able to comfort your child from outside the room, and then you can sneak downstairs.

'I couldn't bear using any method that involved crying,' confesses one mum, 'so I used gradual withdrawal with no speaking, no lights, just "shhh shhh" and retreating – back to the door then outside the door but where he can still hear "shhh shhh" if necessary.'

Getting them to fall sleep by themselves method three: Controlled crying and rapid return

Controlled crying is controversial because it involves letting the child cry and not comforting them. With this technique, you follow your usual bedtime routine, then put the child to bed and leave. The toddler is likely to then start crying but you do not go back to comfort them; instead you return to check on them after (for example) five minutes. Then you increase the amount of time in between each 'checking' – for example, you might leave it six minutes, or ten minutes, or fifteen minutes. Of course, this method involves some noise and stress for the child and/or you and/or the neighbours, depending on your house construction.

'With my son I followed advice from a nanny and basically we put him to bed and stroked or patted him (which he liked) for thirty seconds, then we left the room for one minute. Then we went back in for thirty seconds to stroke him, then out again for one minute. This went on for a few hours. The next night we stroked him for thirty seconds and left the room for two minutes, and repeated that. When we were in with him we didn't chat or pick him up, but just "shhhed" him. It took about a week but he then settled himself.' Mummymybaby

Crying techniques are not as controversial with toddlers as they are with babies – because toddlers have a much better understanding of their environment than young babies, and you can explain that you are still in the room next door, or downstairs, and will be there all night. Your toddler is also likely to tell you if she is feeling ill, or worried, whereas a newborn just assumes that you are abandoning her to be eaten by bears, or somesuch.

Whether this is right for you and your child is up to you to decide. 'Some people disagree with this kind of thing,' writes one mum. 'But if you are desperate then it is highly effective.' Another admits, 'I used crying techniques, but I am a cruel-to-be-kind Mafioso bedtime bitch.' Yet another agrees: 'Crying and rapid return is an appropriate approach for tantrummy sleep refuseniks.' And one grateful mum declared: 'It's not pleasant and you might cry as much as they do for the first night or two, but if it works as well as it did for us it's worth it. Not only did I feel human for the first time in two years but he was much happier and less tired and grumpy in the daytime too.'

There are a variety of approaches to crying techniques, and you can adjust them accordingly.

Unlike babies, some toddlers are able to get out of bed, so when you are using crying techniques on toddlers you need to employ what is called 'rapid return' i.e. return the child rapidly to her bed.

'I sit outside the door and as soon as I hear one foot on the floor I swoop in, pick the toddler up, pop him back in bed and cover him up. I might say "shhh" but no words and no eye contact. About 100 times the first night, 10 the next. Then never again.' Twiglett

Some parents don't actually bother with the 'returning' part – and just set up a baby gate on the toddler's bedroom door so that he can't escape. 'I often find him asleep behind his baby gate,' confesses one mum. 'I pick him up and return him to bed when I go to bed myself.'

Mumsnet sleep statistics

How long does it normally take your child to settle to sleep?

- less than 10 minutes: 8 per cent
- 10–20 minutes: 20 per cent
- 20–30 minutes: 30 per cent
- 30 minutes or more: 40 per cent
- don't know: 2 per cent

The Big Sleep Issue Two: Sleeping Through the Night

As you have probably gleaned from desperately scouring hundreds of parenting manuals on the subject, over the course of a night humans sleep in cycles of lighter and deeper sleep. Like toddlers, we adults also sleep in cycles, but when we get to the 'wakeful' stage of light sleep, we tend to turn over and go back to sleep, rather than screaming for mummy at the top of our voices.

Annoyingly, because your toddler's sleep cycles are not the same as your own, your own wakeful toddler is likely to whack you over the head with Mr Dinosaur just as you are entering deep sleep, so your own sleep cycles are totally disrupted, and you feel like crap the next day, a phenomenon with which many parents are familiar. 'It feels like being on automatic pilot,' explains one mum. 'Today I put the bottles in the washing machine and the smelly babygros in the fridge.'

'Sleeping-through-the-night' has become the Holy Grail of parenting – because parents really want to sleep through the night themselves. Some parenting theorists argue that 'sleeping through the night' means sleeping for a stretch of eight hours or so – but we all know that what *we* mean is sleeping from the time they are put to bed to a respectable time the following morning. And what this really means is that your toddler learns to do what grown-ups do – to turn over and go to sleep again, rather than start shouting for company and waking himself up fully.

'When should a child sleep through the night?' is a frequent question asked by hopeful parents, but despite the prevalence of urban-mummy myths ('When they reach 20lb!' 'When they turn one!' 'When they can walk!') there is no 'set time' that every child will or should start sleeping through. And generally, children tend to start sleeping a little better here and a little better there, as one mum explains: 'I want to give you details of when or what or how things changed, but the truth is, I can't remember; as soon as I get over one "problem" or stage, I move on to the next and the anguish of now becomes the fuzzy memory of yesterday.'

Do I want to deal with it, or do I want to leave it?

So, assuming that your toddler is not 'sleeping-through-the-night', you have the option of doing something about it, or just going with the flow and seeing if things improve over time. Going with the flow might mean co-sleeping, or popping in to comfort your child during the night.

Before you start any sort of sleep training, sit down with your toddler and discuss the situation. Of course, the first words you probably utter each morning are 'Whhhyyy did you wake last night agaaain?' but actually talking about this with your toddler is essential. She might be able to clarify what she is feeling, and articulate her night-time needs. And 'I want a cuddle!' or 'I'm cold!' are different needs altogether. Resolve what you can.

Only you can decide whether you need to take action or not, depending on what you feel is important to you. 'I am a much nicer mummy if I've had sleep,' admits one mum. 'And it doesn't do any of us any good if nobody has slept, so we decided to take action.' Again, once you decide on a plan, explain things fully to your toddler, so that she isn't confused and scared when your night-time responses are different from what she has come to expect.

Tales from the Dark Side: Extended non-sleepers

'Our son is two years and eight months old and has never slept through. He has rarely slept for more than three consecutive hours. In a normal night he will wake around five times, be in our bed around 2 a.m. and be an absolute menace throughout.' *Popsycal*

'Our son is 20 months and has never slept through. He generally sleeps two to three hour stretches, or four to five if we are amazingly lucky. We've tried controlled crying; it was an outright failure. We've tried other methods, but nothing, nada, zilch. Night weaned, no change. Feed nice stodgy supper, no change. Remove milk and wheat from diet, no change. We count ourselves very lucky if he sleeps through the evening and we get some grown-up time.' *GreenGlassGoblin*

'Our son goes off to sleep at 7.30 p.m., and some nights he is awake again by 8.30 p.m. for up to three hours. He used to be awake every night from 2–4 a.m. He has special needs and this causes sleep problems – and his learning difficulties mean it is hard for him to understand – so different reasons to some, but the same long-term sleep deprivation for us both.' *DingdongmerrALYonhigh*

'Our daughter wakes up all the time so by default we have ended up co-sleeping, purely because we're too exhausted to put her back to bed.' *Mgs7*

'Our daughter is three years and four months old. Up until about three months ago she slept fine but now she is a complete horror. She doesn't like being left alone, so I have to stay with her while she falls asleep and then if she wakes in the night I go back to her. Every single night I end up in her bed or she ends up in mine. She wakes at least four times a night if not more.' *TigerFeet*

Bribery

Try this first. See above.

Co-sleeping

Some parents choose to co-sleep as a way of dealing with the night-wakings. If this is what your child wants, then you might already have filed 'co-sleeping' in the 'doing nothing' box, but actually, co-sleeping is a solution for surviving night-time action for some parents.

'If you're looking for tips to survive, I'd recommend co-sleeping if you're not already – it totally saved my sanity.' Gingerninja

The idea of co-sleeping is that the unsettled and wriggly toddler will be more settled in the parental bed, and so everyone will get more sleep. Not having to actually get out of bed to deal with night-time shouting can be more restful, and toddlers often stop waking fully in the night when they find Mummy or Daddy next to them already.

In practical terms this won't work if you are sleeping with your partner in a 1970s 4ft divan; you will need a reasonably sized bed, especially because toddlers have a natural tendency to sleep perpendicular to their parents. One particularly dedicated co-sleeping Mumsnetter has a '10ft family bed' but for most people, a large double or a double with a single next to it is probably a more realistic furniture arrangement.

'My top tip for co-sleeping is to get a big enough bed. For two adults and one extra, super-king-sized; if you're going to have a toddler and a baby in with you, I'd go for a family bed – a super-king/kingsize mattress plus single mattress next to each other on the floor.' Policywonk

To avoid one person being left blanketless, make sure you have enough duvets to cover everyone – a light single duvet for the toddler might be a good idea. If the toddler is sleeping on the outside of the bed, a bedrail can prevent her from falling out and you won't feel bad shoving her right to the edge so you can have a bit more room.

Some parents opt for co-sleeping but in a more fluid way, involving musical beds – for example, lying down and falling asleep in the toddler's bed when they wake in the night. There are a variety of ways to co-sleep, and lots of parents do it, so if it feels natural and a suitable option for your family, give it a whirl.

'What has worked for us is co-sleeping. I put our daughter in her own bed (a double mattress on the floor in her own room) and we take it in turns to sleep in with her. I start off in my own bed and join her when or if she wakes. She's a child that likes the comfort of co-sleeping and I can understand that. She loves falling asleep with her bottom wedged in my stomach (and I love sniffing her head).' Gingerninja

Some parents operate a sort of 'co-sleeping lite', and have a bed available in their bedroom for night-time wanderers to crash in. 'We have a "ready bed" in our room and our son sleeps in that,' says one Mumsnetter. 'We don't have to get up and down in the night but he isn't sleeping in with us. He starts the night in his own bed, and when he does wake up he goes straight into the ready bed and falls straight asleep.'

Co-sleeping: When do you get your bed back?

'We had our daughter in a sidecar-type arrangement next to the bed and found it worked really well. When she was nearly three we talked up having your own bed and bedroom for ages, pointing it out in stories, showing her the kids' rooms in catalogues etc. Then we chose a bed and bedding, went home and set it all up, and she asked us if she could sleep in there. Simple as that. No real problems, and just as well because our son came along a few weeks after that. He's now in the sidecar. Waiting for three years sounds ages but it goes fast, really.' *SputnikEnRegalia*

'My son slept with us until he was nearly three. We only moved him as he is huge and was taking up too much space. He now happily sleeps in his own bed in his room, settles himself to sleep etc. In my opinion the endgame of co-sleeping is when your child is confident enough of your closeness to sleep well. If and when they move to their own bedroom they are confident, good sleepers.' *KaySamuels*

Be boring

The first rule of dealing with night-wakings is to be very, very boring. If you give in to your toddler's demands for warm bottles of milk, stories, or play, then your toddler will learn that making a fuss leads to entertainment.

As one mum chirrups, 'Light time is the right time; when it's dark it is not playtime!' If you are just a very boring person who stumbles in, places them back in bed and tells them to 'shhhh', then, as one mum advises, 'Eventually, they will realise they are getting all they are going to get, and will hopefully settle better.'

'Our son was a brilliant sleeper from an early age, earning us the rabid hatred of our friends. Now, at two years and nine months, he's much worse. He wakes up several times a night and wants attention so he comes up with all kinds of plausible needs, like his top is itchy and needs changing, he needs a wee etc. – things you can't just ignore. We try to be boring and just keep calmly repeating that it is night-time and bedtime, that there is no option of getting up.' Snowleopard

Reasons for waking at night

If your toddler is waking up at night and you want to stop this, then ask yourself why he is waking, and whether you can address any of these issues. Perhaps he is simply cold or uncomfortable.

If you think that the night-wakings might be caused by something that you can rectify, then try to change this before attempting any other approaches. Take things slowly and try to tackle one thing at a time. For example, if your toddler has no bedtime routine, wakes in the night, takes off her pyjamas and screams for a bottle of milk, there is no point trying to deal with everything at once. Start by resolving one thing at a time and it will be less stressful for everybody.

- **Is he cold?** You could try:
  - a sleeping bag
  - extra blankets
  - tucking blankets in
  - leaving the heating on low
  - a hot water bottle (not too hot!)
- **Is he hot?** You could try:
  - using lighter bedding
  - removing vest/pyjama top
  - opening window
- **Is his nappy too wet?** You could try:
  - a more absorbent nappy
  - changing it before you go to bed
  - waking him and taking him to the toilet when you go to bed

(continued)

- **Does he need a wee?** You could try:
  - (as above) waking him and taking him to the toilet when you go to bed
  - restricting him to only water after late afternoon
- **Is he scared?** You could try:
  - techniques to tackle monsters
  - leaving a light on
  - bringing him into your room/bed
- **Do you make night-wakings fun?** You could try:
  - being very boring: no television or stories or talking
- **Does he wake for milk (bottle or nursing)?** You could try:
  - offering water in a cup instead: leave a non-spill cup by his bed, and show him where it is, so that he can get it himself during the night
  - if you are nursing, send Daddy in to comfort during night-wakings
- **Is he over-tired?** You could try:
  - re-instating a day-time nap
  - putting him to bed earlier
- **Is he not tired enough?** You could try:
  - reducing length of / stopping daytime nap
  - more exercise and fresh air

Keeping Toddlers in Their Own Beds

Waking in the night in order to creep (or most likely stomp) into the parental bed is very common, and if this is something you want to stop, you will need to practise 'repetitive replacement' – i.e. consistently hauling yourself out of bed and replacing your toddler in his own bed. 'Every time he wakes wanting to get into your bed, give him a quick cuddle and put him straight back in his own bed,' advises one mum. 'If he gets up again, just say goodnight, give him a kiss and put him straight back to bed.'

'I have used "repetitive replacement" for toddlers. When the little one wakes or gets out of bed you take them back, tuck them in, kiss them goodnight and go back to bed. No other interaction is permitted; you have to ignore the yelling or the tantrum. If they get out of bed you have to put them straight back in. In reality you will have to do it fifty times a night for a few nights (it usually takes about three nights). It's very hard work and very frustrating when you do it but actually works really, really well.' JennaJ

This will take quite a bit of middle-of-the-night resolve, which is not always the easiest thing to come by, but eventually your toddler will realise that getting into your bed is not an option. 'The first few nights he may scream the house down and you may put him back to bed hundreds of times,' warns one mum, 'but it is all about breaking the cycle.'

'Our son started waking in the night at about two-and-a-half. He would come into our room demanding cuddles. I presumed he was having bad dreams and did cuddle him in our bed for an hour or so the first few nights, but it quickly became apparent that cuddle time was going to become a habit so after four nights we changed tack. As soon as he appeared we picked him up and took him back to his bed saying, "It's still sleepy time. Night-night!" Three nights of this and he realised that it wasn't worth getting up.' Frasersmummy

Repetitive Replacement Lite: Staying by Their Side

All children are different, of course, and no solution is right for all toddlers. For some toddlers, it might be necessary to sit with them while they go back to sleep. 'Our son went through a particularly wakeful phase,' remembers one mum, 'and the only thing which helped was getting up very quickly when he woke in the night, giving him his dummy, and stroking his head or hand until he went back to sleep. Letting him cry just seemed to wake him up more.'

Some toddlers – the type to race after you or rampage around the house – can't really be left to it, so lots of parents find that the best thing to do is to stay with them during night-wakings. 'What worked for us was that one of us went into the room after he'd cried for a bit,' says one mum. 'Then we just sat with him whilst he screamed/wailed/wept, "Mummmiiiiiiiee, Daddddddiiiiiie," until he went back to sleep. We held his hand (if he let us), rested a hand against him, stroked his head, but mainly just made sure he knew he wasn't by himself. Once he was asleep, we crept out again. It did take a couple of weeks but he's been fine since.'

Any approach will take a while to get used to, but the crucial thing is to be consistent, try not to give up after a couple of days just because you're too tired. You need to keep at it if you want to stop the night-time wanderings. But most Mumsnetters agree that 'one or two weeks of being really tough is all it takes.'

Should I Let My Toddler Cry?

When you are dealing with your toddler's sleep patterns and trying to adjust them, there is likely to be a not inconsiderable amount of noisy objection to your plans. The sound of your child crying is horrid, and your urge to comfort him strong. However, by this stage in your child's life, you probably know whether he is crying because he is angry and tantrummy, or because he is in pain or scared. 'Don't leave them crying at night if you are not 100 per cent sure your little one isn't in pain,' warns one mum.

'I tried it for one night before discovering a new tooth the following morning and the guilt was awful!'

'I meet their needs for comfort, I am always there, they are never left to scream in fear/distress/pain/loneliness, but screaming in anger and frustration at not being played with is just not going to make me sit up and play. I deal with it by going in, lying child down, and saying "Shhhhh, sleep." And doing it again, and again, and again.' TheAntiFlounce

Another mum writes, 'When encouraging toddlers to sleep, crying is not always distress. Often it is anger and boredom, and I'm afraid I don't care how bored my children are at 2 a.m., it's not my job to stimulate them.' Yet another mum on her first night of trying to settle her toddler to sleep by herself says, 'I am listening to my toddler crying in her bed at the moment, but when I think about it she was just as hysterical at 8 a.m. when my husband refused to give her a chocolate mini-roll ...'

'We got to the point of desperation when our daughter was just over two years old. Despite being very anti crying-to-sleep techniques, there seemed to be nothing else we could try and our sanity was cracking. It took three nights of her crying, during which we kept going in to her to offer as much reassurance as we could, without getting her out of bed. On night four, she just went to sleep. Aside from the occasional "I can't sleep" night, we really haven't looked back.' Smithagain

If your child is sharing a room with a sibling, dealing with sleep issues with methods that involve crying might mean disturbing the sibling (although some will sleep through anything). If this is the case, you can explain to older children what you are doing ('Your sister needs to learn to sleep by herself like you do, and not wake Daddy and Mummy up all the time, so tonight we will be doing this ...'). You might want to consider letting the more settled sleeper bunk down on a mattress in a spare room or in your room while you deal with the night-time noisiness.

'We bought our five-year-old son builders' ear defenders (like road-menders wear) when at our wits' end with our 20-month-old daughter who shared his room. It made him laugh and somehow took the pressure off. Plus he looked unbearably sweet. Once we knew he wasn't going to be woken, we were able to be tough enough with our daughter to try various forms of sleep training.' Onebadmother

When Good Sleepers Turn Bad

If you have been blessed with a good sleeper, who has allowed you to enjoy long hours of undisturbed sleep since their babyhood, then it can come as a huge shock when she starts waking up in the night. And if you are not already immune to night disturbances, you will feel utterly terrible after a night or two of this, and sink into a state of terror at the thought of it continuing. But the occasional disturbed night (or period of disturbed nights) does not necessarily mean a permanent change of behaviour. Disturbed sleep can be quite common if your toddler is stressed or ill. Try not to be too severe, and if you can bear it, wait it out with some gentle persuasion about sleeping in her own bed (and perhaps a little light bribery). Sometimes the occasional bad night can turn into a pattern of sleeplessness, as one Mumsnetter cautioned: 'Our daughter slept fine till she was really ill with chicken-pox, and we had her in our bed to comfort her. She then decided she'd like to continue with this arrangement even though she was completely better.' When a good sleeper seems on the verge of turning permanently bad, you may need more drastic actions (such as those described so far) to get them back on track.

Monsters in the Wardrobe: Night-Time Fears

It seems quite common for children around the age of two or three to develop night-time fears. These might be fears of the dark, monsters or witches. One Mumsnetter confesses, 'My son is going through a phase of being stalked in his bed by 20ft octopi.'

> 'Night-time can be very frightening for young children. As a child I slept with the landing light on and the door wide open, and used to lie awake, gazing in terror at heaps of clothes that looked like monkeys, despite sharing a room with my sister!' FrayedKnot

It is important not to pooh-pooh your toddler's fears. Although they may be irrational and silly to you, they are very real to her, and as one mum explains, 'It will do no good to say that the monster is not real if he believes that it is.' Another mum says, 'I found that if I actually acknowledged my daughter's fears, rather than saying they didn't exist, it worked better. So instead of rejecting the idea as not possible, we behaved as though it was perfectly reasonable and came up with a solution.'

In terms of solutions, fear of the dark can be eased by giving your child a torch (wind-up ones are ideal if you don't want to spend a fortune on batteries) or leaving a night-light on. Some parents have a night-light that turns on when it is pressed, 'for scaring monsters away'.

When it comes to monsters, you might need a different approach. One mum explained that the monsters were actually very sweet and quite benign: 'When the monsters are mentioned I say things like, "Do you mean the big blue furry one with a huge smile that giggles a lot?" or make up other random funny-looking monsters that are totally gentle and harmless.'

Generally you need to identify the monster in question, then find out its weakness and aim to get rid of the beastie as efficiently as possible. Your toddler may be able to assist with ideas.

'We hung a fairy over our daughter's bed that chases monsters away while she is asleep and in case one ever comes when the fairy is not there we taught her a magic word to say which always gets rid of them. It seems to have worked. (She also uses the word to try and get rid of her brother, although with less success.)' GooseyLoosey

If you have tried everything, but your toddler is still very scared and doesn't want to be left alone, you might want to consider bringing her into your bed for comfort (if that is what she wants). As one mum explains, 'What worked for us was allowing them to sleep in our bed until the phase had passed. With my eldest it was a very short time. With my second it lasted longer, about six months, I have to say. But I think that it is something to help your child through, rather than it becoming an issue of discipline.'

Practical tips for ridding bedrooms of monsters

- anti-monster spray which is sprayed in the room every night (water in a plant spray bottle)
- chase them down the stairs
- flush them down the loo
- stamp on them
- use a dream-catcher

- keep the light on (monsters hate light)
- magic fairy dust (monsters hate glitter)
- put a sign on the door prohibiting entry of monsters
- catch them in a big box and then hoover them out of it
- open the wardrobe door and shoo them out
- place a (cuddly) guard-dog, or tiger, by the bedroom door
- send the monsters off on holiday – somewhere 'really far away' like America or India
- give your child a fairy wand to sleep with

'We have a set of "tingers", small Tibetan cymbals which make a lovely ringing sound. When our son gets spooked we go around the room with the tingers, and the noise fills up the room and chases away the scariness.' *Meemar*

Night Terrors

Night terrors are very different from nightmares, although at first you might confuse the two. A nightmare, as we all know, is a very bad dream and your child might wake from such a bad dream and talk about it – but they are quite conscious and you can (hopefully, with a bit of a cuddle) reassure them so that they can go back to sleep.

A 'night terror' occurs when your child does not actually wake up properly, and appears extremely distressed, crying out and possibly kicking out or running around. It appears as though they are acting out a scary dream. They may have their eyes open or closed, but cannot respond normally to you trying to calm them – in fact, your attempts to reassure them will probably be useless.

'My daughter often has night terrors an hour or two after going to sleep,' writes one mum. 'She will sit up in her bed, screaming and fighting off unknown assailants. She doesn't wake up, although her eyes are open, and she becomes so hysterical that she sometimes makes herself sick.'

'My son wakes up two or three times a week, always between 8 p.m. and midnight, screaming, shaking and moaning. He won't talk to me or tell me what is wrong; sometimes he won't even open his eyes! After five or ten minutes he just lies down, and shuts up. I won't say that he goes back to sleep, because I'm not convinced that he wakes up at all! He can never remember having bad dreams in the morning.' Colditz

Because the child doesn't remember the experience, the 'terror' is mostly suffered by the observer, who isn't able to do anything about it. As one mum writes, 'All I want to do is pick her up and cuddle her, but this just makes her kick and scream even more.'

There isn't much you can do about night terrors, although making sure that your child is not over-tired can help. You need to keep them safe if they are thrashing around and you can try to reassure them, but they probably won't respond to you, however good your intentions.

'I've been told my son will grow out of it in his own sweet time,' says one mum and another agrees that there is not much to be done: 'The best thing to do for the dreamer is simply to stay by them. If left alone it usually passes fairly quickly without any distress for them, but it's nice to have someone there in case they wake up and are confused or worried.'

Moving to a big bed: Softening the blow

If your toddler is still in a cot, now is the time to think about moving her to a big bed. Unless you have lots of money that you like spending on amusing furniture, toddler beds are best avoided – they will need to be replaced in a year or two and can't be used by visiting guests (unless your friends are particularly short). Just invest in a normal single bed.

Some toddlers don't toss and turn a great deal but others roll back and forth all over the place. If your toddler is amenable to it, a toddler sleeping-bag (or Grobag) can stop too much rolling and running around. But you might want to think about investing in a bedrail if the thunk and scream of a falling toddler becomes too regular a night-time sound.

There is absolutely no need to rush the move from a cot to a bed. One mum says, 'We waited until our toddler's toes were sticking out through the bars because we feared the moment we put him in a bed he would realise he could go walkabout – it had never occurred to him to try and escape from his cot.'

Alternatively you could make the landing softer by using a duvet or similar on the floor. 'My son didn't have a bedrail when he moved to a bed at two years old,' writes another mum. 'He fell out a few times to begin with, and we put a duvet on the floor to soften the blow, but he normally didn't wake up when he fell out so it must have been fairly soft.' You could think about using her old cot mattress instead, as recommended by this Mumsnetter: 'We put the cot mattress on the floor by her bed, and shoved it under her bed during the day.' Cushions are another option.

You could also try tucking them in securely so that they can't easily roll out. Another mother suggests 'putting the duvet on sideways and tucking it in firmly under the mattress on either side, so it feels pretty snug and secure.'

Bedtime Routine

For many toddlers, a bedtime routine is an essential part of encouraging a good night's sleep. Keeping things calm and restful in the hour or so before bedtime will make your toddler more peaceful than if she is racing around the lounge playing football with the dog at 8 p.m.

Some toddlers do reliably sleep without any sort of bedtime routine. 'We generally just have an hour devoted to naked pegging it around,' confesses one mum and another agrees: 'Sometimes our son falls asleep over dinner if the day has gone tits up – in which case our routine is me frantically trying to do nappy, teeth and put him into vaguely comfortable sleeping clothes while he reels around sleepily.'

However, most parents rely on some structure to get their toddlers to bed. Most bedtime routines involve doing the same things at the same time every day, ending with sleep. The idea of the bedtime routine is that your toddler will get used to doing the same things and will understand that X follows Y and then eventually it is time to go to bed and sleep. A typical routine would be something like: tea, bath, pyjamas, stories, milk, cuddle and sleep. There are lots of variations on this theme. One mum describes her typical end-of-the-day winding down:

5.00 p.m. – I start getting stressed and clockwatching for the magical hour.

5.01 p.m. – Shout at daughter just because it is 5.01 and it gives me a sense of comfort to do the same thing every day at the same time.

5.02 p.m. – Put tea on.

5.30 p.m. – Partner comes home to find teary, stressed mum, untidy house and child dancing without a care in the world.

5.45 p.m. – Have tea.

6.00–7.00 p.m. – Something magical happens while I drink wine and eat chocolate: my partner takes daughter upstairs to the bath. They play a quiet game, have stories and it is bedtime.
A sense of calm starts to fill the house

7.15 p.m. – I go upstairs telling myself what a fabulous mother I am for having such a calm household; prayers, kiss goodnight.

7.30 p.m. – Sit downstairs with fingers crossed and another glass of wine. Nikkim

'My son is three,' writes another mother. 'We have supper at 6 p.m., then he plays for a bit while I wash up. About 6.30 p.m. it's upstairs to tidy his room, clean teeth and put PJs on. Then into bed and lots of stories and a chat about the day, then lights off and I lie with him until he falls asleep. Between 7.30 and 7.45 p.m. I'm back downstairs for some time to myself! It all sounds quite good and organised when written down like this but as you all know the reality is somewhat different and the times vary a bit!'

Other cues can be built into the routine, such as a special soft light or relaxation music, or taped stories. 'We have a "bedtime light",' writes a regular Mumsnetter, 'which is a lamp rather than the normal room light. Sometimes we get all hippy and instead of a story we switch on his glitter lamp and relaxation music and all sit on the floor in the semi-darkness! It's very chilled!'

The main point of a bedtime routine, repeated each night, is to get your toddler into a relaxed state, so that they are ready to fall asleep by the time they are tucked up in bed. It does require a certain amount of discipline to maintain a bedtime routine day after day, but most parents think that the payoff of calmer evenings is worth the monotony. 'Keeping to a routine can be a bother,' admits one mum. 'But I just do my very best not to let it slip and try to keep it all quiet and subdued – and it seems to work.'

Losing the Daytime Nap

Toddlerhood is, sadly, the stage when the daytime nap may start to be phased out. One day you will be sitting down with your coffee and the lunchtime news, and the next you will be by their bedroom door begging them to close their eyes while they jabber on to you about Humpty Dumpty. The loss of their daytime nap is not the real problem, of course; the problem is the loss of your precious me-time, when you can relax and/or wash a few dishes in luxurious silence. The change from the two-shift day to the long, hard, relentless slog of 12 hours with a toddler can be a very hard adjustment to make.

None the less, toddlers seem to grow out of their daytime nap any time from 18 months upwards. Every child is different, and some will still need a rest in the day right up to school age (lucky parents!). However, if your toddler is simply not going down for a sleep at his usual time, then this transition may be occurring.

'My son is 20 months old. He naps like clockwork every day at lunchtime. Yesterday and today he hasn't wanted a nap. Today I tried to get him to go to sleep but he just wanted to play with me. I really think he still needs a nap and more to the point I need a bloody nap! I'm not ready to let naptime go!' Eenybeeny

However, it is normal for toddler to resist the urge to nap at lunchtime, so don't feel that you have to cave just because they are not interested. Some children do need to continue with a daytime sleep. 'My son has been through several stages of "not wanting to nap" for a week or so but I always persevered,' writes one mum, 'and at three and a half he still naps for two-ish hours every day, which is a godsend to me.'

One mum recommends 'putting them into their room with a kitchen-timer and telling them to play quietly', and it is definitely worth encouraging them to lie down 'for a rest, you don't have to go to sleep' when they are just starting to outgrow their nap; this will give you a break and them the chance to drop off if they need to.

Ditching the dummy

Most parents wean their toddlers off their dummies during the day at first, so that the little suckers only use their dummies to sleep. Don't stress too much about ditching the dummy at night. As one mum says, 'If she only has it at night and it's not an issue at any other time, don't worry too much about making her give it up. It's obviously a comfort object for her. You wouldn't take away a teddy bear so why take away a dummy? She will eventually give it up; you don't see adults sucking on dummies.' If you do want to get rid of it, here are some of the techniques that worked for some Mumsnetters (and see also page 28):

'We cut the teat off the top of all the dummies but gave them to our daughter as normal. She put them in her mouth and said they were broken, so we put them in the bin. At bedtime I spent longer with her and I did offer the dummy with the hole in but she took a few sucks and didn't want it.' *Kbaby*

'We told our son to put his dummy in his Christmas stocking and Father Christmas would bring him an extra present. We told him that Father Christmas needed them for new babies (recycling at an early age!).' *Cornsilk*

'Our daughter stopped having her dummy completely just before she was three. She gave it to her uncle's new kitten who was missing her mummy. It really wasn't an issue at all and it was much easier to get rid of than I had thought it would be.' *Hulababy*

(continued)

'My daughter was three when the birthday bunny took her dummy (for a baby that needed it more) and left her a present for being such a big girl.' *Purplepillow*

'We made a big deal about the dummy fairy coming. We put her dummy in a little box and sprinkled it with lots of glitter and stuck on feathers and pom-poms. The first night she cried at bedtime asking, "Where's dummy?" I reminded her of what we had done and eventually she settled. She got some white chocolate coins from the dummy fairy in the morning.' *Justneedsomesleep*

'My son was three and a half when he gave up his dummy. He gave it to Santa in exchange for some dinosaurs.' *Alwaysthemummy*

Early Mornings

Toddlers and babies who wake early practise a form of horrible torture for which we offer you a good deal of heartfelt sympathy. 'I phoned my childless friend at 9 a.m. this morning to ask about her plans for the weekend,' writes one mum, 'and she shouted at me for waking her up early. We, on the other hand, have already been up for nearly five hours!' 'My daughters both wake at 6ish, and I have just learnt to accept it,' admits one mum. 'But 5 a.m. is definitely still the middle of the night!'

'My son has started waking at 5 a.m.,' sobs one mum, 'and is wide awake, jumping up and down in his cot like it's the middle of the day! He shouts, "Get up, go downstairs!" at the top of his voice.'

Of course, your first approach should be to tell your toddler that it is still night-time and she should go back to sleep. For most parents, doing absolutely anything to get them back to sleep at this time of the morning is perfectly acceptable, whether that means cuddling them or bringing them into your bed.

If the early wakings are coinciding with the lighter summer mornings, then think about investing in some blackout blinds or similar window coverings.

For older toddlers, it might be worth investing in a 'morning clock' which is specifically marketed at parents trying to tackle this problem. The clock will change at a specified hour (e.g. a rabbit face will open its eyes) and you can instruct your toddler not to wake until this transformation has occurred. You can try using a digital clock, and instructing them not to get up until the first number is seven (or similar), but this relies on them being able to read numbers in the correct order.

'The main problem with our plan was the presence of THREE numbers on the digital clock. So apparently 6.27 counts as the same as 7.00. My partner is now suggesting sticking a piece of paper over the two irrelevant numbers.' FrannyandZooey

Alternatively, you can put a lamp on a timer and tell your toddler that if the lamp is off, it is still night-time, and he needs to stay in bed until the lamp is on.

There is one technique that some Mumsnetters recommend trying with persistent early wakers called 'wake-to-sleep'. If you wake them an hour before their usual waking-up time, rousing them slightly from their deep sleep and leaving them to re-settle, then (the theory goes) you might disrupt their sleep pattern so that they don't wake at the usual time. So if they normally wake at 5 a.m., you will need to set your alarm for 4 a.m. (yes, we know it's horrific) and then go in and rouse them. 'You don't wake them fully,' advises one mum, 'just enough so they are almost awake – and you then leave them to re-settle. You can rub their face slightly, or lift the duvet off them.'

After three days you can let them sleep through and see if they will naturally wake at a more respectable hour. If not, you can try it for five or six days in a row (is it sounding like fun yet?) and then let them sleep through.

'I did wake-to-sleep with our son when he had a phase of waking at 5 a.m. It was hideous getting up at 4 a.m. to wake him, but in a funny way it was better than knowing he was going to wake anyway.' RubySlippers

Blackout blinds

The hormone that regulates sleep is called melatonin and is triggered by darkness. Therefore most children (and most grown-ups too) sleep better when the room is dark. When the sun starts to light the room, it signals wake-up time and you are likely to end up with a bouncy toddler thinking it's time for his morning telly at 5 a.m. Of course, all sensible grown-ups know this is still very much night-time, but the streaming sunlight is your toddler's cue to start the day, and you may struggle to persuade him otherwise.

Darkening the room using blackout blinds can help to convince your toddler that it is time to roll over and go back to sleep for a couple of precious hours. As one mum writes, 'A decent blackout solution is worth every penny, particularly when it is very difficult to get a child to sleep during the summer months.' However, as many parents have discovered, truly blacking out a room is not as simple as buying one blackout blind. Except for closely fitted blinds on Velux windows, most blackout blinds will leave gaps between the blind and the window frame which allow so much light to penetrate that they could guide the entire Luftwaffe straight to your toddler's cot. You won't be the first parent to attempt to keep out the light by using a variety of cardboard boxes, pillows, Sellotape and Blu-tack, so here are a few tried and tested ideas from Mumsnetters for keeping your toddler's room dark.

Off-the-peg solutions

- 'You can buy blackout curtains that you can just hang behind your existing curtains.' *Meep*
- 'The "Baa-Baa Blind" is a portable blackout blind which sticks to the window using suckers. It has a sort of frill that extends over the frame of the window and is very effective.' *Vanillapumpkin*
- 'You can buy a blackout blind that is basically a sheet of blackout material that Velcros to the wall outside the window frame. But it makes one hell of a noise when you open it!' *Fizzylemonade*
- 'Try your local blind shop for customised blinds (but remember that they will still leave a gap around the edge, unless you have Velux windows). Sometimes larger blinds fitted on the outside of the window recess are more effective than smaller blinds on the inside recess.' *Stephanie1974*

Homemade solutions

- 'I buy leatherette and make my own blinds.' *Divvy*
- 'If you are handy with such things you can buy a load of blackout lining and make a simple blind yourself. Or even just sew some Velcro to a piece of blackout lining, cut to size and stick it over the window at night.' *Indith*
- 'I cut a blackout curtain to fit the exact size of the window. I then folded down a big hem along the top of the blind so it makes a sort of channel, and hung it up on the inside of the window recess using a sprung shower curtain rod. The blind then fits the window almost perfectly and very little light gets through.' *Mrsmalumbas*

Desperate measures

- 'We hang dark towels at the window.' *Meep*
- 'I Blu-tacked tinfoil on my son's bedroom windows, which worked a treat. You could open the windows and it kept the heat of the sun out in summer.' *Kiera*
- 'I ended up sticking thick black paper directly on to the windows. It worked very well, although it isn't pretty, and means no natural daylight during the day.' *Bijou*
- 'When mine were young, I used black binbags ... I was broke back then!' *Divvy*

And So to Bed

'Sleeplessness makes you totally hardcore.' Gingerninja

Sleep. Nothing is more lovely than the beautiful sight of your perfect toddler angelically at peace with her world.

Sadly, sleep and parenthood are often irreconcilable states, and there is no 'sleep solution' that works for all children, or all parents. There are lots of parents out there in the same boat, struggling to work bleary-eyed and incapable of putting together a coherent sentence before they've spent the morning downing strong coffee. 'I have developed coping strategies and I am used to it now,' boasts one perhaps slightly hysterical mum. 'Sleep is overrated in my opinion!'

When you are groaning into your pillow at 2 a.m. (and not for any pleasurable reason), take comfort from the fact that all over the world there are parents in a similar position. 'People ask me about my baby and assume that my older children sleep through!' shrieks one mum. 'Do they heck! They don't even have the decency to all wake at the same time; they take it in turns all flipping night.' But rest assured, eventually, your children will grow up and will sleep better, or at least leave home so you won't be too disturbed if they don't.

Sleep tight!

Note: All statistics in this chapter cited as 'Mumsnet sleep statistics' are from the Mumsnet sleep survey for Grobag; 1,039 respondents (all parents with toddlers), March 2008.

Potty Training

The Long and Tortuous Road to Coming Home in the Same Trousers

In this chapter ...

Introduction

Pre-children you might have thought parenthood was all about barbecues on beaches and children chortling gamely as they knocked a football around the garden. But no, here you are in your front room facing a pot full of human excrement and wondering how best to scrape it out.

Inevitably there's a frisson of apprehension in any parent who decides to take the plunge and bring out the potty. And it's not just because they're protective about their sisal carpets. Ever since Sigmund Freud declared that incorrect potty training techniques could lead to lifelong personality problems, parents have fretted that if they mess this up they'll condemn their poor, incontinent children to a lifetime of expensive psychotherapy.

Some psychologists still maintain that toilet training is a formative experience in the development of a child's personality, because they say it is the child's first introduction to the idea that social obligations can take precedence over bodily desires. (Clearly these psychologists have never been confronted by a hungry baby demanding their breasts when they have just sat down to a steaming hot latte and a plate of brownies at the local café.)

The general consensus nowadays is that toilet training is a process that needs to be undertaken as a project of mutual cooperation, at a time when the child (rather than the parent) is ready, and with as little stress as possible. So grab hold of your chocolate buttons, and to hell with Freud (and your carpet).

Which Approach?

There are two main approaches to potty training: the gradual method, which starts at any time between nine months and two years; and the 'cold turkey' method, which is tackled when the child is around two to three years old.

The gradual method is the more traditional way to toilet train, and introduces young children to potties in much the same way as knives and forks are introduced – i.e. when they are too young to really understand what is going on and everything is most likely to end up smeared down their fronts and/or clattering to the floor. The gist of gradual training is that the young child will slowly begin to learn how to go to the toilet himself by gradual encouragement and taking 'baby steps'. The gradual method takes a long time and has fairly low expectations of immediate results.

The more favoured and commonly used approach by parents these days is to go 'cold turkey' at the point when you think your child is physically and emotionally ready. This happens sometime after 18 months, but usually between two and three years of age. This method involves deciding that your child is ready, talking it through with them, and then putting them in pants and dealing with whatever happens until hopefully, within a week or two, your child uses the potty or toilet instead of his nappy during the daytime.

There are, of course, many approaches which combine both methods and some other more extreme ones (of which more later). Which you choose is entirely dependent on how you and your partner (if you have one) feel about it. Neither is better or morally superior to the other. Just do whatever you can summon the most enthusiasm for – and don't feel pressured by what 'everyone else' is doing. Bear in mind that most studies suggest that whether you decide to train gradually or go 'cold turkey', it won't make a huge amount of difference to the age at which your child is reliably continent.

Early starters

There is undoubtedly a pretty wide potty-training spectrum. At one end, you have four-year-olds still being wrestled on to potties, and at the other, you have tiny babies wearing knickers with nervous-looking parents hovering nearby.

Some parents are big fans of extremely early potty training. This is also known as 'Elimination Communication' (or EC). ECers maintain that there are various signs that indicate that their baby is about to do the deed, at which point they hold the infant over a toilet, often making a 'sssss' noise when the baby pees. Over time, the adult becomes better at recognising the baby's signs, the baby becomes better at associating the need to wee with the action of going-in-the-correct-place, plus the baby becomes better at communicating its need to go to the toilet in a more conscious way.

As one experienced ECer explains, 'ECing is a traditional method of raising babies which millions of mothers worldwide use today. Disposable nappies were invented in 1941; before then people used a combination of cloth nappies and ECing depending on culture and environment.'

'My daughter is eight months old but hasn't done a poo in her nappy for about two months now. She gives a certain look and then a grunt. I put her on the potty and nine times out of ten she will poo.' Carwillin

It's a slow process and the aim is not to have a 'potty-trained baby' in the commonly understood sense of the word – meaning a baby wearing knickers – but to build up a rapport between the carer and child. 'Don't get hung up about the number of catches versus misses,' says one mum who successfully used this method. 'It really doesn't matter. The thing that matters is that you are communicating with your baby; some days you'll communicate better than others.'

The gradual method

A less extreme approach starts with a slow introduction to the potty from an early age and just encouraging a bit of potty action when the child seems interested. This is probably the way that most of our grandparents potty trained their children, introducing the potty as early as possible in the hope of ending the daily chore of washing terry nappies. To start, you need the potty to become a familiar object, perhaps using it in the context of imaginative role play (although quite how imaginative you can be with a potty only you will know).

If you are gradual training you need to make it as stress-free as possible. Encourage your child to sit on the potty whenever she wants to – perhaps during nappy changes, when she already has her nappy off. You can also encourage her to use the potty when you are going to the toilet, so you can sit side-by-side and witter away with a commentary about what is going on (best not to do this too loudly if you have house guests).

Time spent on the potty should be fairly short – a minute or two at most – perhaps with a short story or a song to keep things laid-back and enjoyable (your child might like it, too.). You can put her on the potty as often as you and she want, but to start, it might just be once or twice a day.

You can also put your child on the potty if you think that they are just about to go to the toilet. Young children often wee or poo after naps and meals.

'I started by putting my daughter on the toilet when she was naked during bathtime and she began to poo. Later on she started telling me that she needed to go by pointing at the toilet. At 14 to 15 months she was telling me when she wanted to wee as well – not every time, but some of the time. By 17 months she was totally dry in the day.' MagicalMay

Many mums followed the advice in the popular *Baby Whisperer* book by Tracy Hogg which advises potty training from ten months. As one happy customer explains, 'You can put baby on the potty when they wake up, 20 minutes after a meal/drink (or whenever they usually go if you are already aware of this), before and after naps, before a bath etc. You sit them for no more than a few minutes, and if they do something in the potty, then you go overboard with praise. After a while they may start to signal when they need to go, or keep dry/clean in between. Once they've been dry/clean for a week or two, you can safely put them into pants, although this didn't ever happen for us so we just made the transition to pants at 16 months.'

The gradual approach to potty training from an early age should be taken at a slow pace and, most importantly, it should be fairly stress-free. Grabbing your child and screaming hysterically, 'Hold on!' before charging to the loo and thrusting them on to the toilet seat might be a perfectly natural reaction to preventing a poo plopping on your best rug but it probably won't help save it in the long run.

Cold turkey

Judging by the Mumsnet mums this is probably the most widely used potty training method these days. Going cold turkey means deciding that your child is ready to become a fully fledged knicker-wearer, and dispensing with the nappies in one fell swoop. Every child will be 'ready' at a different time, so don't worry too much about keeping up with the Joneses and their children – sadly, your child's bowels will not respond purely to peer pressure.

'I tried my daughter at two-and-a-half years because everyone else was trying and as she is very tall I felt pressure from others who thought she was older. It was a disaster. I tried again at three and it still took weeks with lots of accidents.' Jasnem

Making the decision to start potty training is daunting. You have just got the hang of the basics of parenting – food in one end, cleaning up the other end – and suddenly you are expected to have acquired the ability to potty train, a whole new skill. It can feel a bit like being asked to tame a lion (we'd imagine). But you can do it, and one day soon your child will be the master of his bladder – so invest in a nice new mop and try to remain calm at all times.

So How Do You Know the Time is Right?

Pretty soon after your baby celebrates his first birthday, older female relatives are likely to start muttering about getting him out of nappies – most likely claiming that you were toddling around in proper pants by the age of nine months. It is true that our generation tends to start potty training later than previous generations. This is most likely because our mothers spent much of their lives dealing with buckets of messy terry nappies, a chore they were undoubtedly keen to dispense with as soon as possible.

These days, there is less of an incentive to potty train, with disposable nappies and scented nappy sacks whisking all the nastiness away with very little effort (although perhaps a little more environmental guilt) and it is generally advised to wait until the child is ready.

'My son is nearly two, but he has started to wee in things: the mop bucket, my shoes. He even weed in my cup of coffee.' Fawkeoff

Children who are starting to wee directly into your morning brew purely for entertainment purposes are probably ripe for toilet training, as are those who start telling you that they need to go, or tug at their nappies when they've gone. If you're not sure whether the time for big-boy pants is nigh but think it might be, the general advice from mums is to give it a shot – to go cold turkey for a few days and see if you progress.

'OK, it's probably too early to get smug. But he was in the garden all day today, running around with no clothes on as it was so warm, so I got the potty out and gently suggested he used it. For the rest of the day he did all his wees (about 12!) and poos (3) in it, without any prompting. No accidents, no fuss, although he was quite pleased with himself. He's 23 months and although I was vaguely thinking we might try training this summer I wasn't prepared for him doing so well at the first attempt! So ... what now? Is it likely to be a one-off or do I need to stop using daytime nappies outright?' Thinktoomuch

'Many children are ready before the age of two. Be prepared that even though he is clearly

ready for pants, he will still have the occasional accident. All part of the learning process and not a reason to put him back in nappies.' Belgo

Potty training: Signs of readiness

- Over 18 months in age. Unless you are feeling adventurous and want to have a go at very early potty training, wait until your child is at least 18 months old (and in most cases over two years old). Generally before then, their bladder and bowels are not under their control.
- Ability to comprehend and follow simple instructions (such as, 'Please put your teddy on the chair').
- Interest in potty.
- Awareness of doing or having done poo or wee (for example, concentrating, telling you, or trying to remove nappy).
- Going to a certain 'safe' place to poo or wee in her nappy (behind long curtains seems curiously popular).
- Frequent dry nappies when waking up from naps (this shows they are starting to gain some control).
- Weeing in your coffee/shoes/mop bucket for comic effect.

When deciding on the right time to train, it is worth giving some consideration to the time of year, for practical reasons. Summer is best, because the child will need fewer clothes or can run around naked, plus the washing dries more quickly.

However, there may be good reasons to buck the trend, if you think your child is ready. One mum took action at Christmas, because her son was physically ready if not quite willing: 'He was ready. He knew when he was going, he could dress and undress himself, and had the language. But he just could not be bothered. So we put out all his cloth nappies, liners and wraps for Santa on Christmas Eve. Santa left lovely presents (including underpants). He was trained for wees quite quickly.'

Let's Go Shopping

'What do I need to start toilet training?' is a frequent cry heard on Mumsnet. The answer, as summed up by one potty-training veteran, is simple: 'Patience – lots of it.' And then she adds, 'And floor cleaner – lots of it. And Dettox – lots of it. And pants – lots of ...You get the idea!'

Choose your potty

Don't worry too much about the type of potty you choose. As one mum of two puts it, 'A potty is a potty! Take your child with you and let them try a few for size, fit and colour.' You might want to look for a larger size if your child is an older toddler or has the mother-in-law's genes in the bum department, and you might want to buy a few, particularly if your house has more than one storey.

'Make sure that the potties are big enough. Mine were all quite late training and I bought a baby one by mistake with a tiny little seat, which was the cause of much whinging and wriggling.' OrmIrian

Many mums advise encouraging your children to take a leading role in the potty shopping trip, as it will hopefully encourage them to think of the potty as an exciting new toy that they will want to use and play with. Some also choose to have a special 'toilet book' to while away the hours with a bit of literary distraction while encouraging sitting on the potty for longer periods waiting for loo action.

'We opted for a pet-potty in the shape of a turtle, although our daughter became rather attached to it and we had to buy an identical one to have at her grandparents' house.' Kteepee

Some choose not to use a potty at all and go straight for the toilet option with a toilet seat fitted inside to prevent the child from disappearing down the loo. 'I didn't bother with a potty with my third son,' reminisces one mum. 'I had learned from my girls that they liked to show me what they had done, which was not very pleasant.'

Bums on the run: Travel potties

It's a good idea to have a potty on hand pretty much all the time in the early stages of toilet training, because small bladders are not always able to accommodate the trek to the nearest public toilet. Travel potties are small potties, some of which fold up so they are quite compact and discreet (or as discreet as possible considering that you are going to dangle a naked bottom over it to defecate in a public place).

A travel potty is small enough to fit into a changing bag, but it is not the most glamorous of yummy-mummy accessories and you will need to brace yourself for strange looks from members of the public who will think you have slipped a sanitary towel into a freezer bag.

'Our travel potty was used a lot in the early days, and with everything being "done" straight into a bag it was easier to clean up and get moving again afterwards.' Loopymumsy

If you are wary of the dangers of bumpy roads and potty-spillage, there are potties with well-fitting lids on the market, which come in handy when you are camping, too. You don't want to take the kids trekking across a field in the middle of the night for a wee.

'Get a potty for the car as well as one for home. Mine was £1.74 from Asda. (Potty, that is, not the car.)' Gingerbear

On the other hand, you may take the view, as one mother of three does, that 'anyone who drags a potty around town with them needs their head examined.' If so, you can buy handy folding toilet seats, which are small enough to fit in your handbag but large enough to cover a normal lavatory seat to prevent your small child from slipping in and drowning. (Alternatively, your child may be quite happy to perch on the toilet seat while you hold on to them.)

Other toilet-training paraphernalia

For night-time training, waterproof sheets, pillow cases and duvet covers are available (although most people would recommend using nappies if night wetting is a persistent problem). Plus you can buy a little plastic step for the loo which encourages independence for small children who can't clamber on and off the toilet by themselves.

A nice way to incentivise your little trainee is to take them on a special shopping trip to buy their own 'big boy' or 'big girl' pants. Many pants feature familiar faces from children's television shows, which are very popular with most toddlers and help to encourage them to use the toilet. After all, no one wants to pee on Dora the Explorer. Set aside a special 'knicker drawer' and make this rite of passage part of the toilet training ritual.

'My daughter is very proud of her "knicker drawer" and loves to choose which knickers she is going to wear in the morning.' Callisto

Training pants are super-absorbent pants made of towelling which some parents feel are useful for the early days when accidents are likely – they allow you to whisk away a wet child for clearing-up, thereby saving them the embarrassment of leaving behind a crowd of people staring at a Puddle of Shame.

One mum of girls dressed them in boys' pants for early potty training: 'They are generally made of two layers of thick absorbent cotton – whereas girls' knickers are made from flimsy thin poly-cotton and lacy bits, which wee just streams through. Wearing boys' pants and absorbent flannel-lined trousers, my girlies are ready to go out and about without me stressing about the possibility of leaving puddles in the M&S food hall.'

Going Cold Turkey: How to Begin

Once you have made the decision that your child is ripe for potty training, make sure you have your partner on board. You need to agree on an approach and both of you need to be consistent and remind each other not to over-react when things get messy (and wet).

The next person you should sit down and talk to is your child. Small children understand a lot more than we tend to credit them for, and a pep talk at this stage is crucial. After all, you would be a little confused if you woke up one morning and your partner had hidden all your underwear. It is much the same.

Potty training boot camp (by Mumsnetter Cod)

Rules

- Children must be over the age of two (the best age is two to two-and-a-half)
- There is NO going back. Do not start if you are going to poof out. You go COLD TURKEY. This is vital.
- Remember it is hard work – that's why it's called 'training'. Yes, life WILL be more difficult for a couple of weeks.
- Do NOT use pull-ups for daytime naps or anything short of a two-hour journey.
- The child must be well and not poorly or miserable.
- Night training is a wholly separate issue.

Procedure

- Preparation. Explain to your child that he is a big boy by now and soon he will do his poos and wees in the potty or toilet, and not in his nappies. Let him go shopping to select his own pants.
- Choose your day. Get your head around the fact that you are starting properly tomorrow; have your partner on board; gather together your gear (new pants, large basket of spare clothes, chocolate buttons or appropriate bribes, potty or potties).
- Stay at home for the first couple of days.

Now we begin

- Put child in fabbo pants of choice (or leave naked).
- Take don't ask. Take them to the loo as often as you see fit – say every thirty minutes. When you go to the loo, make sure you take them with you to sit on the potty (if you are using one) next to Mummy while you wee in synchrony.
- Put him on the potty and, if necessary, distract him with a story.
- Reward with extravagant whooping (and sweets, if necessary) for weeing in the correct place (or telling you at any time they need it even if they then miss the loo).
- Important! When they perform you must go crazy with whooping and clapping. Also you must pretend to ring people up (or actually do so if you have understanding friends) to tell them of the good news. A chocolate button may be awarded if deemed necessary.

- If they wee on the floor just remind them (through gritted teeth, if necessary) to go in the loo next time. ('For God's sake' to be muttered UNDER YOUR BREATH.) Just say, 'Where do we wee? On the loo.' The weeing on the floor can go on for a couple of days if not a week.
- Put a care-mat under him at nap-time.
- When you go out take several changes of clothes. Better a wet outfit than a nappy.

Feedback from boot camp graduate

Cod, I followed your advice in your last potty training boot camp and it worked brilliantly well. I think I was very lucky in just happening to choose the right moment and my daughter understood almost immediately what was required of her.
Callisto

Timing is everything. Not only should you feel confident that your child is physically ready, it's also good to ensure you're not starting toilet training during a period of stress, such as moving house or nursery, or a new sibling being born. If possible, avoid times of stress in your own life, too, because this will help you not to over-react when things get tough.

Manage your expectations (and those of your partner). Expect *at least* two or three days of puddles, and pooey pants, if not more. When accidents do happen take him to the potty and sit him on it to make sure there isn't any more (sometimes children stop themselves mid-flow). Give him a quick wipe or swish with a flannel and put him in some clean pants. NB Don't flush wipes down the loo, a blocked loo and a potty training child is a lethal combination.

'The first two days are GRIM but hang on in there!' advises a veteran potty trainer. 'On day three it will really come together.' The ratio of wees-on-floor to wees-in-toilet should definitely improve over a few days. Within a couple of weeks, you should expect only occasional accidents and can start to relax.

Not everyone can cope with losing nappies at nap-time/for long car journeys straight away. The possibility of losing precious me-time, travelling for an hour or more in a wee (or worse) smelling car and/or coping with a grumpy toddler who has been woken prematurely by being wet is not worth contemplating. Although the 'boot camp' routine of complete cold turkey will have speedier results, there is no shame in using the odd 'insurance' nappy for sleeps and car journeys. Make sure the toddler uses the potty before putting the nappy on and as toilet training progresses, you will find their 'insurance' nappy is increasingly dry post nap/journey. Once you've had a few dry nappies, you can feel more secure about losing them altogether.

Accidents will still happen, even in a toilet-trained child – often when they are totally engrossed in an activity. Expect this during the early months (and even years), and try to remember not to make a big deal of it. And, above all, don't spend too much on nice carpets and sofas if you have young children.

Mumsnetiquette: Do not empty your potty in your host's kitchen sink

Just as one would not encourage one's husband to whip out his todger and urinate on the dirty dishes at a dinner party, it is most definitely not acceptable to empty potties down friends' kitchen sinks when on playdates. Go in search of a bathroom or visitors' loo. You will find that they will have a room furnished with a lavatory for the handy disposal of bodily fluids. Empty potty, rinse and dry with toilet paper (not on the guests' hand towel). Employ a handy antibacterial wipe if they have them (but don't flush wipes down the loo, they cause blockages). Wash your hands. And with any luck, you will be invited back.

The Great Pull-Up Controversy

Pull-ups are nappies shaped like pants which children pull up themselves. Some, however, argue that pull-ups are not helpful because they don't let the child feel that they have wet themselves, and so are no different from nappies. As such, they just delay the toilet training process. 'Pull-ups make them immune from the consequences of weeing,' explains an old hand. 'They need to have a few accidents to get the point. Be gone with your devil's pull-ups.'

'After using pull-ups for a while I decided to go cold turkey: no nappy, no pull-ups, half-hourly toilet visits at first – and we did it in about a week. You were right. Pull-ups ARE the work of the devil, a complete waste of time and money and very confusing.' Donbean

Sometimes, though, there are occasions where you just need to be 100 per cent, copper-bottomed sure. Weddings, christenings and visits to the in-laws come to mind. At times like this a temporary pact with the devil is entirely understandable.

Bribery and Corruption

There are not too many toddler behavioural issues that cannot be resolved with chocolate buttons, which pass as currency for children under the age of three. Bribery is generally recommended as the tool of choice for luring small children on to the toilet and doing their business there, and sweets are the number-one bribe of choice among Mumsnetters.

Bear in mind that it doesn't last for ever; we give you our word that you won't still be handing out jelly babies when your 12-year-old has his morning bowel movement.

Many use chocolate as a bribe, although for one trainer this proved so desirable that it had the unfortunate result of her son constantly straining to poo: 'Weeing was fine – stickers did the trick for us. Poos were a bit more of a problem and I eventually offered chocolate. That backfired as he then decided to try to poo at every possible opportunity, and I'm sure nearly ended up with piles! I caught him sitting on the loo, swinging his chubby legs, chanting to himself, "Do a wee, get a sticker. Do a poo, get some chocolate."'

'My daughter got a jellybean for wees and a choice of three different sweets for a poo. Once she had got the hang of it she stopped reminding me (and I quite often forgot). Then I decided if she had no accidents all day she could choose her treat at the end of it. Then we progressed to over 24 hours (she went night dry very quickly). Then it just passed and going to the toilet got so much of a habit that it didn't come up.' Chuffed

If you're shrewd and health-conscious, and your child is easily pleased, you can go for wholesome fruits by way of a bribe instead – grapes, blueberries and raspberries seem to work well – and no doubt lead to healthy bowels as well as well-trained ones.

As well as confectionary (and the odd berry), stickers and sticker charts are recommended. These are basic charts (often in the format of a calendar week) where the child receives a sticker 'reward' for every incident of the required behaviour (in the case of potty training, a poo or a wee in the desired location). Websites for children's channels often have reward charts based on popular television characters that you can download and customise.

'I've found a good way of getting them on the toilet is to put one of those coloured toilet blocks in the cistern and their reward is to flush and watch the bubbles – "see how many bubbles they can make" sort of thing. Although I recommend supervision. My son tried to scoop the bubbles out with his hands.' Flip

Toddlers are as close as they come to being praise junkies and potty training is a time when you can use their addiction to pleasing Mummy to your advantage. Some people advise not to go overboard with praise because it makes the process into too much of a big deal. However, most seem to agree that lavishing them with praise for producing the goods is an essential part of the process.

Freud would no doubt have something to say about one Mumsnetter's unique approach: 'We send the wee-wee down the toilet to granny and then phone to make sure she's got it.' Broadcasting the good news by phone is also a popular choice. One mother-and-daughter combo habitually call Dad at the office to tell him the good news: 'We ring Daddy, and she informs him in a long, rambly manner how she did a poo in the toilet. For some reason my partner finds this wonderful. I guess he must have a terribly boring job.'

Techniques for Reluctant Trainees

Unfortunately children are not quite as responsive as dogs to the command 'Sit!' When you *know* your child needs to get on that potty but they are adamantly refusing, things can get stressful. The solution in one case was cheery distraction: 'I just picked him up and sat him on the potty regardless of his protests and then distracted him with chatter about what was happening on the TV. He produced a very large wee that I'm glad he didn't do on the rug.' Another mother opted to sing 'I Hear Thunder' and 'Pitter Patter Raindrops' – 'to get him in the mood'.

Techniques for Boys

While little girls obviously sit down to learn the potty business, what exactly does one do with little boys? The consensus from mothers of boys is that for very practical reasons it is best to start by sitting down, as a boy needs to learn to push his willy downwards to avoid spillage. You might also like to contemplate that in the early days of potty training they can't always distinguish between letting out a wee and a poo – not a mistake you'd want him to be making while standing up. What's more, in the early days, when you're trying to encourage them to sit on a potty until they've done their business, it's easier to keep them in a leisurely seated position than standing at a toilet.

Some boys do start to learn standing up, however, including one little boy who at the same time learnt the art of manly competition from his father: 'He follows his dad's example. They do "wee-wee races" together.'

> 'I tried to start my son sitting down but he was having none of it. He is two years and three months and kept saying, "Wee-wee like Daddy"… grrrr. It made for a lot of fun while he was learning on the potty as his aim was rubbish. However, we are now three weeks on, and he is using the toilet standing up and is really good at it.' Nemo1977

Eventually, all little boys will realise that standing up is The Thing, and will start to wee just like Dad. Once they do, there are various tricks to teach boys to aim correctly and avoid nasty puddles and drips around the loo (although if your other half is the culprit then it might be little late in the day for aiming training). One Mumsnetter used a spot of food-colouring magic: 'We dripped some food colouring into the toilet and he was amazed at how he could change the colour of the water.' You can also buy a toilet training ball that you place in the toilet for the child to aim at. (Thrifty parents can opt for a homemade version – a ping-pong ball with a X drawn on it.) Others recommend floating a Cornflake in the toilet – just make sure that younger siblings don't fish it out thinking it's a handy snack.

Dealing With Accidents

'This weekend we had just checked into a posh hotel and were in the garden when I noticed a tell-tale sag in her pants. But when we got to the toilet it had gone! It had fallen out of her trouser leg and was in the hotel corridor.' Gemmamay

Accidents will happen. Lots of them. On your carpet. On your sofa. And on your very expensive top-of-the-range car seat. The most important – and hardest – thing to do is remain calm. It is easy to say, of course, but not so easy when you are cleaning up poo from every corner of your house, as one put-upon mum explains: 'My son has so far pooed in his baby brother's play nest, the ball pit and on his bedroom carpet. Today I met him en route to the bathroom carrying a poo to put it in the toilet.'

Sometimes a grown-up chat can make all the difference when repeated accidents are becoming a problem. One mother explains her approach: 'It's a bit of a project management talk! We go through the day and talk calmly about accidents, when she had them, what she was doing, what she might do to ensure it doesn't happen again. I can tell my daughter feels supported as she isn't embarrassed to discuss her accidents now.'

Buy some carpet stain remover and lots of cleaning equipment. Mop up the worst of the puddle as soon as it happens – don't leave it to soak in. It is better to confine your trainee to a space with wood or laminate flooring rather than carpet if you can. If your child is on the sofa, sit them on a washable cushion, as sofas can be really tricky to clean and dry. It is definitely worth postponing a new carpet until the training process has been successfully concluded.

In the early days, expect accidents rather than continence – and take a deep breath before you react. Go into another room to swear, and then go back and keep saying, 'Where do we wee, darling? On the potty!'

Out and About

Charging around the house with a potty and a mop is all well and good, but eventually you will start running short of basic provisions and will need to go out. Some opt for pull-ups or training pants for the very early days (see page 143 for pros and cons) but there are other things you can do to minimise the stress of those first, nappy-free trips outside.

The thought of spending half a day stripping a wee-soaked car seat can reduce a grown mum to tears. 'Care-mats' to place under potentially wet bottoms and a potty in the car at all times can be a comfort for those embarking on first car journeys without nappies. And as one mum says, 'It's not too difficult to stop the car and whip out the potty wherever you go. Or, in our case, pee at the side of the road/down a drain/up against an ancient monument.'

Mumsnetiquette: Do not poo in your local Bistro

You have just settled into your seat at the local café with a pot of Earl Grey and a toasted crumpet when your darling child announces, 'I need a wee!' The correct response is not to whip out your potty and let him publicly pee while everyone enjoys their elevenses. Restaurants and cafés do not generally sport 'No Peeing' signs but that doesn't mean it's OK. Let's face it: it's not very sanitary and it puts people off their food. And worse still, it might turn into a poo and you will all be scarred for life (and possibly banned from the café). Ask a waitress or nearby table to watch your things, grab your handbag and take your child to the toilet. Or better still, employ a bit of forward planning and take him to the loo beforehand. That way you can both wash your hands before you eat. Perfect!

Out and about checklist

- Go to the toilet before you leave the house. Your granny was right. This advice applies to women of all ages, but particularly those who are under five years old or have had one or more children.
- Take regular toilet breaks. Stop at regular intervals and give your child a chance to use the loo. Children can be lured into uncharted toilets by promises of exciting discoveries: 'Oooh, I wonder what sort of toilet this will be? I wonder what colour toilet-paper they will have?'
- Take spare clothes. Lots of them. If possible, also take a spare pair of shoes. Walking in wee-sodden sandals is not very enjoyable at any age.
- 'Finish' after accidents. If your child has an accident, stick him on the potty or toilet before dressing him in dry clothes. They might have just done 'a bit' and then clamped up again, so the rest might follow shortly afterwards. Give them a chance to finish.
- Take a potty or toddler toilet seat. Some children feel a little anxious in strange toilets and a familiar toddler seat will help them feel more at ease. Of course, if your child is happy to wee anywhere, then don't bother with this.
- Be sensitive to their worries. If they are anxious about any aspect of going to the toilet in public, don't try to force them. Distract if necessary with cheery banter or enthusiasm for the tiling, but you are better catching a wee in a potty than dragging a terrified child into a public toilet. There are a few adults who won't use public toilets because they are frightened of the hand-dryers. Take things slowly and respect your child's concerns.
- Good Mummies Remember Baby-Wipes! These can be useful for removing squished-on poo from bottoms and carpets, and also for cleaning up dirty hands in the event of a sink shortage. Lovely!

Anal Retentives: Holding It In

'My daughter is three and will not poo in the toilet or potty. This afternoon she has managed to poo in the swimming pool! The pool had to close.' Glucose

It is very common for small children to have worries about pooing in the toilet or potty. Some will manage wees quite happily but insist on pooing in their pants or a nappy. This can result in them holding on so that getting anything out can be stressful, which makes them even more reluctant to poo. And so it becomes a vicious circle.

If this happens, the first thing to do is to talk to your child and find out exactly what they are worried about. It might be something that you can resolve together. If it is pain from expelling poo, try rubbing 'cream' on their bottom beforehand – this will help ease the passage of the poo and also reassure them that Mummy is Doing Something About It. They might be worried because they misunderstand the process – children are sometimes worried that if they poo on the potty it might get on the carpet (not realising that their bottom is well over the potty) or they might not like the feeling of splashing water on to their bottom when they poo on the toilet (a sheet of toilet paper popped in the toilet bowl can reduce splash-back). Talking to your child about their worries can often reveal easily solvable problems, which will help to reassure and relax them.

'If he didn't go for several days, I would give him "poopy juice". It was actually prune juice, and he disliked it so much that if I told him he was going to have poopy juice, he would somehow manage to squeeze one out.' Colinandcaitlinsmommy

To keep your child's bowels healthy and regular, ensure that their diet contains fruit and veg and also lots of water. A gentle tummy-rub on the toilet can also help get their bowels moving, as well as reassuring and distracting them, as can a book. Before you resort to laxatives, always see your GP. Lactulose, which is commonly prescribed, isn't a laxative but a stool softener and can help to soften poos that have been building up for a few days, so that they are less uncomfortable to pass.

Going Backwards: Regression

Just when you thought you'd cracked it, the awful shame of an 'accident'. And another, and another!

'The week before last I'd have said we'd cracked the toilet training. She was doing brilliantly and going all by herself for both poos and wees, washing her hands, wiping her bum, the lot. In the last week she has: taken her night-time nappy off, pooed in bed then smeared it all over her cot, peed all over the sofa three times incurring major cushion and cover wash each time, peed all over the floor in the bathroom instead of actually doing it in the toilet, taken her night-time nappy off and taken her poo out and put it on a shelf "so everyone could see it" – and today, the best of all, pooped on my husband's guitar, not just the body of it, but in the hole, and smeared it all over the strings. She'll be three in September. What the heck is going on? PS Any tips for cleaning crap out of an acoustic guitar?' VoluptuaGoodshag

It's possible that a regressor is just attention-seeking in which case the trick is to offer positive attention for good behaviour and little or no attention for accidents.

Another solution to regression is to resort to bribery ... again. One imaginative parent conjured up the Toilet Fairy: 'Every time she went to the toilet "like a big girl" the Toilet Fairy came. She would hide a very small treat somewhere in the lounge (like one Smartie or one chocolate raisin). She loved looking for it, and it became a sort of game. It took a while to wean her off this. One day Postman Pat sent her a letter saying that now she was a big girl the Toilet Fairy would only come when she had a poo. After a while another letter arrived stating that the Toilet Fairy had to go and help the little girl down the road who was still a baby and wearing nappies – not like her, she was a big girl now, and big girls didn't need the Toilet Fairy blah blah. By this time she was well into it and has never looked back.'

It's Not Working

'My son is two years and seven months old, has been interested in the toilet/potty for a while, likes to sit on both, loves to flush the loo. We have had two attempts at potty training and got nowhere. He just doesn't seem to get the idea that the potty is for performing in, and will sit on it, then say, "Finished", and a couple of minutes later fill his pull-up pants. I am using pull-up nappies because I cannot face three or four pairs of dirty pants per day. Any hints or should I just give up on it for the time being?' Madamez

When a child seems interested in the potty but doesn't seem to recognise the urge to go, or connect this to sitting on the toilet even after a good go at training, the general advice is to give up and try again a bit later.

Remember, giving up doesn't mean that your child will be in nappies for ever. As one frustrated potty trainer says, 'My daughter would sit on the potty but not do anything – it was all just a game.

I was starting to think that she'd never be potty trained. Then all of a sudden last week she announced that she was wearing big girl pants today. And that's it – she seems to have trained herself.'

Dry Nights

Children are usually dry in the day long before they are dry at night. Night-time continence generally comes with time, rather than with training. There is also a strong genetic element to night-time dryness – so if you or your partner were late to be dry at night, your child might also follow this pattern.

Your child will not be dry at night all the time until she starts to produce the hormone which suppresses urine production at night (vasopressin). The other element of night-time dryness is the body's ability to send a signal to the brain to wake up when the bladder is full (Enuresis Resource and Information Centre; www.eric.org.uk). Both of these things come with time. There is little point trying to encourage your toddler to be dry at night before they are ready, because it is generally a matter of physical development, rather than learnt behaviour or wilfulness.

'My son was dry during the day at 22 months, but not dry at night until four years and three months.' Cod

'My children were dry at night at five years, two-and-a-half years, two years, eight to nine years, and around three to three-and-a-half years. A bit of a mixed bag really. Your child will be dry when she's ready.' Juuule

'My daughter was 24 months when out of nappies in the day. She is now five years old and only recently consistently dry at night, and even now has lapses.' Hulababy

'My step-daughter was out of her daytime nappies by the time she was three-and-a-half years old and was out of her night-time easy pants when she was six-and-a-half years old.' Biglips

A Day in the Life of a Potty Trainer

'Possibly one of the more humiliating and frustrating days in my life!

'My three-year-old daughter is having bottom problems as she has bad nappy rash and is now scared of going to the toilet, so is wetting herself frequently and needing the toilet very quickly if she does confess to needing to go.

'I have a small and unattractive travel potty, lined with a plastic bag and a sanitary towel to absorb any wee, for her to squat over. Despite it being a shop-made invention, whenever I get it out it looks so homemade that I am practically dying with the thought of some childless passer-by assuming that I have been sticking these gigantic pads on to scummy plastic bags in my spare time.

'Anyway, I was taking my daughter to see the doctor today about her nappy rash, when she announced in a worried voice, "Oooooooh, Mummy, I need the toilet." So I got my contraption out beside a busy main road and she waved her bottom slowly over the pot. And nothing happened so we packed it all up and moved on, and I, probably slightly paranoidly, felt that the traffic started to move freely again.

'To get to our doctors' we go down a very steep hill. My daughter once again announced her need for the toilet, so I set the whole thing up again rather precariously on the steep slope and she lowered herself down by which time the poo was already poking out of her bottom at the poor young man coming up behind.

'Soon enough one of my daughter's enormous poos came out and it was so enormous that the wee that followed didn't have a chance of staying in the tiny pot and flowed down the hill in front of her with bits of sweetcorn and red pepper in it. Meanwhile she was sitting on this tiny pot and I was holding her legs in the air to try and stop the wee-poo from covering her shoes and ankles. I thought the wee would never stop as people were walking up the hill towards us and having to avoid the stream of wee and sweetcorn. My daughter was delighted by this: "Look, Mummy, there's sweetcorn running down the road in my wee!"

'Unfortunately the bag ties that normally sit neatly beneath the potty were covered in poo and wee and then so were my hands. Then it started to rain very heavily while my daughter did a commentary on the mucky state of my hands and I dropped wet wipes everywhere. My son was in his pram screaming because he was getting wet and the pram has been still for too long and I was late for the doctors'. Could things get much worse? Yes.

'Afterwards we were walking through the shopping precinct when she calmly and happily announced, "Mummy, I am doing a wee in my knickers." Arrrrrrgggggggggggggggggg!!! I managed to say very calmly, "WHY are you doing it in your knickers? WHY didn't you tell me you needed the toilet?" before my voice changed to something that sounds slightly like a deranged animal and I marched her to the public toilets and changed her into a nappy to the sound of her shrieking, "But why can't I wee in my knickers? I don't want to wear a nappy."

'It was for the above reasons that I needed a large portion of chips for dinner and also one tube of Smarties, a packet of pretend sugared cigarettes, and a small packet of Haribo chewy fruit things just to try and forget the humiliation of the day. I am now feeling cross with myself for being cross with her for wetting herself, but that was the third time she'd wet herself today and although I know it isn't her fault, it still tested my patience, and I lost. I also feel mortified for my daughter. The whole town saw her bottom, her poo and my weird potty thing that I make her sit on. But most of all I feel mortified for myself!' *Ellaroo*

'By Jove! I Think She's Got It!'

'Yay! My daughter came home from nursery in the same trousers she went in!' Dollybird

After the stress and the mess comes victory. It will not be long before your little child is continent and proud, so try to remember this and to keep calm while you weather the early storms of toilet training. As one triumphant Mumsnetter expounds, 'Not one accident! He has pooed or weed in every blimmin public toilet around and is extraordinarily pleased with his pants. I have no idea what flipped the switch in his brain but my son is now a fully paid-up member of the pants brigade. I hope our tale of triumph gives hope to strugglers. It will happen one day. Just like that!'

Health

A Spoonful of Sugar (NB No Longer Recommended)

In this chapter ...

Introduction

Remember the days when a 'sick day' was the result of too many Tequila slammers and consisted of a morning under the duvet before popping out to read the papers over a full English breakfast? Well, they're long gone. Toddler sick days are intense and stressful, and will see you juggling thermometers and sick-bowls, and scrubbing the floor with the carpet cleaner on a depressingly regular basis. And then there are the nights.

'They are like walking Petri dishes, aren't they?' moans one mum, and from coughs and colds to parasites at both ends, there always seems to be some medical crisis keeping you from your work or putting you off your dinner. Short of installing sheep dip by your front door, there isn't much you can do but accept that this is all part of growing up and strengthening immune systems. In the meantime, there's lots of good advice from mums who have learnt the hard way never to sleep face-to-face with a poorly child ...

When to Keep Them Off Nursery

It can be a tricky call to know whether or not to keep your toddler away from pre-school. In the first instance, of course, you should take the advice of your GP who will let you know best practice. Your childcare provider will also have rules about returning or attending while suffering from certain illnesses, so make sure you have a copy of their sickness policy.

'My feeling is, if they're well enough to run about, and not ill with something contagious and evil (measles, for example), they can go in,' suggests one mum. Another agrees: 'I only keep my kids off pre-school if they are actually "unwell" – for example, with a temperature and not themselves, or if they have something contagious.'

If your toddler is particularly clingy and not his usual self, 'he won't like being at nursery when he's ill,' says one Mumsnetter. 'Nor is it fair on the staff or the other children. Keep him at home.' If he has a temperature or is off-colour, bear in mind that he might flag during the day. If you do decide to let him attend pre-school or nursery, make sure that the staff are informed of the situation, and stand by the phone ready for action if he takes a turn for the worse.

If you are lucky enough not to have work or other commitments, then you can probably be a little over-cautious and keep your toddler at home if they are under the weather. After all, as one kind mother points, 'Mine always wants his mum when he's feeling grotty.'

Colds: What Can You Do?

Toddlers' immune systems are still developing, and it won't be long before you realise why a cold is referred to as 'common'. Toddlers are likely to get several colds in a year. Symptoms might include a running nose, red eyes, a sore throat, a cough and even a fever, and can last for up to two weeks. Your toddler may also be irritable and fractious, although it is hard to tell the difference between a toddler with a cold and one without based purely on that particular symptom.

Colds are not usually serious and will pass in time, although it is horrible watching your child feeling miserable. Colds are caused by viruses, which antibiotics don't treat. However, occasionally, a cold might result in more serious complications. You should seek medical advice if you are very worried and your toddler:

- has a cold that lasts for more than ten days
- is coughing up multi-coloured sputum (green, yellow or brown), is complaining of sinus pain or has a fever – this could be a sign of a bacterial infection which needs treatment with antibiotics
- has earache
- complains about a sore throat for longer than three or four days, or their throat pain seems very bad
- develops symptoms such as a headache, or a pain or swelling in the face or chest
- seems to be getting worse rather than better

Of course, all parents are worried when their children are ill, and this is perfectly natural. Being filled with terror at the thought that they do not have a cold but are actually suffering from a rare form of deadly jungle fever is a normal parental reaction. So don't worry about seeking advice from a doctor. They will have seen their fair share of over-protective parents, and it is their job to determine whether your concerns are realistic or not. Doctors can also check for things that you can't see, such as throat, ear and chest infections. So if you have a niggling feeling that something is not quite right, don't feel guilty about ringing your GP.

Other than that, dealing with a cold is largely a matter of waiting for it to pass, so don't rush your toddler and enjoy a few days of quiet, sofa-based inactivity.

'Keep the baby sheets from your Moses basket and lay under an older baby's head when they have a cold. You can just change this daily instead of the whole sheet if it gets dirtied with snot.' Indie

Ways to ease a cold

- Over-the-counter cold and pain relief. Children's Ibruprofen and paracetamol can be taken regularly when your child has a cold and you can alternate the two. Take as recommended.
- Baby chest rub. You can let your toddler 'help' by rubbing this on their own chest.
- If your toddler is hot and feverish, then sponge them with cool damp flannels (or let them do this themselves).
- For stuffy noses, try warm baths and humid bathrooms. Fill the bath from the shower head if possible to make it extra-steamy, and keep the doors closed.
- To ease and prevent cracked and sore skin under the nose, keep a supply of Vaseline to hand and rub it into the upper lip area.
- Use drops of eucalyptus oil in bowls of strategically placed hot water, or on hankies.
- 'To help with blocked noses and nasty coughs invest in a humidifier that has a reservoir for essential oils/decongestants.' HayleyJ
- 'If your child has a cold put a few drops of lavender and eucalyptus oils on a damp flannel and place on a hot radiator at bedtime. The aroma should ease the congestion.' Cupcakesgalore

- Slightly raise the the head end of their bed or cot (using books or blocks) to help night-time breathing. *Biza*

Getting fluids into a poorly child

Children with bad colds or fevers really need to keep their fluids up, although they might feel too poorly to drink. Try these ideas to get your child to drink more:

- Explain to them that drinking will help them get better.
- Don't worry about your normal 'rules' – offer a variety of drinks, including squashes and fruit juices.
- Warm drinks with lemon and honey (or just honey) are often popular. Blackcurrant squash is a favourite, but you can also try warm apple juice or herbal teas such as camomile. The addition of honey will soothe a sore throat.
- Offer sugary drinks for energy: flat lemonade, for example.
- A smoothie is a good way of combining nutrients with fluids.
- Try offering drinks in different containers. One mum suggests a sports water bottle, or even a baby's bottle; they might enjoy the role play of being a poorly little baby.
- Suggest a straw.
- 'Try making ice lollies from fruit teas. No sticky puddles to mop up and no tooth-rot, either!' *Mammalove*

Entertaining a Sick Child

When your child is very poorly, you need to dispense with the usual rules and surround them with home comforts until they feel better. Now is not the time to stick primly to your hour-a-day television rule, woman. Sick days should be spent slobbing on the sofa gazing at something banal on television. (You can read a magazine.) 'There should be advantages to being sick,' advises one mum. 'Vegging in front of the TV is certainly one of them. We are pretty much a zero television household here. But if the kids are ill, well, all bets are off.'

As far as post-illness recovery is concerned, let your child set the pace. There is no point trying to persuade a toddler that he needs to rest on the sofa if he is desperate to get up on his wobbly feet to play with his kitchen set. On the other hand, don't drag him off to the park unless he is bouncing off the walls. Take things easy until you are quite sure he is back to full health and driving you batty again.

A spoonful of sugar: Persuading your toddler to take medicine

- Before you descend with a spoonful of the nasty stuff, explain what you are doing and that the medicine will help her get better.
- Try letting her self-administer the medicine with a syringe (suitable syringes are available from pharmacies). A toddler can control the medicine herself if it is given with a syringe. Practise a few times with juice or water first. She may enjoy being in control and be more willing to take the medicine than if it is just 'forced' on her with a spoon.
- 'When struggling to get a child to take some less-than-tasty medicine, try mixing it with a few drops of concentrated blackcurrant squash. This will make it taste better and the pink colour might look more like their favourite medicine.' *Mo2*
- 'After struggling to convince my two-year-old to take her antibiotics on a spoon and having her spit it everywhere, my husband disguised it by putting it in fruit juice and she drank it with no problems!' *Ellamum*
- 'If administering medicine is a problem, do the evening dose while they're in the bath. If they spit it out, you can easily wipe it down.' *Fms*
- 'To keep track of when a poorly child had his last dose of medicine, stick a Post-it note on the box and a pen inside to keep a note of the time it was given.' *SorenLorenson*

Coping with Chicken-Pox

Chicken-pox is a highly infectious disease that most children will get at some stage. The incubation period is 10–21 days – i.e. it takes 10–21 days after you have come into contact with the virus before you start showing symptoms. You are infectious from two days before the rash appears to approximately five days afterwards (until all of the blisters have – yuck – burst and crusted over). As far as chicken-pox is concerned, it is coughs and sneezes which spread diseases, because the virus is spread through saliva and nasal mucus – that's why it's so infectious.

The most commonly recognised symptom is a rash of small, very itchy red spots, which develop into fluid-filled blisters. There may also be flu-like symptoms a few days before the rash appears but in a toddler it is always hard to know whether they are under the weather or just crabby.

Once the pox has struck, you are stuck – and need to stay in quarantine until the blisters have (sorry to repeat this) all burst and crusted over. No mixing with children (unless of course they've already had the pox), so no pre-school or nursery. After a couple of days trapped inside, your toddler will probably start getting stir-crazy. It can be particularly hard if they have no symptoms other than the spots (and are therefore not pinned to the sofa and television with fatigue).

Most Mumsnetters admit to trips outside, but keep their children away from other people. 'Luckily, we live in a rural area with plenty of deserted places for fresh air,' says one mum, and another admits visiting a local playground 'which always seems to be deserted anyway.' 'My two both had chicken-pox at the same time at the end of summer term last year,' writes a regular Mumsnetter. 'It was imperative that we went out before I started opening the wine before 11 a.m. – but fortunately I live in a rural coastal area so we settled on a quiet corner of the beach most days and dug our way to Oz.'

Fortunately, once you've had chicken-pox, it is pretty rare to catch it again because you will have developed immunity to the virus – and getting it when you are young is usually far less serious than when you are older. So take heart from one wise mum who advises, 'It's a bore, but at least she will have had it and got it out the way.'

'When your child has chicken-pox, buy a packet of red dot stickers and put them on their favourite toy. My son spent his spotty time cheering up his teddy by reading him books and telling him not to scratch or he'd scar!' Hausfrau

Chicken-pox: How to ease the pain

Some children get chicken-pox very mildly and are not particularly itchy or crabby. Others have a tougher time. As with all illness, keeping up fluid intake is essential, although this is only usually a challenge if your child is feeling very fluey or poorly. The bigger challenge is making them comfortable when they are constantly itching.

Painkillers

- Use suitable painkillers (such as liquid paracetamol) if your child is in pain or has a fever.
- You can also try antihistamines for the itching (these might be particularly useful at night as they often make children sleepy).

Itching

- Keep fingernails short so that children don't scratch themselves too badly (as this causes scars) – and put socks over their hands at night (or once they are asleep) so they don't scratch in their sleep.
- Dress them in loose clothing or let them go naked – cool air on the skin will help reduce itching.
- Calamine lotion is the usual recommended standby for dousing itchy spots. For extra soothing keep it in the fridge to cool.
  - 'If you're finding it a battle to get the calamine lotion on your toddler, try making it a painting game with cotton buds.' *Lojomamma*
  - 'When our daughter had the pox, we gave her a little pot of calamine and a brush and let her dot her own spots which seemed to help.' *Scootergrrrl*

(continued)

- 'I've found a calamine CREAM not a lotion – and it's great.'
  Cremolafoam
- 'I bought Aloe Vera gel from a health shop and it worked really
  well.' *Scootergrrrl*

Tepid baths

- 'I'm on day five of chicken-pox and am finding a salt water bath
  the greatest thing. I use a bag of sea salt from the supermarket.'
  Cremolafoam
- 'I put a couple of tablespoons of bicarbonate of soda in the bath
  and it seems to help.' *Themoon66*
- 'Put a big wadge of porridge oats in an old stocking or sock, tie it
  to the taps so the water runs through it – it makes a nice soothing
  bath. Don't use instant oats unless you like bathing in glue.'
  MehgaLegs
- 'Bicarb of soda is great, and with any leftovers, you can clean the
  teapot!' *Bemyv*

Diarrhoea and Vomiting

The dreaded 'D&V' is one of the most ghastly of toddler afflictions,
partly because it's so horrid watching your baby suffering but also
because they are projectile vomiting on to your sofa cushions. D&V
also creates a whole new scale of laundry problems when you are
already stressed and panicky.

'Sick is one of things that I always thought, "Oh
when it's your child you won't mind it." Turns out
it is just as gross when it's your child, plus YOU
have to clear up!' K74

Meticulous hygiene is essential when dealing with D&V if
you want to reduce your chances of spreading it around the

family (which you most definitely do). Wash your hands and your child's hands after every trip to the toilet and every vomiting incident.

If your child is suffering from D&V the most important thing to do is to keep up fluid intake. Most cases of D&V pass after 12 hours or so, but sometimes they can go on for longer. The main worry is that your child might get dehydrated if they are not taking in enough fluids to replace the fluids they are losing.

Signs of dehydration

- no wet nappies/wees for 10 hours
- weak with no energy
- dry mouth, tongue or lips
- faster or slower breathing
- cold to the touch
- irritability (always hard to discern in a toddler)

If you are worried about your child or they develop these symptoms, ring your GP. If a child becomes seriously dehydrated, they may need to be admitted to hospital and given fluid either intravenously (via a drip) or through a tube up their nose.

Feeding a child with D&V

It is recommended that you avoid dairy products, because they are hard to digest – not to mention that they smell disgusting when regurgitated across your living-room rug.

After your child vomits, let him rest for a few minutes and then offer sips of water. You can use special hydration powders from chemists to replace lost sugar and salt – ask your pharmacist or GP for advice. There are various flavours and they dissolve in a glass of water.

As far as food is concerned, health professionals always recommend the BRAT diet – Bananas, Rice, Apples and Toast – but it's probably best just go with your toddler's appetite, offering small amounts of plain food that is easy on the stomach.

Once he is on the mend, treat him gently. Although toddlers often appear to bounce back to full health he might still be weak for a few days, especially after not eating and drinking, so pamper him as much as you can and unearth the old buggy for trips out of the house. Be gentle with tantrums and offer lots of regular snacks.

Housekeeping tips

Don't just throw a heaved-on sheet into the washing machine without rinsing off (I'm sorry to put it this way) the chunks. You will just end up – as many Mumsnetters have discovered – with a washing machine full of very clean sick. Rinse off the big chunks in the bath and throw them down the loo or shove them down the plughole.

'If your child is ill and vomiting, dress them in an adult-sized T-shirt so that when they are sick you can pull the T-shirt over their head without getting vomit all over them.' Jaynewilk

One thing you really must never do is to just hoover up a pile of vomit. This is probably obvious to most people, but there has been more than one Mumsnetter-husband who has considered this to be the most effective method of clearing up vomit. And definitely don't try it with a bagless cyclonic vacuum cleaner – witnessing a whirlwind of sick will definitely be one of the low points of your parenting career.

Vomiting: Cautionary tales

'My child hurled in the post office,' admits one mum. 'Thank God lots of old ladies with tissues were in the line.' (Helpful for you perhaps, but not so great for the ladies.) And be careful what you feed a potentially poorly child, as one mother discovered after giving her son a nutritious supper of spinach and sardines: 'We were snuggled up in bed later that night when he vommed the whole lot on to our heads; it was in our ears, eyes, up our noses, you name it. My husband still won't eat sardines.' And another mum warned of the hazard of taking a poorly child to an electrical retailers after her daughter threw up all over the feet of the salesperson in Currys: 'I felt obliged to buy the more expensive dishwasher.' I should think so, too.

Going into Hospital

Whether your child is prone to launching herself off sofas or develops a scary mystery fever, at some point you are likely to find yourself sitting in A&E with a toddler on one knee and a bucket on the other.

There are two types of hospital stays – planned and emergency – and you deserve vast amounts of sympathy for either.

It's a good idea to have a 'doctor's kit' as part of your toy-box content, and to make occasional role play of Teddy visiting the doctor or, say, breaking his arm falling off the sofa. This will get your toddler familiar with the stethoscope ('Listening to your heart-beat'), mouth exams ('Say "ahhh!"') and the other instruments of the doctor's bag. There are also lots of books about visiting the doctor and going into hospital that should be part of your home bookshelf to make your child familiar with these ideas and places. 'Try not to speak in a "reassuring" manner too far in advance or you will panic them,' warns one mum. 'Instead make it sound like an exciting adventure.'

If your child has to go to hospital for an operation, contact the hospital in advance to see if they will allow you to visit a few days before, as one Mumsnetter recommends: 'A visit beforehand really helped my son understand what was going to happen, and meant I was less nervous about it.'

Prepare yourself to feel tense and upset, too – seeing your child in a hospital bed can be extremely distressing, as one mother writes: 'When my son had his tonsils out I was totally unprepared for how emotional I would be about the whole experience.' Try to be gentle with yourself – crying in the toilets is permitted – or allow yourself some private time at home to cry and unwind.

> 'Seeing your baby asleep on the big trolley is very emotional. Have your partner or best friend or ANYONE waiting for you!' Blu

When your child goes into hospital, you will probably need to stay with her all the time. This can be hard work, because if your toddler is admitted for several days it will involve 24-hour care and probably a lot of complicated shift-changing with your partner (if you have one). Don't be afraid to ask for help from friends and relatives.

'My son has been in hospital twice and both times he really enjoyed it (play workers, new videos etc.). Meanwhile I was going demented because I was trapped on a ward with no grub, tea or coffee, or anything to read. Pack stuff for yourself or you'll go nuts! And if you can arrange for someone else to come and stay with your child while you go and get a shower or coffee then do so – you'll really appreciate the break.' Zippy539

Your toddler might be stressed by the experience, so this is the time for treats. Be gentle with behaviour that you might not normally tolerate – tantrums are to be expected in a confused child, so cuddle and reassure as much as possible. Lots of mums recommend having a present to open (with some assistance) after coming round from a general anaesthetic.

As far as your child's care is concerned, you have the final say – so don't be afraid to ask questions, and if you are unsure about her treatment plan ask to speak to more people. No good doctor will mind you asking for a second opinion.

Packing a hospital bag

For your child

- clean clothes/lots of spare pyjamas
- slippers
- wash things including several flannels if feverish/vomiting
- a favourite blanket or quilt
- favourite toys (a willing nurse might be happy to name-tag Teddy when they tag your child)
- snacks (one Mumsnetter suggests mini cereal boxes, milk and bowl, and cartons of cold juice in a coolbag)

- favourite or new cup and straws (to encourage fluid intake)
- simple games such as colouring books and pencils, jigsaws (you should have a bedside table that swings over the bed so your toddler can draw etc.)
- children's magazines

'Do face painting while in hospital; that will get him loads of attention from the staff!' Tiffini

For you

- money – for car-parking, and hospital shop and café
- credit card – for buying television and phone time on bedside entertainment systems
- telephone numbers that you might find useful
- snacks
- painkillers (if you are prone to stress headaches!)
- magazines/books for when child is sleeping
- notepad and pen for writing down questions for doctors etc. (expect your brain to be mush due to lack of sleep and stress)
- clean clothes/wash things

Planned hospital stays: Advice from Silentterror

- Most hospitals allow you to be with your child in the anaesthetic room. It does help the child and the parents, but be prepared to feel very tearful when he falls asleep and you have to leave him!
- As well as the time in theatre, allow time for the recovery room as well. A nurse from your ward (hopefully one you and he have already met) will tell you when he is ready to come back and you should be able to go to theatre with her to collect him.
- Be prepared for him to be irritable and crying when you see him, this is very common after an anaesthetic and once he has slept a bit more on the ward he should be fine.
- After a general anaesthetic, a lot of children are sick once or twice, that is normal.
- If he's had a broken bone or is uncomfortable or constricted in some way, for the journey home you might need to forgo his

usual car seat if it is a 3-point seat-belt and use a booster seat and seat-belt instead (don't forget to check safety guidelines for height and weight).

- Make sure you have a contact number for problems, and know if you have got to attend for a follow-up visit. Also make sure you have lots of children's painkillers available at home if necessary.

Alternative Therapies: What's Worth Trying and What's Hocus-Pocus?

Mumsnetters are a fairly savvy bunch so it's rare that there is a discussion about arnica or homeopathy without hearing mutterings about the placebo effects and discussions of double-blind studies.

Of course, there are certain therapies that everyone is in favour of – most mums like an aromatherapy massage every now and then, and some toddlers like a post-bath massage, too.

And despite their general scepticism, there are Mumsnetters who will testify to the success of certain alternative therapies on their young children: cranial osteopathy and homeopathy seem to come up most often as being 'worth a shot'.

As far as finding a practitioner is concerned, quality can vary greatly, so word of mouth is the best indicator of a reliable outfit. 'As with most stuff to do with our babes – trust your instincts!' advises one mum. 'If you think it's helping, if only to calm them down, carry on.'

'Do consider having a treatment yourself, as it can perk you up no end, and you get a sense of what it feels like for your little one.' Meysey

Cranial osteopathy

Most people have heard of osteopathy and have a vague idea that it is about the manipulation of the muscular-skeletal system (which it is!). Cranial osteopathy focuses on the bones of the head, and its practitioners maintain that gentle manipulation of these bones can improve the function of the body.

The cranial bones are relatively flexible in newborns – in order to facilitate the birth process – and harden over time. You can see therefore why cranial osteopathy might be considered useful for small children, whose cranial bones have recently undergone a physically extreme experience (yes, I know it was worse for you but bear with me).

If you can cope with the onslaught of doubt ('Are we being duped? I can't really understand what holding her head can do'), then cranial osteopathy might be worth a try. 'There was no improvement at all,' says one mum cheerfully, 'but at least we felt that we were doing something by trying all these different treatments!'

Cranial osteopathy is sometimes recommended for small children who are suffering from colic or digestive problems, sleeplessness, restlessness and irritability, eczema and ear, nose and throat problems. In theory all the grim parts of toddler health and well-being can be healed by the gentle manipulation of a trained cranial osteopath. Maybe.

'I took my son who's three and a half to a cranial osteopath yesterday as he's been having a few problems with behaviour at pre-school. I was amazed that he let the guy touch his head straight away and was so relaxed on my knee. At the end he fell asleep and was out cold!' Juniper68

'We took our son to a cranial osteopath for several sessions before the age of four, owing to his "headaches" and general grizzliness, possibly caused by head deformation during long labour. He found it very relaxing and it eased his pains.' AlanP

'We saw a specialist in paediatric osteopathy for my son's glue ear. All the gunk from his ears drained away the night after the first treatment!' ShinyHappyStarOfBethlehem

'I used to take my daughter to a cranial osteopath. She cried all the time, while I perspired all the way through and cried at the end of each session, too! It didn't work for us.' Dorisdaisy

'Cranial osteopathy was one of the many alternative therapies we tried to ease our daughter's toddler eczema. The explanations they offered as to why she might have it and why this treatment might help sounded plausible, but sadly there was no improvement.' Munchpot

Homeopathy

Homeopathic treatments are extremely diluted 'remedies' that are generally considered suitable for use with children. The theory behind homeopathy is hugely controversial and critics claim that the theory is nonsensical and any efficacy of the treatments is due to the placebo effect.

Some homeopathic remedies can be bought over the counter in pharmacies and health food shops, or you can visit a trained homeopath, who will take a detailed medical and personal history, before choosing a suitable remedy or combination of remedies. Follow-up consultations are usually required.

Many mums take a 'suck it and see' approach to homeopathy (often quite literally). It can't do any harm to give it a whirl, and some sceptics have been converted as a result, including one mum who admits, 'I used to be a non-believer but have seen some amazing results with my son.'

'My son had terrible eczema when he was young. I tried all the creams etc. prescribed by doctors but they didn't work. I eventually took him to a homeopath and he prescribed tablets. It took a few weeks but it cleared up completely.' Lorne

'I have a three-year-old who had eczema from about five months and was starting to develop asthma from about two years. I thought we were getting nowhere with constant trips to the hospital for nebulisers and use of inhalers. So I tried homeopathy. In six months, I have used no creams and no inhaler. The eczema has totally gone and we have had no asthma all winter so far.' Wuliej

'We tried homeopathy for eczema after friends had had some success. The practitioner was so confident it would work. Even when it got worse, they said sometimes it has to get worse before it gets better. It never got any better and we went back to steroids.' Munchpot

'The first time I used homeopathy I was scathing (and desperate). I used it on my severely autistic son aged two. The results were astounding. If it stops working I'll stop using it.' Gess

'I used homeopathy and found that for my children it works wonders. I then wasn't worried so much about the fact that it couldn't be explained.' Jimjams

'An ex of mine used to really believe in homoeopathy and paid his homeopath quite a lot of money for visits and potions. When he moved far from her he would consult by phone and she used to tell him to write the name of a remedy on a piece of paper and sit a glass of water over it and the water would become suffused with whatever was written on the paper and he would then drink it and feel much better! That particular relationship did not last very long.' Jasper

Threadworms: 'And His Name is Wiggly-Woo ...'

Another delightful part of life with small children is their natural ability to charm various parasites into your lovely house in the manner of the Pied Piper. Chief squirm-inducing parasite is probably the threadworm.

Threadworms (sometimes called pinworms) are small white worms that infect the intestine. They look like tiny pieces of white cotton. The worms lay eggs around the anus and genitals during the night, which makes the victim itch crazily – the classic symptom of an infestation. Scratching the affected area scrapes the eggs under your nails. They can then be easily transferred to your mouth, and so the infection cycle continues. As well as itching, you can sometimes see the worms at night (when they lay their eggs) or they may appear in the infected person's poo.

'My daughter decided to come and do a poo in my bathroom, nice and sociable-like. She announced she has the runs. Nice. Gets up, wipes bum, looks in loo and screams, "There are WORMS in my poo!" I look in – yes, there are. And they are waving at us.' Princesspeahead

Treatment aims to get rid of the parasites and prevent re-infestation. Strict hygiene methods alone can do this if you are fastidious, but usually medication is required (as well as strict hygiene!). Re-infestation occurs when the eggs are swallowed, and the eggs are extremely hard to eradicate – changing the bedclothes can toss squillions of them into the air.

'Threadworms are really, really common. It's really not anything to do with how clean you are. Kids pick them up from one another by putting their fingers in their mouth etc. It's just one of those things that children get. Honestly, it's not a big deal, although I know it seems a bit yucky. Try not to stress!' Mrsmalumbas

Eradicating threadworms

The life span of the threadworms is approximately six weeks so these hygiene methods should be followed for this amount of time. Everyone in the family needs to follow these precautions and take medication, even if they are not exhibiting symptoms.

- cut your children's nails short
- discourage nail-biting and thumb-sucking
- wash hands frequently, scrubbing under fingernails
- wear close-fitting underwear at night and change it in the morning
- wear cotton gloves at night

- bath or shower in the morning to remove any eggs laid overnight
- make sure everyone uses their own flannel and towel
- vacuum regularly and thoroughly to get rid of eggs
- take medication

Mumsnetiquette

Deal with your worms and nits. There is nothing more despised at the pre-school gate than a parent who won't properly de-parasite her child. Be fastidious and deal with infestations or risk a shunning on the playdate circuit. And definitely don't announce to your mummy-friends that you are a strict vegan and won't kill threadworms, as one mum did, because you will meet a chorus of disapproval.

'What you can't beat is the double whammy: nits and worms. You're never sure which end to scratch first.' Foxinsocks

Headlice

As soon as chat turns to headlice, you can guarantee that you will feel the urge to start scratching. Nits are small insects (about the size of a sesame seed) that live in your hair and suck blood from your scalp. They are a common visitor in houses with children, because they are spread by jumping from head to head of people in close contact with each other, as children often are.

'Decided to check children for nits. I grabbed my daughter. I saw eggs. Argh! Attempt to comb through – her hair is waist length – I hate it

– much arguing about cutting it – can't comb it – so I chop it to mid-shoulderblade and spend the next HOUR combing out about 5,000 tiny lice and about 50 huge ones the size of woodlice. I can't believe it.' Princesspeahead

You will generally suspect headlice when your child starts scratching her head (particularly at the nape of the neck and behind the ears) or when you get a warning letter from pre-school announcing that lice are doing the rounds. Check your child's hair by using a 'nit comb' – a special fine-toothed comb – in order to trap the tiny eggs and bugs. To check for nits, use long strokes from the base of the head right to the end of the hair. Check the comb after each stroke. It's a good idea to do this fairly regularly.

The practice of dousing your children's heads with a vat of pesticides at the first sight of one of the little critters is rather out-dated, not least because it doesn't work very well and headlice are remarkably resilient.

Wet-combing is the favoured method these days, which simply involves slicking your child's clean hair with conditioner, and combing repeatedly in order to remove the lice and eggs. This must be repeated every three to four days for at least two weeks in order to break the cycle. And you must be thorough (spend at least 15–25 minutes depending on hair length and thickness) because if you leave just one egg behind you'll be back to where you started in a few days.

'The lice are not easy to see on some of the nit combs, especially the steel ones. Use a jug of water to rinse the comb after each stroke. The lice and eggs will sink to the bottom after a few minutes. You can check your haul 10 minutes after you have finished combing.' SlightlyMadShrek

Conjunctivitis

The dreaded 'pink eye' is a common affliction of toddlers. It is an inflammation of part of the eye, and while it can be caused by allergies and irritants (such as chlorine), the most annoying form is infective conjunctivitis. This is caused by viruses or bacteria and can be spread extremely rapidly, particularly with young children who wipe their eyes and then smear the gunk over anything or anyone within reach. Because it's so infectious, children with conjunctivitis are often excluded from pre-schools until their infection has cleared up.

You will notice that the eyes are red and inflamed and may be 'oozing' yellowish pus, particularly when your toddler wakes. Sometimes their eyes might stick together after a sleep. If this happens, don't force the eyelids apart, but reassure your toddler and give them a couple of warm flannels or cotton pads to hold against their eyes which should loosen up the gunk. (Stick the flannels straight into a hot wash.)

In most cases, infective conjunctivitis does not cause any complications. Official advice is that it rarely requires any medical treatment and normally heals by itself, usually within one to two weeks. However, some GPs will prescribe antibiotic eye-drops or eye-ointment.

'If your child gets conjunctivitis, ask the doctor for the ointment, not the drops. The ointment can be pasted into the eye from the tip of a clean finger. We have found the drops completely impossible to deliver into the tightly clenched eye of a very wriggly, screaming toddler!' Lal

The best way to prevent conjunctivitis is to be careful with hygiene – wash hands (particularly after applying eye-drops to your toddler), don't share towels or pillows, and be really careful how you deal with your toddler's eyes. 'Use a piece of clean cotton wool for each wipe,' advises one mum. 'Wipe from inner edge of eye (near nose) to outer edge with a bit of cotton wool dipped in lukewarm water. If you need to wipe again, use a fresh piece each time and for each eye.'

If you are still nursing, breastmilk is recommended for clearing up conjunctivitis, because of its natural anti-bacterial properties. 'Don't be delicate with the breastmilk,' advised one lactivist. 'Give a good squirt till it runs out the corners of their eyes. I found it easiest to do with my daughter laid flat on the changing mat.' Or you can chase your toddler around the house squirting furiously in the direction of their eyes. Probably best not to do this if the in-laws are staying.

Molluscum Contagiosum: Warts and All

Many parents of toddlers will come up against the wart-like molluscum contagiosum, a viral infection of the skin that seems particularly prevalent among the toddler youth of today. Molluscum appear as tiny, firm, wart-like raised spots on the skin, which are whitish in colour; they often appear in clusters. After a few weeks or months, the individual spots burst, and release the infected part, a white fluid. The spots then start to heal. They may leave a tiny scar or white patch, or there may be no marking at all.

The virus is contagious and children have a tendency to scratch their skin and then pass on the molluscum to other parts of their body – or to other toddlers. 'Keep nails short to prevent too much scratching or scarring,' counsels one mum. Although it is mildly contagious there is no need to keep your toddler in quarantine or to stop them going to nursery or pre-school (which is fortunate because it may last for a year or two!). You do, however, have to be a bit careful about sharing baths and towels, which is a pain if you are used to bathing siblings together. Swimming pools seem to be fine, but paddling pools and regular baths are probably not worth the risk.

'My daughter has had molluscum for ages
– about two years now – but the last blobs are on
their way out, hurrah! On the advice of the GP,

I didn't do anything with them. The bigger ones got red and burst and that was a prelude to their disappearance. The smaller ones just seem to vanish.' Suedonim

The molluscum may take several months to clear up, but they will do so of their own accord. There is no need for specific treatment unless the spots become inflamed or your toddler is in discomfort – in which case, see your GP for treatment or advice. He or she may recommend squeezing the spots (perhaps after a bath) to burst them, but don't try this without advice about the right way to do it so that you don't damage or distress your toddler.

There isn't a great deal you can do to help the spots heal, although various remedies have been hailed as successful by Mumsnetters: Manuka honey, tea tree oil, homeopathic pills, topical creams, Echinacea and even certain best-selling anti-wrinkle creams. Although posh face cream is probably best left for Mummy's crow's feet, smearing your toddler in honey might be worth a try. Just don't let him roll on the sofa afterwards.

Lots of people have immunity to the virus, and the good news is that once the molluscum have run their course your child will be resistant to further outbreaks.

Car Sickness

There is not much worse than a stream of warm vomit down the back of your neck as you are driving. Some children are particularly prone to car sickness. There is no magic cure, but you can try some of the following:

- Looking out of the window. Avoid activities that require looking down (such as books or games).
- Fresh air can help. Sit your toddler by an open window.
- 'Travel sickness wristbands' can be bought from chemists. They apply pressure to 'key pressure points' according to 'acupressure' theories.
- Traditional remedies include ginger and peppermint.
- Some toddlers seem to feel better if they suck on something

sugary, and tiny sweets like Tic-Tacs are always popular. Just make sure you're confident they aren't going to choke. Performing the Heimlich manoeuvre at 70 mph from the front seat is no easy task.

- You can buy over-the-counter medicines for settling travel sickness in young children. Some also have a sedative effect. Ask your pharmacist or GP for advice.
- Have one adult sit in the back to entertain the travel-sick child (which can help distract from nausea) and also to spot heaving and thus avert maximum damage.
- Put plastic down under the car seat (bin bags are much cheaper than the purpose-made stuff) and cover the car seat with a towel under the plastic.
- Always bring changes of clothes and lots of wipes.
- Take lots of carrier bags or zip lock bags to put pukey clothes in.

'My son gets very carsick. The only thing we found helpful was to schedule car journeys around times that he would nap (he was exceptionally good at falling asleep in the car). He is now seven and gets sick a lot less. And even if he does get sick he can get it all neatly into a bag now.' SofiaAmes

Glasses Refusal: How to Convince Children to Wear Their Specs

'Big up cool glasses-wearers. Postman Pat is a popular myopic role-model of choice.' *Gigi*

'You must persevere. As long as you are consistent they do realise in the end that you mean business. And I think when they twig that they can actually see with their specs on it is a lightbulb moment!' *Sidge*

(continued)

'To get her used to wearing them, I'd put them on her for an hour, then I'd take them off, and increase the time each day (the optician told me to do this with my own glasses, and figured that a few more days of her not wearing them constantly wouldn't matter). If she did the time without taking them off, she'd get a treat. If she took them off before I did, they'd go straight back on again.' *Deepbreath*

'We also turned the TV off if she took her glasses off, or took her book away and told her she could have it back when she put her glasses on.' *Sidge*

'I found a single sweet treat has done the trick. Box of jelly babies comes out, glasses go on, lid comes off box and a single sweet is chosen.' *West3*

'It took my three-year-old a week of continually having her glasses put on her every time she took them off. And I mean constantly putting them back on. EVERY time she took them off. Thousands of times a day (well it felt like thousands!). And then something clicked and now she wears them constantly.' *Sidge*

What to Do When YOU Are the Patient

Before you have children, you know there are downsides to parenthood, but tiredness and saggy bosoms come most easily to mind, rather than, as one mum rants, 'the constant stream of parasites, vomiting bugs and mystery viruses! I was NEVER sick before having children.'

If you are the primary carer, the first time you are ill post-baby you are hit by the awful realisation that you can't take a day off. Those long, idle sick-days that were available to you when you were a busy 'working person' seem akin to a luxurious spa break in comparison with the demands of juggling a small child while feeling crap yourself. 'Being ill just takes every tiny scrap of pleasure out of parenthood,' moans a poorly mum, and another agrees: 'It'd be nice to "rest" but who has time for that with a three-year-old?'

'Do not wake up at 4 a.m. with a cold and decide to take a night-time cold and flu tablet even though you know you have to get up at 6 a.m. To say I was zombied would be an understatement.' Nemo2007

As one wise Mumsnetter says, 'Sometimes you can soldier through, sometimes not.' If you are very poorly and can't survive the day directing battles from the comfort of the sofa, try to arrange things so that you can spend some time resting; see if you can book your child in for an extra day with childminder/nursery, or if your partner can take a day's leave, or if you can persuade Granny to look after your little one for a few hours.

If your child is going to nursery or pre-school, think whether you can ask a friend to do the nursery run for you, or a neighbour if you have children attending the same pre-school.

If you have to survive the day on your own with your toddler, Mumsnetters recommend fresh air – even if it's just via open windows. 'When I'm feeling ill,' writes one mum, 'I open the windows in the bedrooms, no matter how cold it is – just for a few minutes even. The fresh air perks me up.' Keep your standards of hygiene high so that you don't pass on your bugs. 'WASH HANDS LOTS!' shouts another mum, 'and if you have a cold, as soon as you use a piece of tissue get rid of it straight away – it really helps stop germs and passing them on to everyone else.'

Other than that, revert to the rules for When Children Are Poorly, i.e. get out DVDs and let them watch as much television as they like. 'I hide in bed or, if I must, lie on sofa vaporously while kids watch telly non-stop,' confesses one mother.

It's fine to be a slut in the kitchen when you are feeling ill. One Mumsnetter recommends home delivery pizza, and others suggest ready meals or beans on toast. 'We eat microwaved freezer meals or beans which everyone likes more than my cooking anyway,' admits another mum. 'Sometimes I have just piled it all on a plate in the middle of the table, assigned the eldest (who is four) to dish out grub to herself and sister, and gone back to the sofa. The kids love it – I let them do whatever they want as long as they don't bug me.'

Above all, don't worry about the usual housework, which your healthy partner can do on their return. As a particularly sensible mother advises, 'Go slow, breathe deeply and leave the million jobs for another day.'

Alternatively, another mum suggests taking it like a man: 'I cope by developing Man-flu and making my partner wait on me hand and foot.'

Now that's a bit harsh, isn't it?

Special Needs

Onwards and Upwards (But Definitely Not Backward)

In this chapter ...

Introduction

There are many different types of special needs (SN), ranging from physical disabilities such as cerebral palsy to Autistic Spectrum Disorder (ASD) and Attention Deficit Hyperactivity Disorder (ADHD). Some of these may be diagnosed when your child is a baby; others only start to become apparent when your child is at the toddler stage. When one thinks of toddlerhood and special needs, ASD and ADHD probably come to mind, but there are also quite a few physical special needs that become noticeable at the toddler stage: anything that interferes with walking (like connective tissue disorders) for example, or hearing or speech problems (many children are diagnosed with hearing problems when they fail to develop speech).

The toddler years can be the time when a suspected special need starts to take shape in a more tangible way – certainly a more public way. 'Now my son is a toddler,' says one Mumsnetter, 'I am starting to see how his life will be different, whereas it was only theoretical before.'

Toddlerhood is also the stage at which a lot of parents become aware of the lack of childcare options for many children with certain special needs. 'You might find yourself filling out the forms for carer's allowance and ditching your hopes of combining your fabulous career with motherhood,' says another mum.

Whatever the situation, for many, the toddler years can be particularly gruelling.

Before we go any further, a note: For the purposes of this chapter, we will not look at specific conditions or signposts towards particular diagnoses. If you have worries about your toddler, please see your GP or your health visitor. Our aim here is to show how mums of children with special needs have felt, how they have coped with 'the system' and how they have sought support. Some of the advice in this chapter will be relevant to all situations; some may be more pertinent for parents of children with needs such as ASD, which is the most common special need on the Mumsnet boards.

'It would have been nice to know we were not alone.' Fiofio

'I Think Something is Wrong': Respecting Your Gut Feelings

For some special needs, you may have a diagnosis from very early in your child's life, or even from birth. But others may only become apparent with time, perhaps as developmental milestones are not met or other markers of potential problems are noted.

As a parent, you are the expert in matters concerning your child. You know your child better than anyone else. 'If you think something is wrong, trust your gut feeling,' is the most commonly cited advice for parents of toddlers. 'Don't be put off by people telling you that all children are different.'

'My fourth son was very different from my others from the word go. We were quick to realise all was not well and sought expert opinions very early on.' MehgaLegs

'Those early days were probably the worst time,' writes one mum. 'I felt guilty that I was trying to convince people there was something wrong with my son.' Lots of parents suspect that there is 'something wrong' even from the birth of their child, but warn that it may be years before that suspicion is confirmed by the medical community. Trusting in your own feelings and instincts is important, particularly in the period when your concerns may not be shared by the people who are responsible for diagnosing your child. 'I knew something was wrong but I was told it was all OK for ages,' says another mother. 'I started to think I was going mad.'

'I was assessed time and again for post-natal depression when I took my daughter to the clinic, convinced there was something wrong with her. I think I could have ended up being assessed for Munchausen's, as the health visitors really did see nothing wrong with my daughter.' Silverfrog

Before you have a diagnosis, other people may be surprised that you think there is something unusual about your child, and that, as one mum writes, 'you are having what appears to be unacceptable thoughts about your child – namely that they are not perfect.' Again, this can be very isolating and lead to you questioning yourself. 'There is such a big element of self-doubt when you start questioning if there is something atypical about your child,' says a regular Mumsnetter. 'One of the things that always niggled me was whether he really did have a problem, or if it was my imagination. It was a big relief for me when I found out that my feelings were normal and his problems were not something that I was projecting.'

Seeking a Diagnosis

In practical terms, the first thing to do if you have concerns about your child is to arrange a talk with your health visitor and your GP. 'The system is confusing, but nothing to be scared of,' advises one mum.

'Getting a diagnosis will be hard,' warns another. 'Some doctors think it's not on to "label" children – but this is the only way to get appropriate help.' A third mum agrees: 'There have been times when I've felt like telling the doctor I'd be happy for my daughter to have her diagnosis tattooed on her forehead if only it meant we could get some bloody help!'

Many parents of children with special needs say they felt guilty about pressing for a diagnosis, as if they were somehow 'making' the child disabled. But Mumsnetters are in agreement that you need to push for all the help you can get, including a diagnosis, and not see this as confirming your worst fears – but as helping your child. 'Do not be fobbed off by professionals who talk about the perils of "labelling" your child, as if this was somehow going to wreck their life,' advises one mum. 'It's not a "label" it's a "diagnosis", and a diagnosis is the gateway to therapy and services which can change your child's life.'

'Most of the time, the only way to get any help for your child is by being the parent who asks loudest. Not necessarily in a stroppy manner (although this can work sometimes), but being the person who phones to check an appointment has been made, then phones again when it hasn't. And then phones again, and again.' Silverfrog

Sometimes finding the right person to give the diagnosis can be hard. You may know that there is something unusual about your toddler – maybe they don't quite seem to be walking, moving, talking or interacting like other toddlers – but what is clear to you, living with your child 24/7, may not be quite so apparent to a GP who sees them for a ten-minute appointment. Ask for a referral to the specialist that understands the particular issues that you have concerns about. One mother writes, 'The best bet is to read up enough to convince your GP that you know more than they do. They'll refer you up the food chain to a specialist soon enough.'

What is the CHAT Test?

'I've heard a lot of people say things like, "I don't think my child is autistic because he is affectionate/has good eye contact/is bright." None of those things necessarily rules out autism. At the same time, just because a child likes to line things up or spin round in circles it doesn't necessarily indicate autism.' Coppertop

CHAT stands for 'Checklist for Autism in Toddlers' and is a checklist for markers of autistic spectrum disorders, which may indicate if a child requires referral for more detailed assessment. CHAT is not a diagnostic tool – it just aims to identify absent behaviours which may indicate that the child may possibly be at risk for ASD. These behaviours are things like joint attention (such as pointing to show something to someone) and pretend play (such as pretending to pour tea from a toy teapot).

The CHAT is not definitive and failing to exhibit these behaviours does not necessarily mean that your child is autistic; they just might not be very keen on pouring tea. If your child fails the CHAT, make sure you are referred to a paediatrician for more detailed assessment.

How You May Feel

When you do get a diagnosis that your child has special needs, it is like having the rug pulled from under you; your assumptions and hopes for your family life and your child's future – growing up, moving out, having a career and relationships – are thrown up in the air. For many parents it can be like a grieving process; you have to deal with the loss of the dreams you had for a 'normal' child – as one mum puts it, 'a child who walked at the right time and did everything in the way it was supposed to happen.'

'It all just hurts so much,' says another mother. 'I just want to wake up and find that she's walking and can do everything that she wants to.' The grieving process is normal, so don't beat yourself up or feel that you are going mad if you get upset watching the little girl next door playing in her garden.

'The diagnosis was like a brief period of mourning for me – for the future I thought he would have – and then a slow realisation that he probably would have a future, just a different one.' Luckylady74

'Be warned that you can think really nasty things about your child, about not wanting them or feeling that they have ruined your plans,' cautions one Mumsnetter. 'It is normal and does not mean you are bad.' This is all part of the grieving process and coming to terms with changed goalposts.

Counselling is recommended by a lot of parents as a helpful tool to get through this stage. It can be hugely beneficial to talk to someone outside your circle of friends or family, who want to 'say the right thing' but who are also struggling with their own feelings.

Don't feel that you are a failure for not coping as well as you think you should. 'I would hazard a guess that we all think everyone else is doing better than us at the coping game,' writes one mum. Parents of children with special needs are not automatically blessed with naturally saintly qualities.

'There is a stupid notion, oft spouted in books and on television, that caring for a child with difficulties makes us special. As if one day we get a diagnosis and turn into some self-sacrificing, jolly Mother Earth who relishes meeting the needs of our "special" child. Bollocks. We love our children and we get up every day and do our best, and gradually the good bits seem brighter and the hard bits seem easier to manage.' Pagwatch

Some parents find birthdays quite emotional times, because people often measure progress in terms of age, and you will find it hard not to dwell on what a two- or three-year-old 'should' be able to do. But as you start to understand and come to terms with your situation, you will begin to feel acceptance. You will get used to looking at your child's progress within their own framework of abilities, rather than comparing them to their peers.

'The first couple of grieving stages are denial and anger; later comes bargaining, then depression, and finally acceptance. It's a long road and it's not easy, but you do get there. You will get through this and your child will make you proud. I promise. My daughter makes me proud every day.' Cappuccino

Reactions from Friends and Family

It can be a difficult time when friends and family learn about your child's diagnosis. Their natural reaction will be to ask, 'But he will be OK, won't he?' Don't feel that you have to reassure them, or even to tell them as soon as your child is diagnosed. You may not feel ready to announce it to the world immediately.

A diagnosis of special needs can be a huge shock for grandparents, who have a tendency to idolise their grandchildren. Mumsnetters admit to finding grandparents' negative reactions extremely upsetting. Given the choice between believing that you are a bad parent and thinking that their beloved grandchild is disabled, they may choose the former. 'It's just human nature to go with the most painless option,' explains one mum, 'but it means you'll be undermined by your own mother when you least expect it.'

'Be prepared for friends and relations to let you down when you need them most.' R3dh3d

It is also a struggle for people outside the family to come to terms with your child, and there can be a massive social impact of having a child with special needs. Playdates may not be the respite that mums yearn for from a toddler play session with the children disappearing to make mud pies while you sip Martinis on the deck. And when playdates are hard work, parents aren't as keen to cultivate friendships; it simply adds to an already stressful life.

Among closer friends, there is a natural tendency amongst parents to be reassuring: 'Oh yes, it's OK, little Archie does that all the time.' But as one mum sighs, 'It's comforting if you are talking about licking the window to see how it tastes. It's not comforting if you are talking about licking the window for hours and hours. In fact, you will feel belittled and possibly want to kill them, but until you have an SN child yourself you don't realise the difference.'

Toddlerhood is a time when competitive parenting is rife; when Jacinta's mummy boasts that her darling can draw faces and when Julian's daddy shows off that his mini-me wears pants at night. This is harder to deal with when your toddler is not meeting the usual milestones. 'It can be painful when your children's contemporaries are outstripping them,' admits one mum, 'or even worse, when younger children are outstripping yours. No, I don't want to compare toilet training problems when your child is literally half the age of mine, thank you.'

Your social life is not completely doomed, however. Although it can be hard for you when you are at a low ebb, keeping up communication with good friends will help them to understand your situation and accept you back into the social circle. There's still a huge taboo around special needs, and some people find the whole matter uncomfortable or embarrassing. 'To them, however tactful they are, a tragedy has happened and your baby has turned into a freak,' explains one Mumsnetter. 'Good friends will get over this and quickly move into the same space as you. Others won't. But again, the initial reaction is just human nature and generally leads to a period where no one speaks to you for fear of saying the wrong thing. Keep talking to the good friends and educate them gently.'

'Sometimes friends without children can be surprisingly supportive. You get understanding and compassion in the unlikeliest of places.' Totalchaos

Managing the Challenges of a SN Toddler

Social isolation is a huge problem for parents of 'different' children who may be hard to handle in social situations. Health professionals often recommend that you attend mother and toddler groups as a means of socialising, for both you and your child, but running the gauntlet of mainstream groups can be daunting.

Most mums recommend at least giving them a go. 'Don't hide away,' says one. 'Get out there to the toddler groups and learn to live with the fact that it is always going to be different. You can't pretend that nothing is wrong and hope no one will notice.' However, although it can be a tough experience, you may find that you make new friends. 'Yes, some people are incredibly stupid,' writes another mum, 'but others are wonderful and it will sort out your friends from the pillocks.'

But one Mumsnetter also warns that there will be times when you come out of mother and toddler groups 'and feel sick and awful and more upset than you were when you went in'. If you keep feeling like that, give yourself a break and don't go, or try other groups. Some mums say they feel more comfortable going to groups run by organisations such as Surestart. Workers at these sorts of places should be trained in awareness of SN and the groups are likely to be more diverse than your average privately run, singing-with-mummy class.

There are also groups and activities that are specifically organised for families with SN children, although it may be hard to find them as there isn't often a central hub of information. If you are the enterprising sort and can't find available groups, you might want to take matters into your own hands. 'Ask the local rag to run an article saying that you're hosting a coffee morning for parents of kids with disabilities. You'll be overrun!' assures one mum.

Support groups specifically for families with SN children can be a real boon, especially in educating you about what you can expect in terms of living with a SN child.

'What's been most useful is speaking to people with older kids who have the same diagnosis as our son; someone who can tell me about their child, rather than a doctor reeling off a list of facts.' Bigcar

Mumsnetiquette: Be SN Aware

Try not to exclaim loudly, 'Look at the size of the child in that buggy!' It might be a special needs buggy, rather than a fat spoiled child being lugged around by a lazy mother. Try also to avoid the question, 'Have you considered potty training yet?' to a mother whose idea of fun is probably not changing the nappy of her thrashing four-year-old, and has very possibly succeeded in instilling continence into previous children. And don't tut loudly and mutter about treating children like dogs towards the parent with her excitable child on reins – it might be the sensible course of action, particularly at a carnival where there is the small matter of multi-tonne floats chundering past. Finally, as one Mumsnetter can advise, don't comment on your SN nephew's 'annoying humming' just in case one day, when you are whining about something or other, he walks in the room and tells his mother, 'Mum, you should start humming; that's what I do to drown out the sound of her voice.'

Special Educational Needs: 'Statementing'

When your SN child becomes a toddler you may begin to get involved with the education system – much earlier than you would for a child without special needs.

At this stage you may need to start thinking about getting a Statement of Special Educational Needs for your child. This is a legal document which sets out your child's Special Educational Needs as assessed by the Local Education Authority (LEA), and sets out the provision which the LEA feels is needed by your child, including the name or type of school or facility that will provide this support.

The aim of the statement is to ensure that your child gets the right kind of help to enable him or her to progress within an educational environment. A school, health authority or parent can request a statutory assessment under the terms of the 1996 Education Act. The request needs to be in writing, although some LEAs have online forms that you can use.

You can apply for a Statement of Special Educational Needs from the age of two years. The system can be complex and one Mumsnetter advises that 'you need maximum lead-time to understand the situation with its local oddities and to sort out something acceptable by the time your child is ready to start school. You also need time to gather tips from other parents and sound out all the possibilities.'

Who's who in the system

- **Educational psychologists** help children who are experiencing problems within an educational setting with the aim of enhancing their learning. They can advise about school placement and getting the right support within a school environment.
- Depending on the type of SN, a **geneticist** may be involved in diagnosis, and a **genetic counsellor** may be involved in planning further children.
- **Occupational therapists** assess and treat physical conditions with the aim of promoting better or independent movement and related life-skills. They work with children with sensory problems

and dyspraxia-type problems. 'OTs can be absolutely invaluable in evaluating a child's day-to-day situation and coming up with practical solutions to physical problems,' says one Mumsnetter.

- **Orthopaedists** help treat children's musculo-skeletal problems; for some children this may include special footwear.

Onwards and Upwards

'All children are wonderful and all children are different,' writes one mum. 'But for some, the differences are more pronounced.'

It's possible that at this point in your child's life you might not know exactly what is different about your child, but you do know they are harder work than your friends' children.

The toddler years are tough and dealing with a toddler with special needs is even harder work, both emotionally and physically. 'It is bad, to be honest,' admits another Mumsnetter. 'Being housebound in holidays, having to constantly plan, trying to juggle siblings in the midst of all this. Years and years of lack of sleep. Fighting for services. And so it goes on.'

'But ultimately you have a child who you love just like your other children, and you adapt and your life is very different than expected – almost certainly a lot harder than you expected – but it can lead to new careers, new ways of looking at things and an understanding of what really matters in life. It's hard, bloody hard, but if life is about experiences (and I think it is) then you can make the most of that. And however difficult the day-to-day is, you still have a child you love.' Yurt1

Having a SN child is a life-changing experience; you cannot plan for the future the way other parents do. There is so much you take for granted as a new parent; with a child who has special needs all of this goes out of the window. But some parents say that once they have accepted their situation there is a certain gift of *carpe diem* that comes of living with a SN child. One mum writes, 'You have no option other than to think "sufficient unto the day is the evil thereof". It can be surprisingly liberating.'

'Having a child with special needs can have its advantages; one of them is not having to queue to use rides in playgrounds, because one excited scream from my son sends all the kids running!' TeeJaye

During the dark days of toddlerhood, when everything is up in the air, it can be impossible to imagine that there will be happy family times ahead. But there will be, although they will be differently happy to the times you daydreamed about in the past. 'I wish I had been reassured that things actually are not that bad, and they are still your children and you do still love them,' writes another mum, looking back on her feelings during the toddler years. 'I could never have imagined how lovely my daughter was going to be.'

SN items to Google (or to ask about on Mumsnet)

'Please beware of the dangers of consulting Doctor Google. You have no idea how many times I have scared myself stupid!' *Bigcar*

The following list gives an idea of the various kinds of help that may be applicable or available to you and your child.

- ABA (applied behaviour analysis)
- biomedical approach (for children with SN)
- blue badges (parking benefits scheme)
- carer's allowance
- council tax rebates
- DFG (disabled facilities grants)

(continued)

- direct payments for disabled children and young people
- disabled parking spaces outside houses
- DLA (disability living allowance)
- exit passes (for fast-tracking of SN children at tourist attractions etc.)
- free or reduced-price entries for tourist attractions
- higher rate (mobility component) of DLA
- insulation grants (for homes with disabled children)
- PECS (picture exchange communication system)
- portage
- respite
- water meter cap (for homes with disabled children)

Back to Work

I'm a Mother, Get Me Out of Here!

In this chapter ...

Introduction

Planning your working life up to the birth of your baby is relatively easy, vomiting and back pain notwithstanding: you announce your pregnancy to your work colleagues, you sit around getting fatter and fatter while cups of tea are brought to you and collections and cards are made, and you leave in a blaze of pregnant glory with kind words, a brand-new baby bath and good intentions to return when the maternity pay runs out.

After the birth, everything is different. Your attitude to work is different. Your feelings about motherhood are different. You are different. It turns out that your entire universe revolves around what was just a bump in the tummy. You haven't plucked your eyebrows in months, and can barely shoehorn your old work trousers over your thighs. Things you thought you knew during those care-free pregnant months are as cringe-worthy as those old Goth chains at the bottom of your wardrobe.

When it comes to life as a parent, the best-laid plans are nothing compared to the real experience of being a mother or a father. You may enter your maternity leave convinced that you will make one decision regarding work, but you might well change your mind.

'As a full-time working-mum I have complete admiration for stay-at-home-mums. I always thought I would want to be one but was surprised to find that I was actually quite keen to get back to work after nine months at home. I love hanging out with my son – but for me, working is much easier.' Fluffymummy

Of course, it is not just the mother who can choose to stay at home. Mumsnet is also home to several dads who have given up their paid day job into order to be at home with their children.

However, in most households, the decision more often than not is whether the mother will go out to work. Maternity leave provides an exit from paid working life, and it seems that in most families, extending this period of leave seems to happen more naturally than deciding that Daddy will take leave from paid working life as well.

'I am a stay-at-home dad. The wife is now concentrating on her career and is progressing really well. She enjoys the fact that she can relax knowing that one of us is with the kids and taking care of the house stuff rather than a nanny or childminder. My mates will rib me occasionally about it – but they also tell me that they wish they could do what I do.' EricL

As much as we argue about the validity of the model, the traditional Jane-and-Peter notion of dad out to work while mum stays at home playing with the children and cooking (or reading the paper and arguing on online talk boards) remains statistically popular. For most of this chapter, therefore, our language will answer the questions of returning to work from a mother's point of view – although the issues will, of course, apply to either parent staying at home or returning to paid work.

'The wrench is between your mummy life and your non-mummy life – and both are very appealing in their different ways.' BK78

The stay-at-home mother versus the work-out-of-the-home mother debate is perhaps the most bloody of all topics that come up on the Mumsnet discussion boards. All of us fall somewhere on the spectrum between the militant bra-burners and the PTA scone-bakers, and of course we all want to be reassured that our decision is the right one. As one Mumsnetter explains: 'This is a highly emotive subject because every parent wants to feel they are doing the best for their child.' Once you are responsible for a small child, the question of what to do 'for the best' overshadows every decision you make. No one wants to be a bad parent. But as another Mumsnetter says: 'There is not a definitive Golden Way in which families best work, but many different solutions depending on the individuals and circumstances involved.'

Some mothers will need to return to work in order to qualify for all of their maternity leave and if they do not, they may need to return some of the money. Financial considerations are perhaps the most significant part of the decision-making process.

'I desperately want to be at home with my son and we have tried every which way to balance the books – but no, I can't.' PanicPants

Big fat mortgages are most commonly cited as the reason that both parents need to work (rather than holidays in the Bahamas or posh private schools and ponies). However, before you make the decision purely on financial grounds, take some time to work out the sums involved. Weighing up the costs of childcare, the cost of annual or unpaid leave to look after poorly children (or step in for poorly nannies) and possibly calculating the reduction in the tax credit benefits can make for a complicated financial picture.

There are other reasons to return to work, of course. Some women return to work for a break. The treadmill of laundry, housework and constant attention required by a baby can feel physically and mentally exhausting, and the idea of actually sitting down at a desk talking to real live grown-ups – perhaps even with a hot drink – may seem like a vision of paradise after months of maternity leave. 'I love that I get time away from the home,' writes one mum. 'I love the break from the children.'

Other women don't want their role as a mother to take over their whole lives, and they feel that participating in paid work is a positive part of their identity.

'I know some mothers who gave up their working lives and then when their kids were teens their lives were empty. It made their teenage years very hard because the mothers couldn't let their children go. I will keep my

career going somehow so that my kids are not my only reason for being.' Artichokes

For a number of mums, financial independence is crucial. 'I feel really uncomfortable depending on a man,' says one Mumsnetter. 'I am the product of divorced parents and of course I very much hope that my husband and I last the course. But I need to be sure that I can support myself if I ever need to stand alone.' And going out to work also means that partners do not shoulder all the financial pressure.

And of course, many women enjoy working. As well as financial independence, for some there is nothing like the satisfaction of doing a (paid) job well and being recognised and rewarded for it.

'Earning, working, forging a career, the adrenalin you get from doing a deal or whatever your work is – that is the spice of life for many working women who would rather lose an arm than be a housewife.' Xenia

The decision to return to work, however, is not an easy one, and needs to be made with a lot of consideration and thought. It's important to make the decision that is best for you and your family – and that decision is different for each family, depending on their financial position, the dynamic of the parental relationship and the satisfaction that you may or may not obtain from working in paid employment and the sort of people that both of you are. 'Women who stay at home and become depressed are not helping their children by doing this,' writes one mother, and equally, some women find juggling family and working life impossible, and would much rather be at home.

And finally, a word of warning from one battle-scarred Mumsnetter: 'Take great care when passing judgement on the choices other families make.'

Should I return to paid work?

PROS

- Going to the toilet without spectators.
- People making you cups of tea.
- Paid employment can make you feel more valued.
- Adult company and conversation.
- Financial independence.
- Family is not dependent on one income – everything does not depend on the partner 'in work'.
- Pension payments can continue.
- No 'career break' so long-term job prospects are improved and there are no worries about getting back into the job market once children are at school.
- Having a life/identity outside of your children.

CONS

- If both parents are working, someone else will need to raise your children during the day.
- Nursery runs can be exhausting.
- Days off for children's illnesses or childcare crises are stressful to manage and may use up your annual holiday leave.
- Once children are school-aged, taking leave to cover school holidays can be very difficult to organise.

Part-Time Versus Full-Time

'I'm part-time and I love it. I work one day a week from home when the children are in bed and two days in the office with a lovely secretary making my coffee – and no playdough in sight! It's lovely.' Corblimeycharlie

In 2003 the right to request flexible working was introduced in the UK, and this has given parents a greater degree of control over their working and home lives. Flexible working encompasses part-time work, flexitime, job-sharing, term-time working, school hours working, or working from home. Many parents have amenable employers who recognise that parents can do a perfectly good job without sitting at a desk from 9 a.m. to 5 p.m.

Many mums feel that part-time work is the best of both worlds, as they can keep one stiletto in the world of work while keeping the other slightly sticky Croc in the home camp. It means that children do not have to be in full-time childcare, and have a shorter 'working week' of their own at nursery.

The main downside of working part-time is that you may feel that you are doing both 'jobs' half-cocked. 'I am grateful to be able to work part-time,' says one mum, 'but am suffering bad terminal guilt for not being at home when at work and not being at work when I am at home.' It also seems frustratingly common for full-time colleagues to be rather envious of part-time working parents, even though they can clearly see that you arrive with snot and porridge on your trousers every day. 'My colleagues keep telling me how lucky I am to be able to work part-time,' writes one mother. 'I think they want me to beat my chest and admit that *yes*, I am a *sponger*.'

Despite the downsides, part-time work is becoming increasingly popular among parents who feel that it results in a better 'work–life balance'.

Working full-time

Pros

- Some careers can only realistically be continued if you work full-time.
- Will keep up with peers regarding pay-rises and promotions.

Cons

- May only see child during the week for breakfast and bedtime routines (or even when they are asleep).

Working part-time

Pros

- 'Best of both worlds' – still in paid employment but also get to spend days with the children.
- If you find staying-at-home hard work, you may find that a few days 'off' makes you more relaxed and better able to deal with life at home
- Flexibility. You may be able to make up hours if you need to cover for emergency childcare.
- Children don't require full-time care.

Cons

- You may feel that you aren't doing either 'job' properly.
- And/or feel that you are doing a full-time worker's job in part-time hours.
- Colleagues may be jealous or feel that you are 'having your cake and eating it'.
- May not be perceived as an 'equal' colleague to those who work full-time.

Being Self-Employed

There are several advantages to being self-employed and having a family, the main one being flexibility. You can take days off if your child is sick, or time off for doctors' appointments and dentists without worrying about upsetting your boss.

Being self-employed may be suitable if you have the right skills and a network of contacts from your 'previous life'. However, the downside is that you only earn money when you are actually working. You can't spend a bad day faffing around looking for a new leather armchair on Ebay, and still claim your pay-packet. Self-employed people also don't have benefits such as holiday pay, maternity benefits and a company pension.

Forward-planning can be tricky, especially if you are just setting up your business. Obtaining work and keeping up the momentum with new clients and projects can be tough. 'The fact that there is no guarantee of work can lead to some slightly scary moments,' confesses one self-employed mum. 'I had three months without any work last year but then had six months which were totally frantic.'

And sadly, you cannot currently claim nursery costs as a business expense!

Self-employment

PROS

- Flexibility. You can take days off to cover your child's sickness.
- You can keep up National Insurance contributions. (Useful if you get up the duff yet *again* and need Maternity Allowance, or other social security benefits.)
- You can continue to pay into a pension.

CONS

- No guarantee of work.
- No guarantee of regular income – invoicing and payment delays can be problematic.
- No holiday pay or company benefits.
- If taking days off for sickness, you might let down clients.
- Working alone can be lonely – you may miss adult company.

Location, Location, Location: Working from Home

A common misconception amongst the childless is that mums who work from home are sitting in a sunny garden teleworking on a laptop while their child plays merrily on a rug under the apple tree. 'I've just heard a pregnant friend tell me that she won't need to give up work because she works from home!' is a common shriek heard on Mumsnet, and we all fall about laughing at the first-time mum's naivety.

Mumsnetters are in agreement that if you are working at home then you need childcare. 'Let's face it,' says one, 'if you worked in an office, would you take your kids with you? Looking after children is one job; doing a paid job is another. You definitely have to have paid childcare.'

Some mums occasionally try to fit in an hour or two of work while the children are around but otherwise occupied with television, but most warn against this. 'Trying to work with unsupervised children in the house has bad effects on every aspect of my life – health, marriage, housework and how I treat the children,' says one wise sage. 'You need childcare, unless you're working in the evenings when they are asleep.' Another work-from-home mum says, 'If my daughter is pawing at me to get me off the computer, it's a double whammy of guilt. I can't do my work properly and I'm not spending time with her properly.'

Some parents work from home in the evenings and weekends, but this relies on you having a lot of energy and little downtime. It's logically possible, but again, most think it's a bad idea in the long term. Some amount of quality time, couple time and family time is a necessity, not a luxury.

So, now that we have demolished the possibility of working while the children play at your feet, and you have arranged some child-free hours in which you can get your nose to the grindstone, then yes, if you can master the urge to dust the lounge or make a cheese toastie every ten minutes, then working from home has other practical benefits.

For a start, you won't have any commuting time (especially if you can persuade your partner to do the nursery run) so you can sit down and start working as soon as you hear the pitter-patter of feet disappearing up the garden path (or the nanny coming in the front door). You never have to waste annual leave and spend hours on the phone to a telecoms company because the engineer failed to turn up on the right day. You will always be in to pay the window cleaner. And you will never miss a Recorded Delivery item ever again – hurrah!

However, you do need to be extremely disciplined. It takes a certain sort of person to be able to step away from the housework and start working, and some people are just not cut out for it. If you have a dusty pile of unread books on your bedside table bearing titles such as *How to Stop Procrastinating and Start Living!* then now is probably not the time to hand in the keys to your office. Dithering and procrastination are not compatible with home-working.

You will also need a proper space to work – ideally a fully appointed luxury garden office in shady tropical shrubbery, although a dedicated and organised corner of the dining room is better than nothing. It is easy to fall into the trap of faffing during the day and then worrying all evening because you are not making up your hours. Setting firm time and spatial boundaries helps minimise the stress and will allow you to enjoy both spheres of your life.

If you choose to have childcare at home, you also need to work out ground rules with your nanny/au pair about how accessible you are.

'I love it that my two-year-old pops in on her way in and out to activities, has a two-minute cuddle, but then she goes off happily with the nanny. I also like being there when the older children get in from school, but when she's there the nanny is in charge. This means that what she says goes. If I disagree I'll talk to her about it later when the children aren't around, but never undermine her authority.' Munchpot

What kinds of jobs do Mumsnetters do at home?

- headhunter
- journalist
- fundraiser
- sales rep
- illustrator
- writer
- proofreader/editor
- I.T. support/consulting
- web designer
- translator
- clerk to governors
- finance manager for small charity
- book-keeping
- accountant
- market research analysis
- researcher
- civil service
- linguist
- Avon rep
- sports P.R.
- market trader
- humanist weddings celebrant
- childminding
- ironing
- voluntary work

The hardest part about working from home is actually doing the work. 'I know I'm rubbish – a real procrastinator,' confesses a mum. Another advises to 'keep off Mumsnet', although she admits, 'I usually crack by about lunchtime.' It is very easy to find yourself staring at an Untitled Document at 4 p.m., and realising that you only have ten minutes before you need to leave for the nursery run.

'Some days I work from home but really cannot be arsed. I end up spending most of the day surfing the net, doing chores, maybe even having a snooze. Today I had a sore back so I had a bath at 2 p.m. ... shh, don't tell my boss.' Gingersj

Make sure that your work space is away from other distractions. A separate 'office' is ideal – a room that is not piled high with ironing boards, dirty dishes and sticklebricks. If you can't ignore housework, one mum recommends tidying up the worst of the filth before the children leave the house:

'I fly around in the mornings before school and get the kitchen tidied, washing on, dishwasher emptied, that kind of thing. If I feel I've "cleared the decks" I concentrate much better on work while my son is out of the house.' Anorak

Another work-from-home mum advises no faffing once you are back from the school or nursery run if a ten-minute tidy-up is likely to drift into an hour's procrastinating, 'I go straight into the study as soon as I get back from drop-off. I don't go near the kitchen.' Someone else uses a timer: 'When I get back from the school drop-off I set the kitchen timer for ten minutes and tidy up. When the timer goes off, I start work.'

Once you are at your desk the internet means that procrastination is ready to hand in the form of the news, chatrooms, social networking sites and online strip poker. 'I get the most work done when the computer is broken,' confesses one mum. 'I hardly ever need to use it. If I did I can't imagine how I would resist surfing the web and silly games every five minutes.'

Some mums restrict their internet time to 'breaks' only, while one Mumsnetter takes more drastic measures: 'I unplug my router. It takes five minutes to reboot so I can't just switch windows and then get distracted for 20 minutes.'

It's a good idea to timetable working at home. One mum advises: 'Schedule breaks so that you feel justified taking them – one hour on this task, then take a break and do the laundry, then come back and do task B.' Or: 'Take a break every hour or so just for five minutes, wander round the garden or make a cuppa. It refreshes you so you can go back and work more efficiently.'

Breaking your day into chunks of work can also help. 'I use the twenty-minute rule and that's really helped me,' writes one mum. 'Tell yourself you'll work only for twenty minutes at a time, which is very manageable. Then you can break off, but more often than not after twenty minutes you will be quite well into it.'

'I find that giving myself lots of mini-deadlines with breaks helps. For example, I will write 200 words (not worry about the quality for now, easier to splurge first and edit later), then put a load of washing in. Then I will write another 100 words and have a cup of tea. Then I will write 200 words and pay that gas bill etc. This got me through my PhD (500 words a day for a year) and is still useful now for sermons, book reviews etc!' Miranda2

You can also keep a timesheet, which is often a requirement of the job if you work for someone else, as one work-from-home mum says: 'I keep a timesheet and clock up around 40 hours per week "whenever"! If there's a great coffee meet-up I go, then catch up with four hours on a Saturday evening.'

Working on a Saturday evening is fine if you have consciously planned it that way, but most Mumsnetters recommend getting stuff done in 'work' hours. So no baths at 2 p.m., slacker, and don't even think about checking Mumsnet Talk active conversations ...

What Kind of Childcare?

Once you have decided that you are going to return to work, you need to decide who is going to look after your children. There are several options available to you: a nanny, a nursery, a childminder, an au pair, a friend or a grandparent/relative. All have their advantages and disadvantages, and as one Mumsnetter says, 'Your choice of childcare depends, ultimately, on what is most important for you, your partner and your children.'

Some parents organise their lives so that they don't need to outsource childcare at all because one of them is always at home, as one mum explains: 'My husband works full-time and I work part-time, but we don't pay for childcare as we work "opposite" shifts.' If you can manage this, and don't mind not spending much time as a couple or family it can be the ideal solution for some families. However, most jobs require work from 9 a.m. to 5 p.m., so this solution is not available to many.

Some parents are quite sure what sort of childcare they want – perhaps they have always had a hankering for a nanny, or are very keen on the social side of life at a nursery. Maybe you have a friend who raves about their childminder and you really want to grab a piece of that action. Recommendation is very important and gut instinct is also rated highly among Mumsnetters.

If you are feeling clueless about your options and are starting to look for the first time, ring your local council and explain that you are looking into local childcare options. They usually offer a 'child information service' and will provide you with a list of registered local childminders and nurseries. If you are working for a company that offers Employee Assistance Schemes, these can also provide information. It is also worth asking your HR department for advice: some employers offer childcare voucher schemes with local childcare providers, which might help reduce your costs. For nannies and au pairs you can try agencies, or stick up an ad at local nurseries or pre-schools/playgroups – anywhere where nannies gather. You can also ask on Mumsnet for nannies/nanny shares or childminder recommendations.

It is worth bearing in mind that good childminders and nurseries may be booked up well in advance, and one super-organised Mumsnetter confesses, 'We put the deposit down on the nursery just after our fourteen-week scan!'

Once you have found the right kind of care, it is fantastic to skip off to work knowing that your child will have a lovely day with his new carer and friends. And when he wakes at 3 a.m. shouting that he wants a cuddle with the childminder, you can feel reassured that you have made the right choice.

And remember that, if the childcare you have chosen doesn't seem to be working out, you can always change it at a later date: and by then, you will be in a better position to decide what you need, because you will have had some experience of childcare shopping.

Childminders

Childminders look after children in their homes. The number of mindees that they look after can vary from one child to several, although there are rules about the numbers depending on the ages of the children (the younger the child, the fewer they can look after). Childminders are usually parents themselves, and may have their own children to look after, too, or their children may be school-aged.

'I chose my childminder because on our first visit, I had to prise my son away from her when it was time to leave!' Stephanie 1974

While childminders may seem a more informal option than a nanny, they have to have a basic level of qualification, a Criminal Records Bureau (CRB) check, a valid first aid certificate and training, and be registered and inspected by OFSTED. They are usually cheaper than nurseries. Parents who use childminders often do so because they want their child to be looked after by one carer in an informal home environment. There can be more of a 'family' feel to a childminder set-up, often with children of different ages to play with.

The disadvantage of using a childminder is that you are dependent on one person – and will need to find emergency cover if she is sick or on holiday. Personal recommendation is invaluable, but it can be hard to find a childminder with spaces. Activities may be less structured than at nursery (as they tend to be in a home environment), and mixing with children of various ages means that not all activities will be age-appropriate. Younger children may spend time being ferried to and from school or clubs for older children.

One mum advises: 'Visit a few childminders and get references, read OFSTED reports and, above all, trust your instincts.'

Nurseries

Nurseries are usually the most expensive childcare option. The main advantage is that you are not reliant on one person, so you don't need to worry about the carer being off sick or on holiday, and they are usually open 52 weeks a year (possibly with some days off for Christmas or other Bank Holidays).

The advantages of having a large team of staff are not just practical. Some parents like the fact that the child can bond with several people, rather than just one, and also that there are several people to take the strain when the children are all driving everyone round the bend. One Mumsnetter says: 'My baby can be quite demanding and I would not wish eleven hours with him on anyone without sheltered breaks. If there is more than one carer, there is more cover and it is less likely that one carer gets too stressed.'

The nursery staff are there purely to look after, entertain and educate the children; they are not interrupted by household chores or errands in the way that a childminder or nanny may be. This also means that you can drop off and pick up your child at any time – they will not be out doing school runs – which provides a great deal of flexibility: 'My children are at nursery for three days a week, but as I work for myself the times I drop them off and pick them up varies a great deal, depending on how quickly we get out of the door in the morning, and how my day is planned.'

'My son loves his nursery and talks about the staff there all the time. And when he sees them in the street he always gets excited and gives them a cuddle.' M2T

Nurseries are usually structured so that children of the same age are grouped together in rooms, which creates a more age-specific learning environment. Many parents find that a nursery provides a good pre-school environment, and larger nurseries may have their 'pre-school' rooms (for three- and four-year-olds) set out in a way that is very similar to a reception classroom, with little tables, and computer and home corners. The nursery experience teaches the children social skills that are useful for school as well, as one fan explains: 'I chose a nursery because I think it helps learn group skills that are useful for school. For example, group story-telling, queuing up and eating with peers.' You probably don't want to fret too much about academic achievement at this age, although one mum confesses, 'I chose our nursery especially for the Spanish lessons.' (At least she had the decency to be suitably embarrassed!)

However, 'institutionalised' childcare is not for everyone; and some feel that nursery staff tend to lack the experience of older carers/mothers/trained nannies. The quality of food varies, too – Mumsnet is privy to many nursery chip-butty scandals – so you do need to check out their menus and find out whether meals are made on-site with fresh produce. Any menu containing the word 'dinosaur' should flag up possible problems on this front – and don't forget to press for ingredients; Cowboy Hotpot may be nursery-speak for sausages and beans from a tin.

Nurseries have strict rules governing sickness, in order to avoid spreading contagious diseases, so your child will inevitably miss some days of nursery if they are suffering or recovering from certain illnesses. You can't sneak in a conjunctivitis-riddled toddler in the hope nursery staff won't notice the red eyes while you swan off to work. Although if you are tempted to whip out your Touche Eclat to tone down any possible brewing rashes, you won't be the first mum to do so.

Nannies

'A nanny you love is an absolute blessing and worth every penny.' Harrietthespy

Surely every mother wants a Mary Poppins to touch down and transform her children into delightful, engaging little people with her magic tricks and posse of tasty young chimney sweeps? Sadly, as Mrs Banks discovered, it can be a difficult job finding and retaining the right person for the job. None the less, a nanny is the childcare solution that many parents opt for, often because they want their children to spend their time at home.

As one experienced nanny-employer puts it, 'A nanny really becomes part of the family.' Nannies can also work flexible hours, so may be a suitable childcare option if you need to work at times when other forms of childcare, such as nurseries, are not available.

A nanny can be 'live-in' or 'live-out/daily' (self-explanatory) and of course, if you need a live-in nanny, you will need sufficient space – at least a spare room and, ideally, a separate bathroom, too. A separate entrance is also desirable.

Unlike a childminder, a nanny will be dedicated to looking after your child, so there will be no nursery or school-runs for other children (unless they are your own). You are still The Boss (quite literally) so you will have a large amount of control over your child's activities and diet – no danger of Smiley Faces on the menu here (unless of course you are Smiley Faces fan). A nanny will also help with child-related tasks – the remit of which depends on the terms and conditions that you have agreed – such as cooking and washing up for the children, tidying, laundry and maybe a bit of general household management. A nanny could also accompany you on your family holiday.

The downsides of having a nanny are largely those of being an employer: recruitment, retaining staff, and the practicalities of paying a salary, with the implications for tax, National Insurance and pension payments. There are special 'nanny payroll' companies that can help you with the practical side of this, or you can throw yourself on the mercy of your local tax office and they can help you set up your own payment system. One Mumsnetter warns: 'There's a simplified payment scheme, which even I as a maths illiterate could manage, but once my nanny started working more than a couple of days a week, she earned too much to qualify for this and then I struggled. But the tax office folks were remarkably helpful.' Recruitment can be tricky – not just the anguish of deliberating over candidates in order to find 'the one' but also the costs involved in advertising or using agencies.

You are also dependent on one person, so again, like a childminder, you will need to find alternative cover if the nanny is ill or on holiday. As one veteran nanny-employer warns: 'One year I used my entire annual leave covering the nanny's sick days/ holidays. You can't legislate for illness, but it is worth checking with the nanny's referees how much time they take off for illness, and make sure you say when hiring that they either have to take holidays when you do, or give you heaps of notice so you can make alternative arrangements.'

Au pairs

An au pair is a young person from another country who lives in the family home and provides assistance around the house (a few hours a day rather than full-time) in exchange for lodging and an allowance. Like a nanny, an au pair should have a contract.

Au pairs reasonably expect 'light' household duties, so they should not be asked to spend 12 hours a day raising your two-year-old triplets. They may be suitable if you need someone to help for a few hours before and after school or nursery. An au pair is ideal for a larger family (and house), where a 'big sibling' figure can provide help during the frantic moments at the beginning and end of the day, for example coordinating school runs and bathtime.

The extent to which an au pair can provide childcare largely depends on the person and their experience. They will most likely not be trained in childcare like a nanny or childminder, and how they fit in with your family depends very much on their personality and yours.

Like a nanny, a good au pair will become a part of the family – quite literally for one Mumsnetter, whose au pair married her brother, although she admits to feeling some discomfort: 'It is a bit weird that I found my brother's future wife on the internet.'

Another Mumsnetter splutters: 'I got in from work early today and walked into the house to find the au pair and her boyfriend stark naked and shagging on my new silk rug in the living room! They were so carried away it seemed like it took for ever for them to realise I was there. They ran to her bedroom. A packet of condoms and her knickers are under the sofa.'

Grandparents and friends

Once upon a time it was considered quite normal for grandparents to lend a hand in the raising of grandchildren. These days, we have many choices in our lives, and a jolly granny baking in the kitchen while grandchildren gambol at her feet is a less common sight.

Many of us who have our children late in life find ourselves looking after our parents at the same time as our children ('the sandwich generation'). Alternatively we may have a father who is CEO of a global bank and a sixty-something mother who is a professional golfer. Or our parents may feel that they have spent their lives working and raising their own children, and now they want to reap the benefits and lie in the sun in their Portuguese *casa* sipping their Sangrias. *Salud!*

The general consensus on Mumsnet is this: 'Parents bring up their own children and it is their decision how much involvement they have in the raising of their grandchildren.' And if they want to sun themselves on the Continent, it is largely agreed that is their prerogative.

'Grandparents should be there to enjoy their grandchildren, and maybe spoil them a little. It can be a lovely relationship, but it shouldn't be about feeling an obligation to provide regular care.' Inthegutter

If you have grandparents who are willing and able to provide childcare for you, then it can be great. You don't need to worry about 'settling in' periods and whether your child will get on with them, because they will already have a relationship and a bond. It is lovely to know that your children have been left with someone who is there just because they love them and want to look after them. And they will usually look after your child in a familiar home environment – either theirs or yours – so again, there is nothing new to become accustomed to.

However, using a grandparent to provide childcare does change the nature of their relationship with their grandchildren. 'Using grandparents as an occasional babysitter is one thing,' points out one mum, 'but once you get into the realms of every Wednesday afternoon it can become a chore.'

The physical strain of looking after children is quite considerable, and a day in charge of a two-year-old can be exhausting. It is hard enough if you are a fit 30- or 40-something; add on a couple of decades and a touch of arthritis and it can feel akin to climbing a mountain. 'Even though my parents are young, fit and healthy,' says one Mumsnetter, 'they do find it more tiring having my children for an afternoon than they did having their own children 30 years ago.'

Another downside of having your parents look after your children is that you may feel bad about relying on them on a regular basis. You also need to ensure that your parenting approach is similar. If you have very different ideas about discipline or diet, then you will either need to come to a compromise or accept that your parents do things differently and occasionally your daughter will have spam and chocolate cake for dinner.

Overall, unless you have a very good relationship with your parents, they are extremely keen to look after your child, and you broadly agree with their parenting methods, then it is perhaps best to keep their childcare responsibilities to a few hours a week.

Childminders

PROS	CONS
• Usually cheaper than other forms of childcare.	• Dependent on one person (will need cover for sickness/holiday).
• A home environment.	
• Less institutionalised.	• Can be hard to find one with spaces.
• One carer: encourages personal bonding.	
• Older children to mix with.	• Less structured activities than a nursery.
• Babies enjoy interaction with older children.	• Mixing with various ages of children means that not all activities will be age-appropriate.
• Usually more mature than nursery staff.	
• Should offer home-cooked food.	• Younger children may spend time being ferried to and from school for older children.
• Usually plenty of fresh air.	

Some people use their friends to look after their children. Bear in mind again that if you pay your friend to look after your child, then he or she will need to be registered as a childminder in order for the arrangement to be legal. Some parents 'swap' a few childcare hours per week so that you look after their children for a few hours, and vice versa. This can work, although one Mumsnetter warns that mixing personal and professional lives is a tricky balance: 'You will always feel indebted to her and it's very hard to move things on to a professional level with a friend.' And another points out that 'it makes life so much more difficult when they are not available or willing'.

And if you have agreed a swap, then you will also have to look after her children for a few hours a week. If the thought of this makes you long for the days when mothers were allowed a Valium with their cornflakes, then this is probably not the best arrangement for you.

Nurseries

PROS	CONS
• Not relying on one person, so there is always guaranteed cover. Child will mix with same-age peers.	• 'Institutionalised' childcare is not for everyone.
• Bonds created with a number of people.	• Nursery staff may be young and lacking the experience of older carers/mothers.
• Several adults are available. If key carer has a 'bad' day there are lots of other adults to take the strain.	• Quality of food varies.
• Staff are there purely to look after/entertain children; not responsible for cooking/house-keeping chores.	• Strict sickness rules mean that your child cannot be accommodated if suffering/recovering from certain illnesses due to contagion risks.
• You can drop off and pick up child at any time within nursery hours (will not be out on walks or school runs).	• Not much flexibility if your working hours are unpredictable, and potential financial penalties if you are late to collect your child.
• More structured age-specific learning environment.	
• Usually no television.	
• Helps learn group skills that are useful.	

Nannies

PROS

- Professional, qualified childcare.
- Will look after children in your own home.
- No nursery-run (unlike childminder).
- One person to bond with child – will become 'part of the family'.
- You are in charge of food shopping/what child eats.
- Will help with child-related household tasks, e.g. cooking/ tidying.
- Nanny may accompany family on holidays.

CONS

- Dependent on one person (will need cover for sickness/holiday).
- You will need to be an 'employer' and learn about paying tax/National Insurance (although companies can do this for you).
- Can be expensive to hire (advertising/agency fees)
- A 'live-in' nanny will need space: bedroom/ bathroom etc.

How to Choose a Childminder

Word-of-mouth is really the best recommendation where childminders are concerned, but your local council Children's Information Service should provide you with a list of local registered childminders. Ring round a few to see if they have any vacancies for a child of your child's age at the times you need – if so, arrange to visit them at home.

'The National Childminding Association website is a good resource for information about finding a childminder,' advises one mum. 'And always take up references. You could ask for names of other parents to talk to about the service.'

When you visit your childminder, come prepared with a list of questions. 'If there is anything you want to know, don't be afraid to ask,' suggests one experienced mum. 'Good childminders expect you to ask questions and will be happy to answer them.'

'Go with your instinct and look at how your child reacts. I've just seen two – with one, my son clung to me like a limpet (very unlike him), and with the other, he wanted cuddles within half an hour and cried when I put him back in his buggy to leave. It made any questions more or less immaterial.' Shreddies

Choosing a childminder is similar in many ways to choosing a nanny; you need to follow your instincts and go with someone that you *like*. If you feel a rapport developing with someone, then that is a good sign. If you leave feeling concerned or with niggling doubts, then that childminder probably isn't the right one for your child.

Questions to ask your childminder by Mumsnetter Alibubbles

- How long have you been working with children?
- What training have you had? Qualifications/certificates to look out for include: quality assurance; registration; insurance; business use for car; first aid (no more than three years old); food hygiene; childminding practice or NVQ3; other contracts and record forms.
- Do you enjoy being with children and why?
- Can I look around, see the rooms and outside play space? If there is no outside play space how will you make sure my child gets the chance to play outside?
- Where will my child rest?
- What kind of food and drink do you give? Can I see a menu?
- What will my child do all day?
- How do you encourage good behaviour?
- Will my child be with a regular group of children? How old are they? How will their timetable fit in with my child?
- How will you make sure I know how my child is getting on?
- What hours are you open?
- How much do you charge?
- What about when my child is sick, holidays, days off?

- What do you do in an emergency?
- When was your last OFSTED? Can I see the report?

And look for these Quality Pointers:

- Are the children calm, safe, happy and busy?
- Do children play and talk together?
- Is the childminder listening to the children and answering them carefully?
- Is the childminder friendly and proud of her work?
- Is she joining in with what the children are doing?
- Are there lots of fun activities planned to help children learn and play? Can children plan some of these activities themselves?
- Are there plenty of clean toys and equipment for children to use?
- Are the premises clean, well kept and safe for children with a fun outside play area (or will the child go to parks and other places regularly)?
- Do parents have plenty of chances to say what they want for their children?

How to Choose a Nursery

There are lots of different types of nurseries – big nurseries, small nurseries, nurseries owned by national corporations, small independent nurseries, council-run nurseries, and nurseries that may be affiliated to local schools. Each type will offer something different, and what meets your needs will depend on your family and your requirements.

'Both times I have chosen nurseries on gut feeling. I have just felt comfortable with the atmosphere, the children seemed happy, and I "clicked" with the staff straight away.' Fairymum

It is worth booking appointments to view a selection of nurseries so that you can meet the staff and see how the nurseries are run. Most Mumsnetters agree that it is caring and confident staff that make all the difference. 'I liked the nursery where the workers talked to my daughter and not just to me,' notes one mum. 'I know I make the decisions, but it's my daughter going there!'

Mumsnetter and nursery-owner NurseryJo suggests the following questions to consider when weighing up different nurseries:

- Do the children look well-stimulated, sitting down at activities, engaged by the staff?
- How is the day structured and what sort of activities are built into the timetable?
- Does the building look well-kept, safe and secure?
- How many of the staff are qualified?
- Does it have good quality outdoor play areas? If so, how often do children get access?
- Does indoor and outdoor equipment appear of good quality?
- Do they cook food on the premises?
- What are the menus like? Do they include a good combination of fresh (rather than tinned) fruit and vegetables?
- Do you have confidence that the nursery manager possesses strong leadership skills, is well involved and has a 'hands on' approach?

Mumsnetiquette: Don't go in with all guns blazing when your child makes wild claims of deprivation and horror at nursery

Mumsnetters have investigated all sorts of claims from their nursery attendees which have often turned out to be less than accurate. 'The lady at nursery gave me cat food for lunch,' claimed one boy, and a three-year-old girl regularly spoke of all sorts of violent acts and retributions: 'I had a nice day at nursery. I did hit Susie with the hammer. I was on time out because I did hit Oscar with the bat.' One mother worried that her daughter repeatedly claimed that a boy was hitting her, although she admitted, 'I started to get suspicious when she blamed him for her BCG scar as well.' And another mum of a three-year-old was 'informed that she ate crocodile for lunch at the nursery. When I ask what she played with it's usually crocodile. I've never seen a crocodile there.'

How to Choose a Nanny

'Oh Lordy, please let one of them be THE ONE.
This is harder than finding a husband!' Balancingact

When choosing a nanny, your best bet is to opt for the first young
woman who flies in on a talking umbrella and produces a six-foot
hat stand from her carpetbag, then you can leave the children in
her care while you disappear off to your important work fighting
for a woman's right to vote.

Alternatively, there are two main ways of bagging yourself
a nanny: going through an agency, or advertising privately and
doing the detective work yourself. Agencies can have surprisingly
large fees (typically, 15 per cent of annual salary plus VAT), but
should take most of the footwork out of the tasks of finding
suitable candidates and providing references and Criminal
Records Bureau (CRB) checks.

If you want to advertise privately, you can place
advertisements in local newspapers or magazines, on local
noticeboards, or on websites (including Mumsnet). If you have
a local college that trains nannies, you might want to consider
advertising there.

Your advert should include the hours of working and a
brief summary of duties, the number and ages of children, and
where you live. For privacy and safety, it is worth avoiding too
many personal details such as your address. Include a telephone
number and email address. State what you wish to receive – a
CV and covering letter is standard, as one experienced nanny-
recruiter advised, 'I always expect a CV to be emailed to me, and
written references provided at the first interview. I take up phone
references after the first interview.'

'I ask for a CV to be emailed to me in my
advertisement. If I like them, I send them a
questionnaire which is fairly detailed. Then I
select five or so that I want to talk to more, and
I email them. Then we might chat a bit on the

computer. Then, I call them on the phone and speak to their referees (unless the referees don't speak English, in which case I email and get my own translations).' Uwila

The convention seems to be that most advertisements state net wages, but most contracts state gross wages. 'I put gross pay in ads (or something like "good rate of pay" if the pay will depend on nanny's experience),' explains one mum, 'but I also include (£XX,000 net approx). I don't like doing a direct net–gross conversion in case nanny has complicated tax issues.' This does mean that you will need to do a tiny bit of calculation before you advertise, although there are plenty of online tax calculators that should be able to work out the net pay for you (try a few to make sure).

'Always state the gross wage in the contract. This way if or when the nanny's tax rates change, you as employer are not affected as much, and you are able to calculate how much it will cost you to employ the person, as you take the gross annual salary and add employer's NI. Also gross wage is needed for payroll purposes.' Justaphase

It is essential to have a contract and to do everything 'above board'. Although it might be tempting to pay cash in hand, it is illegal and there are considerable financial and legal ramifications for both of you if you are caught. 'If your nanny doesn't pay National Insurance and tax,' points out one Mumsnetter, 'she won't get any benefits if she is sick, won't be paying state pension contributions, and will never get a mortgage, as she won't have any way to prove income.'

Nannies can very rarely be self-employed; although there are certain conditions where short-term nannying may be on a self-employed basis, generally a nanny will be considered an employee.

What to look for in your nanny

Before you try to lure your nanny, you need to think about what you are looking for.

- What will the nanny's duties be? (Childcare obviously, but also decide on laundry, tidying, cooking, the school or nursery run.)
- What hours will they work? Will they be part-time or full-time?
- Will the nanny be a live-in or live-out?
- Do you mind if your nanny has her own children with her while she works?
- How will you pay her?
- What are the terms and conditions of employment?
- Should your nanny be:
- a non-smoker
- able to cook/prepare meat
- multi-lingual
- an animal lover
- experienced with twins
- experienced with children/families with other special needs?
- Does she need a car or a clean valid licence?

When interviewing nannies, it is important to find out where they stand on matters such as discipline, nutrition and anything else that's important to you. An interested nanny should be expected to ask questions about the position and your family (unless you have covered absolutely everything in your two-hour PowerPoint presentation).

Mumsnetters largely agree that while qualifications are great, they are not as important as being the right sort of person for the job, and having 'a positive, can-do attitude'. 'I've had qualified nannies who were a disaster,' writes one mum, 'and unqualified ones who just felt right and were brilliant with the children.'

Choosing the right nanny is 'largely about a gut reaction', 'a feeling of having clicked' and 'warming to the person'. 'The gut-feel factor is absolutely crucial,' agrees one nanny-employer. 'Can you live with her? Will she be "right" for the children? Can she live with you?'

Nanny-sharing

Some families choose to nanny-share, which means one of two arrangements:

- more than one family employs the nanny to look after the children of two families; or
- one nanny works for two (or more) families, but part-time for each family: she doesn't have two or more 'sets' of children at one time.

Obviously, the practical side of the first arrangement is more complicated, in terms of who is the primary employer and how you divide her hours for the purpose of paying her salary. You also need to decide where the nanny carries out her duties (or, as one Mumsnetter described it, who is the 'host mother').

The main benefits of nanny-sharing are that it can reduce costs for each family, and (if the nanny is working part-time for each family) it can be a good arrangement if you only need a part-time nanny.

Nanny-sharing can also throw up some interesting conflicts which need consideration, as one mum explains, 'I turned down one nanny-share because my style of parenting is far stricter than the other family's, and I thought it was a bit unfair that my daughter might be punished for things her friend was allowed to do repeatedly without consequence.'

There are agencies that specialise in nanny-shares and you can also advertise through specialist websites. Or you may know of a local family that is looking for this sort of arrangement, or a local part-time nanny with hours that she would like to fill with additional childcare work.

Ready, steady, nanny

'Woohoo! I've got a nanny, I've got a nanny! Oh, I shall put lovely flowers and a basket of muffins and brownies in her room on her first day!' Balancingact

Once you have persuaded a fabulous and loving nanny to partake in the care of your children, you need to make the right start by making your expectations about her role very clear. Obviously, let her eat a plate of delicious muffins first.

Experienced nanny-employers recommend writing out a sample daily and weekly list of chores for your nanny, so that she can see exactly what she needs to do.

By the end of each day

- children's dinner cooked, eaten and cleared away
- children's bedrooms tidy
- dishes washed, counter wiped down
- children bathed and in pyjamas
- teeth brushed
- children's clothes in washing basket
- school bags/swimming bags/dancing kit etc. packed for next day
- packed lunches made (if required)

Once a week

- bed clothes washed and changed
- school uniforms washed and ironed and hanging in closet
- supermarket shop/restock fridge

Like any employer you'll want to have regular 'supervision sessions' and it is a good idea to make these a formal, ongoing arrangement. 'I have weekly and monthly review sessions with our nanny,' wrote one experienced nanny-employer. 'I take her out for a meal and chat about the kids. I let her know that I value her opinion, but I am also clear that I make the decisions.'

'As a first-time nanny-employer I think that the relationship takes a bit of getting used to. I feel like our nanny is in my house doing my job – and to be honest I feel a bit jealous of her, so it's very easy to be critical.' BirdyArms

Diary planning is also a good habit to get into, working out playdates and activities and making sure everyone knows who is responsible for booking/arranging stuff.

One common complaint on Mumsnet is that the child behaves differently (or just behaves full stop) for the nanny and plays up with you. This can be particularly taxing after a full day at work. If this happens, talk to the nanny and work out your strategy for dealing with it:

'My children will eat all sorts of things for my nanny that they flatly refuse to eat for me. I used to worry that they were punishing me for going to work, but I have finally given up agonising and now just make sure that on the days she's here she feeds them stuff they won't eat with me and I stick to their favourite staples.' Biza

Like any new relationship, it may take a while to settle in and to get to know each other. But once you have found the right nanny, she should make everyone's lives easier.

'I love my new nanny! She really is fab. My son just adores her, and is happily being put down for naps and bedtime and he eats everything she puts in front of him. I'm a bit jealous, of course, of all the lovely cuddles they have together. But BOY I am so happy that he WANTS to have cuddles with her! It means she was such a good choice.' Spudballoo

Going Back to Work: How to Cope with the Loss/Guilt

Although you might have rationally made the decision to go back to work, it can be hard to deal with the feeling of guilt that descends when you actually return. 'I feel guilty when I am at work,' confesses one mum. 'Partly because I feel I should be with my daughter, but also because I am totally relaxed, sitting at my desk drinking coffee and writing reports while I know that my mother is probably running around pretending to be a horse and working much harder than I will all day.'

'You will always be her mum. There are many, many years ahead of you both. She will hopefully have wonderful carers, kind teachers, and lots of other people in her life – but she'll never have anyone else like you.' Hatwoman

'Guilt is part of the job spec of being a working mother,' one mum sympathises. 'But if you are happier then your child will be happier.'

'There is nothing wrong with mothers working,' another mum reminds us. 'If it is bad for mothers to work, it is bad for dads to work! You are also giving your son the message that it is OK for women to work, so just think of the good you are doing for his future wife.'

A big part of the guilt that mums may feel on returning to work is that they are leaving their 'baby' with 'strangers'. However, your child's carer will not be a 'stranger' for very long; they should soon be an important and enjoyable part of your child's life.

'Remember you and your child were strangers when you met, yet you managed!' Aloha

It may help to ease the guilt if you make a conscious effort to be a much nicer mum during the times you are together, after work or on the days you are home. Remind yourself that hopefully you are working for the benefit of your family, and it will not benefit them if you are shouty and knackered when you are at home. Take time to do the things that you might otherwise brush over in favour of getting chores done; sit and do a jigsaw; or have a chat about your respective days.

'I deal with the guilt by ensuring that when I am with my daughter, I concentrate on her 100 per cent. She probably gets more focused time with me than when I was staying at home and would let her play whilst I watched *Trisha*. (Oh, I do miss *Trisha*!)' Prufrock

It seems that the happiest working parents are those who are content to be 'good enough' and not constantly worrying that they are inevitably falling short of perfection. As one full-time working mum-of-five writes: 'I have the ability to be content, to do a good enough job; a good enough job with the children and a good enough job at work. I don't seem to seek or need perfection. If the children are reasonably happy and the people I work for are too, then that's great.'

A Day in the Life of a Working Mother

'I thought I would share my day with you. After two weeks of tonsillitis and a day of D&V with no time off work, I awoke this morning at 6.20 a.m. to remember that I had not prepared my son's nursery bag last night, so stumbled out of bed and prepared bottles, nappies etc. Showered and dressed by 7 a.m., ignoring the fact that my son was clearly awake.

'Was forced to get changed again at 7.30 a.m. due to regurgitated Weetabix and formula adorning black v-necked top. Eventually managed to get my son and myself into car and drive to nursery, quelling feelings of guilt at taking him though he was a bit vomity after a chesty cough. My son pulls enormous mardy face in car all the way to nursery and is only placated by surprise finding of favourite toy under his car seat by me whilst at traffic lights. I throw myself upon the mercy of nursery who agree to have my son despite Weetabix incident earlier.

'Fight my way through rush-hour traffic to get to work by 8.30 (under re-negotiated post-baby hours agreement). Throw self into pile of paperwork. Send memo to entire team regarding team meeting on Monday – spoonfeed them again the dates of future meetings (already issued previously). Pay bills and bank income. Perform a staff appraisal. Manage to ring nursery – son is OK. Guilt abated temporarily. Have meeting. At 12.30 realise have not eaten and succumb to bag of chips provided by caring member of team. Help out with some important data input.

'Take telephone call from husband informing me that he has come home from work sick and gone to bed – can I collect our son by 6 p.m. through Manchester rush-hour traffic (when am not supposed to finish till 6 p.m.)? Throw self on mercy of employer who agrees. Complete an audit, negotiate a contract and placate an upset member of staff at lightning speed, and leave at last possible minute to collect son. All for three-fifths of pre-baby salary.

'Fight through rush-hour traffic again, arrive at nursery to find crying son who has sicked up his tea. Guilt looms once more. Take him home and give him fluids (fear of dehydration at the forefront) and play for half an hour. Manage to pop head in on husband who looks pathetic, but no time to comfort him as son is shattered and crying.

'Bath son and get him ready for bed. Give a small bottle and pray for no vomit. Administer antibiotics and Calpol. Put him to bed. Hurrah! He goes straight to sleep. Give husband drink and paracetamol as he has a temperature of 101. Worry about husband. Clean and sterilise eight dirty bottles. Stack dishwasher, load tumble dryer and washing machine, check on husband again who is feeling better and hungry, so go and make some pasta (putting bottle of wine in the fridge at the same time).

'Collapse.'
Zoe

This Little Piggy Stays at Home

Many couples feel that childcare for their own children is not something that they want to outsource, and that it is a time of unique opportunities to parent at a crucial time of a child's life. There is something regrettably simple and wholesome about the image of a mother-at-home, looking after her fat, happy babies.

'I spent most of the first four years of my twins' life at home and I wouldn't have missed it for the world. It was a precious time that I will never get back, and I have lots of very happy memories of it. My family will always be more important than any job, and our family life is definitely much easier and smoother without me working full-time.' Sandyballs

On the other hand, some women feel that life at home with children is too tedious. 'I gave up work completely when my son was born,' writes one mum, 'but I do struggle with being a stay-at-home-mum at times.' Another confesses, 'I find days at home utterly boring. The constant chattering of my two children drives me completely mad.'

Mingle with grown-ups

Most stay-at-home mums will advise that the number-one rule to survive domestic life is to ensure that you have adult company every day. You can arrange playdates with other young children and their families, or ingratiate yourself with the local parent-and-toddler groups, or even visit elderly relations – do whatever you have to do to ensure that you have chatted about something other than Noddy and wee-wees by the time 6 p.m. arrives.

'Parent-and-toddler groups aren't for everyone, but they can be a lifeline if you need some adult company,' suggests one experienced stay-at-home mum. Most parent-and-child groups are hard to break into, so you need a thick skin to start with.

From the outside, they seem like well-established cliques and the thought of breaking into the inner circle seems both terrifying and implausible. The trouble with these sorts of groups is that, by their very nature, most attendees are concentrating more on the antics of their own charges than oiling the social wheels.

'Don't worry if you go to parent-and-toddler groups and no one talks to you; persevere, and your face will become known and people will start to chat. If you don't like the feel of one, try another until you find one that you do like.' Pinkteddy

If you really don't want to socialise with other mums, take the approach favoured by one steadfastly anti-social mother: 'I can't bear the pressure to make eye contact and chat, so I take a book or a newspaper, and sit and drink my coffee in peace.'

As well as parent-and-toddler groups, there may be a number of different activities you can take your child to – for example, singing or music, toddler gymnastics, toddler tennis, swimming groups, and church toddler services. All of these groups will provide opportunities to meet other parents with children that are a similar age to your own.

The National Childbirth Trust (NCT) is a country-wide charitable organisation that links up families (in real terms, usually mothers with young children) and organises social events and get-togethers. If you join the NCT, you will usually receive details of your local branch's activities, including Open Houses (where you can visit a family's house for an informal drop-in playdate). It is worth checking beforehand whether the other attendees will have children of a similar age to your own – having a lumbering toddler smashing her way through a tidy pile of newborns is never the best way to make a good first impression. You can also, of course, try Mumsnet, which offers a 'meet a mum in your area' facility on your Local site, and is full of great ideas of places to go and things to do with your child, as well as empathetic advice when you've had a rough ride at the local toddler group.

Plan your week

'If you don't do the planning, there is a risk that every day will just drift by in a sea of boring domestic jobs, daytime TV and frustration with your children,' warns one mum. 'Plan your week as if it was a working week (which it is, kind of).'

'Plan all the practical stuff like trips to the supermarket, but also schedule in some fun stuff which you can actually enjoy with the kids, and that should include lots of adult company for you. There is a reason so many "pushy mums" go to a different class every day, and I don't think it's for the children. I think it's so they will be able to talk to other adults and not go mad!' TuttiFrutti

Try to get out of the house every day. Twelve hours of one-to-one interaction with a toddler can be incredibly draining. Fresh air and the chance for both of you to have a run around can be a real break. Feed the ducks in the park, play on the swings and the slide, or take a favourite dolly and pram. (Bear in mind there is a strong possibility that you will be the person who lugs it back home.)

'I survived as a stay-at-home mother by drugging the children with television at breakfast-time, while I read the morning paper.'
Morningpaper

Making time for yourself is a crucial part of motherhood. If you can carve out some identity for yourself over and above that of the knackered parent who spends all day wiping bottoms and tables, then you will be able to face the next shift with a lighter heart. One mum took up running and completed two half-marathons – 'the pride I felt from that was a real boost!'

Develop support networks

When you have opted out of the water-cooler grapevine, you may find you are missing your former colleagues who provided shoulders to cry on, listening ears when you needed to vent, and someone to drag you to a wine bar for life's consolations and celebrations.

Parenting at home can be very socially isolating. It is easy to find that the only grown-up you talk to is your partner. Widening your support network is essential to help both of you deal with the stress and boredom of the everyday, and also just to refresh yourself with some different company now and again. There are, of course, some very useful websites through which you can meet local mums and/or just vent your frustrations (Mumsnet Talk being, obviously, the best!).

The older they get, the easier it becomes. 'Staying at home is hard work when children are young,' one mum sympathises, 'but be aware that you are going through one of the worst bits. It does get better! Very young children are pretty limited in terms of interaction, let alone conversation, but my son is now over two and is so much more fun now than he was a year ago.'

'I quite like being at home and bringing up my lot; they are actually pretty nice.' Hatrick

Top tips for enjoying life as a stay-at-home mum

- plan your week
- seek out adult company
- get out every day
- join the NCT, and/or check out Mumsnet Local
- go to parent-and-toddler groups
- join toddler classes – music is very popular
- do something for yourself

Sibling Rivalry

He Ain't Friendly, He's My Brother

In this chapter ...

Introduction

Apparently, there is no better gift you can give your child than a sibling. It is good to remind yourself of this when they ask for the receipt for the new baby so they can exchange him for a pirate ship playset.

It might not all be about precious sibling bonding in the early days, but when they are poring over the brochures for your nursing home, they will surely appreciate your kindness and generosity in providing them with a co-conspirator.

So while you look forward to that day, there are a few tried-and-tested methods for preparing your beloved firstborn for the little thing that is going to compete furiously with him for Mummy and Daddy's time and attention.

How Do You Tell Your Child You're Pregnant?

Toddlers are very Buddhist about the passage of time, preferring to live from one chocolate button to the next, very much in the present. They have little concept of time, and to them there is not much difference between next week, nine months, or the day they leave for college. So it's best not to start talking excitedly about your plans for any of these events just yet – although of course it will be lovely when you've got your study back.

'In the early weeks of my pregnancy I was very sick. I didn't want to tell my daughter we were having a baby just yet, but didn't want her to worry that I was ill, so I told her that I had the egg at the first stage and it might grow into a baby but it might not and that was why I was being sick.' Pesha

For obvious reasons, it's better to wait at least until you have had your first scan until you announce the news of an impending new arrival to your toddler. Having said that, if you are spending every day with your head in a bucket, you might need to explain a little earlier.

A lot of mums opt to tell the older child that the baby is 'theirs' to increase their sense of ownership and pride. It's not quite as much fun as a spanking new miniature quad bike, but if you can encourage them to think of the baby as something exciting that is arriving especially for *them*, it might actually feel exciting when it arrives.

'Number two was due on number one's third birthday, so the baby became "her birthday present" from the very beginning. This gave her a real sense of ownership, and she announced, "I'm having a baby!" to several surprised friends. Unfortunately, the baby was a week overdue and she was very angry on her birthday morning when there was no baby in the cot. But once the baby arrived, all was forgiven and it was love at first sight.' Stephanie 1974

The language you use can also help. It's better to emphasise that 'you're having a baby brother!' ('something lovely is happening to you') rather than 'Mummy and Daddy are having a baby' ('and you are being replaced'). Try to make your toddler the centre of the news when you talk about the baby ('When your sister arrives ...' instead of 'When my shiny new baby arrives ...').

Don't expect your toddler to react to the announcement with great joy. 'When I told my daughter about her brother she did not immediately comment,' remembers one mum. 'She was too busy smashing her dolly's head repeatedly against the kitchen bin.'

One Becomes Two

Be positive about the new arrival, but also be realistic. You don't want your toddler to start fantasising about a baby that will pop out ready to play hide and seek.

There are lots of toddler books that explain about becoming a big sister/brother and these make useful reading in the weeks beforehand. Depicting what is happening in a visual form should make it easier for your child to comprehend.

'I've picked up a few baby and parenting magazines,' writes a mum-to-be. 'It gives us pictures to talk about to my toddler. It also lets me introduce the idea of breastfeeding.'

Asking for your toddler's assistance in decorating the baby's room is a lovely idea that again reinforces their 'ownership' of the baby and their position as an older sibling who is helpful and clever. You could even frame one of their drawings or paintings to go above the baby's cot. Another mum says, 'We chatted to our daughter about friends of hers that had little brothers and sisters, and she helped decorate the nursery, make up the Moses basket and arrange the cuddly toys.'

A string of 'family photos' in the baby's room can be a useful exercise in teaching the idea of family. You can encourage your child with the idea that he will have to teach his baby sibling who all these people are.

One word of warning from an experienced mum: 'If you are moving your toddler out of his room into a new one for the baby, do it sooner rather than later.' Although it won't be long before your toddler settles into his new room, the stress of having a new baby is enough turmoil without moving rooms, too – which can be hugely significant for a small child. 'Couch it in terms of a "big brother" room, so he doesn't feel like he is being shoved out,' advises one mum.

If you can bear it, help your toddler make a personalised present for the baby. Another mum suggests, 'We found that giving our son a plain white babygro and some fabric pens, so he could "design" an outfit for his sister, definitely helped with bonding. Whenever she wore it, he cooed.'

Having Two: Is It Really Hell on Earth?

There are a number of books about becoming a family of more than one child, but Mumsnetters agree that some of them scare the bejeezus out of you unnecessarily. 'I found the book I read thoroughly horrifying,' confesses one mum, who adds, 'The reality was much nicer.'

Mumsnetters' advice – particularly if you are heavily pregnant, propped up on fat ankles and dripping with hysterical hormones – is summed up by one mum's recollection: 'Hand on heart, looking after a baby and a toddler is EASIER than looking after a toddler while 37 weeks pregnant. Yes, two children are harder than one, but not twice as hard, and the second time around you adjust much quicker.' The general consensus is that having two is hard work but 'quite manageable'.

Another mum of more than one agrees: 'For the last eight to ten weeks of my pregnancy I was exhausted and spent lots of time trying to persuade my toddler to watch television while I semi-dozed on the sofa. About two weeks after the birth, I suddenly found I could run after my son again. I had the energy to interact with him more and be a better mummy. The baby basically just ate, slept and pooed.'

Let's face it, you have already survived the shock of motherhood and losing your pert breasts/leisure time/once-weekly laundry/continence – and those are the big adjustments. You are now a mum and dad, über-managers of all things baby-related, even though you might not feel it sometimes. As one mum reassured a pregnant multigravida: 'I have two kids, I am a totally incompetent mother, and I've managed really quite well for the past three years.'

Of course, the early months with a baby and a toddler can be hard work at times, and require a level of organisation and planning which is more intensive than when it was just you and number one against the world. You need to remember to take two sizes of nappies out with you, for a start, although, as a veteran mother of a toddler, you won't be too stressed out by the thought of finding the ideal designer changing bag, and will just bung a nappy in your coat pocket and stuff a couple of flannels down your bra before you leave the house. 'You have experience now,' reassures one mum, 'You will not be thrown by little problems and will take much more in your stride.'

The smaller the gap between your two siblings, then the harder work the earlier months will be, because younger children are, by their nature, more needy. Your patience will be tested, probably every few minutes, as will your multi-tasking skills, as one mum recalls: 'I remember breastfeeding baby while changing the nappy on the toddler. What fun!'

Some days will be really tough. On the plus side, it won't be long before your two similarly aged siblings are happily playing together, feeding playdough to the cat.

'My son's arrival in our family was great, and from the beginning he fitted in and belonged. His sister loves him to bits and he loves her – it's so lovely to see siblings together. (Yes they have their moments but don't all siblings?!) Try not to worry, it will work out fine and you'll wonder what you worried about.' BettySpaghetti

'Is it easier to go from one to two than to go from zero to one?'

'I think it must be easier because you know what sleepless nights are like. But with the first at least you get to nap in the day ...' *compo*

'Going from one child to two is much easier than being a first-time mum. My newborn is definitely calmer than my toddler ever was and I'm sure it's because I'm more confident and relaxed with him.' *Mgs7*

'I didn't find it easier at all. I expected to know what to expect second time round but I didn't. I had no idea. I also couldn't get

(continued)

my head round the logistics of looking after two small people. It got better after about six months, though.' *franke*

'It's less terrifying but more tiring.' *chicagomum*

'It's more work, but more fun, too.' *sansouci*

'It's easier. When I had the first one I was rarely dressed by lunchtime. When I had the second, we were all up and dressed and dropping my toddler at nursery for 8.30 every morning.' *Tanzie*

'I found one to two much harder than zero to one. With the first, you have all of your time and energy to spend on them and it's all new and exciting. With two there is more than double the work and just don't even ask about the laundry. It's so hard to divide your time between a toddler and a newborn.' *logic*

'You have more of a sense of perspective the second time round. You know that babyhood passes in a flash and that most of the problems will be sources of laughter/anecdotes a few months down the line.' *Melpomene*

'The size of the gap makes a huge difference. Going from one to two with a small gap was really hard. But then we had a five-year gap before number three and it felt like a doddle.' *Stephanie1974*

'Well, when we brought our first baby home from the hospital, we just sat looking at her saying, "What do we do with her? What shall we do if she wakes up?" With my son, 22 months later, I cooked a roast dinner when I got in!' *rummum*

Falling in Love Again

'How can I love another child as much as I love my firstborn?' is the question that every parent asks themselves when they consider life with two. 'At first I was worried that I wouldn't love the baby as much as the eldest,' confesses one mum. 'Then as time went by I was worried that I loved the baby *too* much ...'

It will take a while to adjust. Once you have spent a few hours with your tiny newborn in your arms, your ancient firstborn will seem huge and rather clumsy. 'The first time my son walked into the ward to see us I thought, Wow, he's so big! It seemed like he grew in one day.' Compared to the transparent little-bird thighs of your newborn, your toddler's chunky, clunky legs will come as something of a shock. Don't be surprised if you find yourself prodding and poking and wondering how your firstborn got so vast and ungainly overnight.

Suddenly your first baby isn't your baby any more. 'Her status as my baby went out the window when a new baby turned up,' admits one mum of four. 'But that feeling didn't last. We all settled down together in a few weeks. I've found that each baby changes your feelings towards the next one up, but it is more to do with everyone finding a new place in the family, I think.' Another mum of three agrees: 'I couldn't imagine that I had any more love left, but the babies just bring the love with them.'

It's not all rose-tinted, though. 'I find the elder one far more irritating than I used to,' confesses one mum. 'It's hard not to drool over the cute baby all day.' But although everything changes, some things do stay the same. 'I still enjoy the moments when it is just me and the eldest together – when the baby is asleep for example. It's nice to recapture the magic of the first flush of our romance.'

First Impressions: Introducing the Newborn Sibling

Give a bit of thought to what you will do with your firstborn when you give birth. If you are lucky enough to have willing grandparents nearby, then an overnight stay at Granny and Grandpa's will be ideal for your big day (or night). Near your due date, or when you go into labour, you can pack a special small suitcase for your tiny traveller to make him excited about his trip away too. Explain exactly what is going to happen: 'The baby is coming, so Mummy is going to the hospital with Daddy and the midwives will help welcome the new baby and get him all dressed ready to see you! Then hopefully tomorrow you can meet him and introduce him to Granny and Grandpa!'

If you don't have a ready or willing relative, ask your friends if one of them would help look after your little one while you are in labour – most will be extremely happy to help out at this exciting time.

You don't get a second chance to make a first impression – a cliché that is of utmost importance when introducing your child to his new sibling. If this is your second child and you have an uncomplicated delivery, you might be home pretty sharpish, so the introductions may occur at home. Or it might be the case that Daddy or a relative brings the new Big Sibling to the hospital.

It is generally recommended that the first glimpse of the new baby is not in Mummy's arms under her adoring gaze. When the older sibling comes in, offer him attention first (and a cuddle) – then he can approach the baby at his own pace. Chances are that having a cuddle with Mummy at this point is more important than meeting the new baby.

'When my son came to the hospital I made sure that the baby was in the cot and I cuddled him and introduced him to the baby. Then I let him hold his sister immediately and asked him to help with nappy changes and choosing clothes.' MrsMiggins

Alternatively, if you are coming into the family home where your toddler is waiting, ask your partner to carry the baby into the house to ensure that you have a chance to greet your toddler with your full attention.

Let the new big brother or sister cuddle or stroke the baby. Try to be positive in your language ('Isn't she soft and little?') rather than negative ('Be careful/don't hurt her'). If the baby cries then don't make the older child feel responsible, just explain that babies are a bit crabby when they are tiny as they are worn out from all the excitement of being born.

Presents are always welcome and provide a positive start to the relationship, as one mum of two explains: 'We bought a present for the baby from our son which he chose, and a present for him from the baby.'

'When my daughter first met her new baby sister, I arranged the sleeping baby in her car seat, with a large wrapped bar of chocolate on her lap, in the middle of the lounge. Two years later, my eldest still talks about how she first met her sister "and she came with a bar of chocolate for me!"' Stephanie 1974

If you know you're going to be in hospital for a while – after a Caesarean section, for example – it's a nice idea to have a few small presents wrapped up, so that the baby can give the toddler something to go home with. 'It's amazing how a sticker book can to ease the pain of extended separation,' says one mum.

Presents of dolls are also popular – and enable the new big sibling to have some imaginative role play looking after his own baby while Mummy looks after the other one. 'Our daughter was 24 months when her sister was born,' remembers another mum. ' I bought her a regular, does-nothing doll for about a fiver, a couple of baby doll outfits and some cheap accessories (like a brush for dolly's hair, a dolly's buggy) and she was *delighted*. She loves her doll. We change nappies together; she even breastfeeds her!'

Practical Ideas for the Early Days

In the early weeks, giving your eldest quality, one-to-one time is really important; more so than housework and cooking. 'Say yes to all offers of help,' advises one mum, 'and do all you can to ensure that the toddler gets plenty of attention either from you or Dad or other relations. Let your parents or parents-in-law take your eldest out for a couple of hours in the day, or better still, if you've got the energy, let them take the baby and just hang out with the toddler.'

Your toddler will need constant reassurance that she is still loved and as important as she ever was. Having both parents at home can really help to ease the transition – so make sure that you make the most of Dad's parental leave as well as your own. 'My husband would play with our eldest while I looked after the baby,' reports one mum. 'Then when I'd finished feeding, we'd swap.'

'Where possible, put baby down and give your eldest as much time as you can,' advises one mum. 'And try to spend some time alone with her while your partner is with the baby, or the baby is asleep.' You don't have to spend hours with your older child, but just ten minutes actually concentrating on them rather than grunting in their direction will pay off in terms of reassuring them that they are still Mummy's special little soldier. Ten minutes of quality attention can fuel a child's confidence for hours.

If you're comfortable having relations around they can be a huge help. 'My mum stayed with us for the first five weeks, so our older daughter got attention in that difficult newborn stage,' writes one mum. Babies don't usually mind who is jiggling them about – and will make it quite clear if they do – so play pass-the-baby as much as possible and use your free arms to give some cuddles to your eldest.

If it's possible without coming across as a rude control-freak, encourage visitors to pay attention to the toddler when they arrive, rather than racing to sweep the delicious newborn into their arms. Some will be more able and willing to do this than others. If Aunty Sue rushes in gushing over the baby, try to draw the focus back to the older child wherever you can, 'Yes, this is X's new baby sister! X is being so helpful helping me dress her.'

Feeding times can be tricky, because you are pinned to the sofa by the suckling babe, which makes it hard to give the older child your attention. It can be hard to remotely manage a toddler's activities in this position.

'When breastfeeding my newborn I was watching my three-year-old doing a simple Tweenies jigsaw on the floor in front of me. I had to try and help her just by giving instructions. It was *so* infuriating. "No that's Bella's foot, dear. Where do you think her foot goes? No, not on her head, dear. I think maybe her leg. Her LEG. That blue thing at the bottom. THERE. No, the other way up. No not face down. I meant with the laces at the top. No the top of the shoe, not the top of her head..." Argh!' Fpesha

'Reading and feeding' is a popular activity, whereby you cuddle up together with baby on breast and book in a spare hard, so you can read to the older one. 'Our big feeding trick was to all lie in bed together, with the baby in the middle,' recalls one mum. 'I'd breastfeed the baby and read a book to the older one at the same time. It was great in those early days when the baby wanted to feed constantly. Plus I got to lie down!'

Some parents put together a 'feeding box', containing special books and toys which are only allowed to be played with during feed times. A variation on the idea is a box for 'grown-up' toys:

'I went through the toy-boxes with my three-year-old and we collected together all the "dangerous" small toys, and put them in a special Small Toy Box. I explained that these might be dangerous for the baby, in case she ate them, but that Big Sister was allowed to play with the Small Toy Box whenever she wanted to – but only her, not the baby, because she was grown-up and sensible. She loved this and would play with the Small Toy Box on the kitchen counter for ages.' Sp4

You may find that your big child regresses occasionally, reverting to babyish behaviour – partly because she wants a slice of the mummy-action but also because she is confused about her place in the family, and wants reassurance that she is still your baby. 'We found indulging our daughter's urge to be a baby helped (she did revert and feel insecure despite the doting),' writes one mum. 'Give her as many cuddles as possible, and tell her over and over how much you love her and how she's your special girl.' Of course, there are some things that you should indulge – curling up on your lap or cuddling your breasts – and some requests that are perhaps inappropriate – a toilet-trained child wearing nappies, for example. Try dealing with inappropriate requests with distraction or suggesting alternative ideas: 'Why don't you put the nappy on your dolly while I change your sister? Oooh, I think your dolly's done a poo! Let's change them together.'

It seems to help most toddlers if they keep to their usual routine as much as possible during the early months, so don't feel that just because you are at home again on maternity leave you should take him out of playgroup or nursery. If you can afford it, he will probably enjoy the familiar routine and playing with his peers, who are a darn sight more interesting than his grizzling, dribbling brother or sister. 'It seemed extravagant to keep paying for the toddler to go to pre-school when I was off on maternity leave,' writes one mum. 'But the routine did him a world of good and gave me a much-needed break.'

How to do the bedtime routine with two

When you are coping with a toddler and a newborn the bath and bedtime routine can spiral out of control, leaving all of you in tears. It takes a while to get the hang of the new routine, so take on board these tips for a trouble-free evening routine.

- Take things slowly – even if you have to start preparing dinner at 2 p.m. Rushing and over-tiredness will lead to meltdowns all round.
- The toddler pretty much always comes first; if he has a routine then try to stick to it as much as possible. The baby will fit around the toddler's needs, and might not be in a routine for several months.
- You don't have to do baths every day, unless your toddler has got dirty playing.
- If you want to bath every day, try bathing one in morning and one at night.
- Try putting baby in a bouncer in the bathroom while you bath the toddler (success will depend on temperament of baby).
- Allow baby some naked time kicking on a pile of towels on the floor (make sure bathroom is warm).
- Bath them together. Buy a firm plastic back support for the baby, which allows you to bathe the baby 'hands-free'.
- Make sure your toddler has lots of toys to keep him happy while you take baby out of the bath and get her dressed.
- Feed baby on the loo seat while toddler plays/bathes.
- Don't try to settle them both to sleep at the same time – the baby might need to be lugged around in the sling or cuddled on the sofa for the evening.

'You learn little tricks. For example, I would run the bath while soaking the dinner things and laying out pyjamas and nappies on the big double bed. Then I'd let the eldest strip himself while I placed baby in bath. Make it a game: for every item that they successfully get off baby gets another part of body washed. Then the eldest gets in and they have five minutes sharing a bath, and then baby comes out into a warm towel and you put nappy on. Then wash toddler's hair etc., lift him out and carry him through on to bed, then go and collect baby. Have gentle drying and massage, then curl up with milk in cup for eldest, bottle or breastfeed for baby, and all read a story in big bed together. Allow toddler to go into room and choose one toy to take to bed while you place baby in bed. Then come and read toddler a story on their own, if the baby allows.' *Amyjo22*

'I could never manage getting them both to bed at once so, would get the baby bathed and fed while the toddler watched a DVD (treat) then put baby in the Moses basket and even if the baby was grizzling a bit I'd go and do the whole bath, milk, story, bed toddler routine. It was a really precious time with my eldest and by the time I'd finished and checked on the baby, he was usually asleep so I got a bit of time to myself.' *Biza*

And of course, don't feel bad for resorting to television during these early weeks. 'Get lots of DVDs from the library for him to watch just to get you through the first three months,' advises one mum. 'Oh yes,' says another, 'I neglected to mention telly; gallons of it.'

Mumsnetiquette: When you are a relaxed Parent-Of-Two, never point out to a Parent-Of-One that she is suffering from Precious Firstborn Syndrome

It is for good reason that firstborns have their own acronym on Mumsnet (PFB = Precious First Born) and subsequent children have theirs (NSC = Neglected Subsequent Child). 'My third child points at the photos on the walls and says, "Is that me, Mummy?"' laughs one mum. 'I say, "Of course not; they're all photos of the eldest!"' Your firstborn may well be ferried to music classes and baby gyms, undoubtedly in a matching ensemble that you change for a similar outfit if it is sullied with a drop of dribble, but your subsequent spawn will be lucky if they see the inside of Asda once a week while wearing a grubby sleepsuit. 'When my firstborn went to nursery, she took with her a homemade personalised drawstring bag with gingham patches. All the nursery nurses oohed and aahed over it,' one mum recalls fondly, before admitting that she had just sent her second child to nursery 'with her spare clothes stuffed into a supermarket carrier bag with her name scrawled on in permanent marker.' So don't laugh at parents who use only pre-warmed babywipes, sterilise their steriliser and croon that they are blessed with the most beautiful baby in the world (even though you know he looks like a cheerful potato). It is only with experience that you clean a dropped dummy by licking it yourself.

Talking the Talk

Positive pep-talks are a crucial part of your toddler-coaching technique at this time. 'Try to focus on her, rather than the baby, in the things you say and do,' advises one mum. 'Tell her she's the big sister, she's in charge. Give her control over things like his clothes.' Yes, you might feel a bit reluctant to leave the house with your son wearing a tiara and pink chiffon, but it will give your daughter a sense of ownership and responsibility, which hopefully she will rise to.

Reward her with lots of bribery and fuss when she is helpful, and involve her as much as possible. Let her hold the baby and dress him, and get her involved in the feeding and nappy-changing. Asking for her help stops her from getting bored and makes her feel important, and also enables you to get your jobs done (albeit more slowly). There are few toddlers who do not feel a great deal of satisfaction at being Chief Baby-wipe Dispenser.

Be imaginative in the language that you use, and feed your child's imagination. Daydream together about how big brother will be able to teach his little sister to swim and run and play football in the garden.

'I tried to build a relationship with my son and the new baby by constantly building him up: "Look at her, she only smiles like that at you"; "She loves it when you tickle her toes", etc. I also used a squeaky baby voice for my daughter to "talk" to my son which went down well: "Mmmm big brother your breakfast looks yummy, I wish I didn't just have to have milk." ' Puddle

Some mums use a bit of conspiratorial psychology on their older children, making the baby the common comedy 'enemy'. 'What often works for us is an "adult-to-adult" type moment,' explains one mother. 'I'll raise my eyebrows at my eldest when the baby does something naughty, infuriating or downright mad, and we'll both sigh together. It perversely makes my eldest more tolerant of her baby sister.'

Tips for going from one to two by Mumsnetter Thomcat

- use positive language and encourage a sense of ownership ('this is your baby sister!')
- read age-appropriate books about becoming a big brother/sister
- point out babies in real life and in pictures
- decorate the baby's room together
- help your toddler buy the baby a suitable present
- help your toddler make something for the baby – a picture or decorated shirt
- buy a present for the baby to 'give' to her big sibling (a doll is popular)
- when your toddler meets the baby, place the baby in neutral territory such as a cot or car seat

- accept all offers of help
- give your toddler one-to-one time
- find ways of managing feeding sessions (a special toybox, 'reading and feeding')
- be gentle with your toddler and expect some behavioural changes while you all adjust
- don't feel guilty about resorting to lots of telly
- tell her a thousand times a day how much you love her

Managing Aggression and Jealousy

Imagine that you have just spent the weekend at Granny's house, and you have come home to discover that your husband has a new girlfriend. She's younger than you, and let's be honest, a lot cuter. To make things worse, she is wearing all your nice old clothes that you are too big and fat to wear, and a string of relatives keep popping in to shower her with gifts and compliment her on her lovely eyes and soft skin.

Frankly it's amazing that your toddler doesn't immediately bolt out of the door to his therapist – or solicitor. Insecurity, jealously and confusion about where he fits in are all quite natural reactions.

'My older sister "drowned" all her baby dolls in the loo when I was born. But we're buddies now.' Elibean

Don't be over-protective of your new baby. We know she is small and fragile, and that in comparison your toddler looks like the incredible hulk in floral dungarees, but constantly banging on along the lines of 'don't-crush-my-baby' is going to just provoke jealousy. Just as you wouldn't want your husband telling you how fragile and delicate his new girlfriend was, so please mind your big fat clumsy limbs, your toddler doesn't want you being over-protective of someone else at his expense.

'I have lots of photos of the big one cuddling the little one when she was weeny and she looks absolutely terrified and as if she's being crushed/strangled. I tended to think it was just toughening her up, and she's very tough now at nearly two! She survived! I tried not to intervene if the cuddle was real, even if the baby looked a bit squashed.' Bibliophile

It is quite normal for your normally adorable toddler to become unsettled with the new arrival, and this may manifest in more tantrums than usual, or, as seems very common, passive-aggressive violence towards the new baby 'She pretends to cuddle him but is actually strangling him,' writes one mum, 'and sometimes this affection spills into hitting and eye-poking.'

Ignoring and distracting is the first line of defence. One mum was baffled by bad behaviour for a few weeks until she decided to ignore it: 'It's very hard to ignore bad behaviour, but I've found that if I do, it usually blows over in a few seconds.'

'When she's giving him a special "cuddle" (squeeze), let her do it for a few seconds, so you're not saying "stop it, stop it" straight away. Then maybe try a bit of distraction – "Wow, look at this X over here" – and physically detach her from him. At least then she won't feel like she's always being told no, but the end result will be the same.' Emsiewill

As a new mum, your gut reaction to anything sharp or clumsy coming near your newborn is a mix of horror and fury. Try to overcome your urge to scream and fend off the attack of the giant toddler.

'When my sons are unkind to the baby it makes me rage inside (and outside too, often). I do think this is a natural protective reaction but feel bad that I am expecting too much of my older children who are also very young and unable to display mature levels of self-control.' Amateurmum

Toddlers live in the moment and are blown around by their feelings. Now is a good time to start teaching empathy. Again, cringe-worthy though it may seem, adopting the 'voice' of the baby can help them to understand things from the baby's point of view as one mum explains: 'When the baby has calmed down and finished howling, I say things like, "Ow, big sister. That hurt me. Please don't pinch me, I love you very much. Please cuddle me instead."'

It is quite common for displays of aggression to become more frequent, even directed at family members and friends, as well as the baby. Again, it is best to ignore this behaviour if you can.

'My son is very sweet and good-natured but when his sister was born he turned into this head-butting monster for a month. He used to run at my parents and me really hard. We just ignored it and tried to show him he was still very much loved and after a month, he went back to his loving self.' MrsMiggins

When your toddler is misbehaving or getting crabby, it is worth remembering that although (in your head) he now seems terribly grown-up and mature, he is still a toddler, and tantrums are part of the package. As one mum points out, 'I don't really think her tantrums are necessarily anything to do with me having a baby, as lots of my friends with just one child have told me that their toddlers are doing exactly the same thing!'

If you are disciplining at this stage, be as gentle as possible. 'Give her a warning and if she persists, send her to the naughty step,' suggests one mum. 'But don't get angry with her. For a child who is missing some exclusive attention, it is better to get bad attention than not at all.' Calmly insist that your toddler keeps to the normal rules. 'Stay constant with how you discipline her. Don't let her get away with anything you wouldn't have before baby. She needs to know that the boundaries are still the same and that Mummy and Daddy are also still the same (even if there is an alien invading the house!).'

Don't forget to keep reminding your toddler that you still love them, and be gentle with yourself, too. 'The early stage is knackering,' sympathises one mum. 'She will see his potential when he starts to smile in a few weeks' time. Soon enough he will be an adoring, pliable toy. It does get easier.'

Mumsnetiquette: Supervise your children

Never leave your toddler alone with a younger sibling, Vaseline, emulsion paint or toothpaste, because as many Mumsnetters can testify, disaster can strike 'in the time it takes to turn over the sausages in the oven and turn on the carrots to cook'.

In particular, always supervise:

- *cleaning products* ('My two girls smeared fabric conditioner all over the kitchen floor so they could both slide along the floor naked')
- *sharp things* ('My son and daughter used stones to draw all over my brand-new shiny car – badly')
- *pens* ('My toddler drew a spider on our laminate sitting room floor, and then became hysterical because she was afraid of the spider')
- *nappy-changing equipment* ('My toddler smeared nappy rash cream all over her baby sister's face, having stuffed a bit of kitchen roll in her mouth first to keep her quiet)

And always make sure you know exactly where they are: 'My two hid in the wardrobe in their bedroom and wouldn't answer when I called. I phoned the police and had the police helicopter out before we found them.'

'Mine!'

Sharing does not come naturally to little children. Let's face it, it doesn't come that naturally to quite a few adults, but children are by their nature selfish creatures – the capacity to empathise and see things from another person's viewpoint comes only with age and maturity. The urge for everything to be 'mine!' is a very strong one in small children, but it's essential to teach them to share if you are to avoid years of inter-toddler violence.

One mum recommends having 'multiples of favourite toys around (no one can get possessive over 57 matchbox cars)', but it is probably a tad impractical to have two completely identical toy-boxes, so how do you actually teach sharing?

When it comes to younger siblings, you can take advantage of your elder toddler's advancement in cunning by teaching them the rudiments of negotiation and distraction. 'My daughter is two and has a baby brother who's seven months old,' explains one mum. 'She knows that if she wants a toy that her brother has, she has to give him a new toy in exchange.'

'I have no choice but to teach sharing to my three-year-old and her 18-month-old brother, since they fight over the same toy constantly. I just say, "It's your sister's turn now, give it to her", taking the toy off him if he doesn't volunteer it himself. He screams blue murder sometimes and looks really hurt and put out. I then say, "Good boy for sharing, it will be your turn soon", and insist that my daughter returns it to him for "a turn" after a few minutes.'
Handlemecarefully

In serious altercations, pay attention to the snatchee, rather than the snatcher. 'If my son snatches a toy from another child, or doesn't want to share and says, "My toy, my toy!", which is what he does with his baby brother, I pay attention to the other child,' writes one mum. 'If you pay lots of attention to your child when they don't share, they get the message that they will get your attention when they behave like this.'

Teaching sharing is not easy, but one mum insists that 'you have to encourage it. If they're playing with other children then say, "Let Archie have a go with this toy now" and hand it to Archie. Just keep emphasising that it's nice if everyone gets to have a go with all the toys.'

'I have always worked on the principle that the child playing with a toy gets to play with it until they are finished,' explains one mum. 'So I will say, "Charlie is playing with that car ... shall we wait for him to finish? Or how about playing with this nice red car instead?"'

Be gentle, though, and try to emphasise the positives (everyone gets to play) rather than the negatives (you don't get to play).

'When do they learn to share?' is an oft-pondered question on Mumsnet. Children learn to share at different times, and for some it will be easier than for others. Most Mumsnetters agree that by the time they are about three years old, toddlers should have grasped the principles of sharing and should be emotionally mature enough to share without having a complete meltdown.

'I think they "get it" around three years old. And then at four they use it as a premise for sanctioning taking things off other children.' Suzywong

It is important that children are allowed some things which are their own special items. They might love Mr Lion too much to share him. You can teach them to put some favoured toys away or out of reach if this is easier for them to cope with.

It's important too that your child learns to share by you leading by example. If your child catches you with your head in the cupboard munching on the chocolate animal biscuits it's only fair and right that you give her one, too. Just don't let the baby see.

Taking turns

Toddlers don't understand the difference between (1) Mummy is taking this great toy away for ever and (2) taking turns for everyone's benefit and enjoyment.

Here are a couple of exercises that help teach the joy of sharing. Until your toddler has grasped the basics of taking turns, don't even think about letting them play 'pass the parcel', or bloodshed will ensue.

'We do this exercise at one of our music playgroups and it has really helped my two-year-old understand sharing. We all sit in a circle and the teacher takes a nice cuddly dog out of her bag and gives it to the first child, and we all sing "bow wow wow, whose dog art thou, I am (child's name's) dog, bow wow wow". Then the kid has to pass the dog to the next kid, and we all clap them if they do it well. We all sing again for the second child, the third, and so on.

'The first week we did it most children made a fuss at sharing the dog, but we've now been doing this every week and now all the children share it without a problem. It has helped my son share with his little brother; if he doesn't want to share I sing the song and positively encourage him.' *BlueberryPancake*

'I think that "sharing" is too woolly a term and concept for tiny ones, and we settled instead on the notion of "taking turns". We set up a game of taking turns, and made it very funny – each of them having a turn for two seconds, then the other, then the other. It helped them understand that if another child had a toy, they could have it in a minute, and that if they did let the other child have it, they would get it back.' *Blu*

'If you have a timing device in the oven or an egg timer, these can be used as fun gimmicks to encourage sharing. Get the toddler who wants the toy to help you set the timer, and then when it goes off, it's their turn. If the child who's been deprived of the toy wants another turn, they can be distracted from their deprivation by helping reset the timer, and when the bell or buzzer goes, they get the toy back. This one can run and run...' *Biza*

Twins: Sibling Rivalry Gone Mad

Twin toddlers bring a whole new meaning to sibling rivalry; it's one thing accepting a new baby who, although cute, can't really do anything, it's quite another to feel as if you are in a permanent competition with someone who can do exactly the same as you, and is sometimes better at it. Here are some top survival tips from the Twins Front Line:

- Try to get help at stressful times.
- Give them as much time apart as possible so you can have quality time with just one of them.
- Consider putting them in nursery at different times so you get to spend some not-fractious time with each one
- Hammer in the concept of turn-taking from a very early age.
- Try to praise effort rather than performance – don't encourage competition (which will need no encouragement). Remember that they are individuals and just because one can walk, talk, build a tower of blocks before the other doesn't mean that the other one is slow …
- Don't worry too much – twins will tear shreds out of each other throughout childhood and beyond but can still be the best of friends.

'When my twins started pre-school I specifically asked for them to be put in separate groups. It is a brilliant way of letting them develop their own character without constantly being compared to the other. Also on days out, my husband and I sometimes split up, taking one each, and then we get great one on one time.' TwoIfBySea

'I try to solve arguments by "encouraging" the boys to sort it out between themselves. So if they both want the blue football and fight over it, I remove the ball and tell them to sort out with each other how to share it fairly, "and when you both agree I will give it back". They usually become amazingly nice to each other and immediately work out a turn-taking deal, knowing the ball goes if they don't.' Shimmy21

The Hell-Shaped Room: Sharing a Bedroom

The current advice is that the safest place for a baby to sleep at night for the first six months is in his parents' room. But lots of parents will have a bedroom 'ready' for the baby from much earlier than this, and eventually, many siblings end up sharing a bedroom.

'NO WAY am I giving up my office.' Motherinferior

There are many reasons why you might consider putting your children in the same room together. You might produce more children than there are available spare bedrooms. Or you might want to keep one room spare for your study, for visitors, or for Daddy/Mummy to sleep in when he/she becomes irritated with small night-time invaders kicking them in the head. Or you might just like the idea of siblings sharing a room together.

Some people have positive experiences of sharing a bedroom with their own siblings, as one Mumsnetter writes: 'My sister and I shared a room; I loved sharing and was truly devastated when she left home when I was 14!'

Lots of Mumsnetters speak favourably of their children sleeping in the same room together. 'Initially they were in together out of necessity, now out of choice,' says one mum. Some children just seem to love each other's company at night.

'My son and daughter share a large double bed,' grumps another. 'I keep trying to separate them but they just creep back together.'

Many parents' first worry is that the baby will keep the older child awake, but this doesn't appear to be a problem. 'They seem to be immune to each other at night,' notes one mum. 'If the baby wakes up looking for food, the toddler doesn't even stir.' 'My daughter learnt to sleep through my son's squawks very quickly,' agrees another.

Bunkbeds are best avoided with young children, for practical as well as the obvious safety reasons. As one mum warns, 'You will soon be too old/fat/pregnant/unfit to get up there to change the sheets.' And if you have a child prone to vomiting, definitely never let them sleep on a top bunk, again for obvious reasons.

As well as encouraging sibling bonding, there are other long-term advantages to sharing a room, as another Mumsnetter notes: 'They have fun together in the morning which gives parents an extra few minutes in bed.'

Think Positive

Preparing for a new sibling is an exciting time for everyone, but also a time of huge upheaval for a toddler who hasn't experienced much of life. The first few months will probably have some hellish times when you wonder whether 10 a.m. is too early for a gin and tonic, but there will also be lovely times too (and you will certainly fight back tears the first time you see them both, tousle-haired and pink-cheeked, sleeping together in a bed).

A positive attitude is your best tool for smoothing the path of the new arrival – at least in the things you say and do, even if your inner thoughts are more tumultuous and worried. But once the newborn is a fat, wriggling baby crawling through the house in pilgrimage after his adored older sibling, there will be moments when you will feel like the proudest mum in the world. And then you might even find yourself thinking that another baby would be nice.

'My boys are perfect. I love seeing them together and watching how patient and protective my eldest is with his little brother and how much he's learning. And my baby idolises his big brother and follows him everywhere. I feel proud to have given them the gift of one another for the rest of their lives. Having never really been all that impressed with anything else I've ever done, I look at my boys and waves of awe and adoration course through me.' Greensleeves

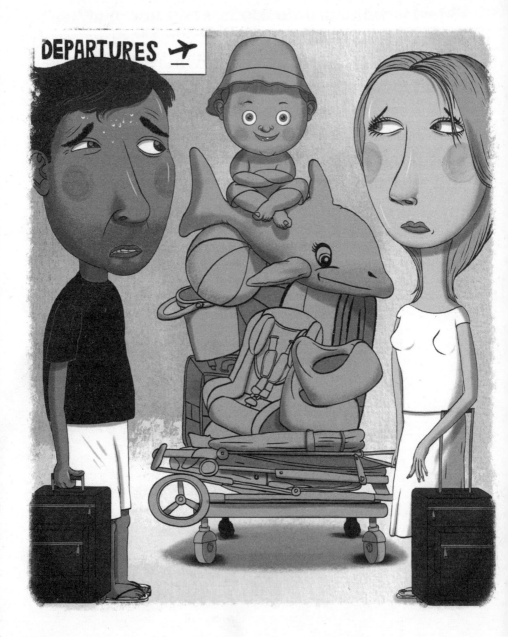

Travel

Trains, Planes and Playmobils

In this chapter ...

Introduction

You've probably realised by this stage in your child's life that your fantasy of travelling around the world in a camper van showing your delighted children the wonders of the world is not going to happen. In fact, given the panic that sets in when you stray more than a mile from the nearest purveyors of white bread and chips, British holiday camps suddenly seem a brilliant idea.

All those novels that talk about parents having adventurous, cocktail-soaked social lives while children gaily frolic under palm trees are peddling evil lies. If you pack your suitcase with such crazy ideas in your head, you will be sorely disappointed. Instead, take heed of the advice offered by one experienced family traveller:

'You will have a great time, so long as you accept that you are paying for a 14-night holiday but will actually get maybe six nights of calm, two nights transferring there and back in the dead of night, two nights on the toilet with D&V, and four nights up all night while the rest of the family vomit all over you. So long as you know them's the rules, you will be fine.' Squiffy

What Sort of Holiday?

When planning your holiday, your primary decision is probably location: home or abroad.

You need to think about whether you can bear flying with your toddler (and whether your toddler can bear flying with you). 'Planes are fine but it is all the waiting around,' points out one mum. 'A two-hour flight turns into a twelve-hour slog in airports and transfers.' And the problem of keeping your child not too messy or shouty in a confined space while being judged by a planeful of other adults can prove a tad stressful.

'Ferries are better from the point of view of waiting around, but my friend has just endured an hour's crossing in rough waters where every damn child in the boat was throwing up.' Slur

One downside of going abroad proper (i.e. where you are surrounded by natives rather than other Brits) is that your toddler might find it frustrating trying to play with other children who don't speak the same language, as one mother writes: 'My daughter spent the whole holiday trying to talk to children she'd spied as potential friends and they just looked at her blankly.'

But the main frustration with going abroad is that young children really like beaches and sweets and as long as those conditions are met, they don't care whether they are in Margate or Mauritius. So spending 24 hours travelling with a small child, when they would be just as happy if you drove down the M5 and stayed in a caravan in Cornwall, seems like a lot of unnecessary hassle.

'We took ours for a six-week tour of the Caribbean last year; we had a great time, and so did they, but when my daughter was asked about the best part of her holiday she said, "I went to the park and had an ice-cream."' Prufrock

It's not surprising then that holidaying in the UK is a popular choice for young families. Generally you know what to expect, and you avoid the hassle of flying. The downside is that the weather can be rubbish, but then again if it all goes horribly wrong you can be back home in a few hours. 'At least in this country I know I can get everything I need,' writes one mum, 'and if they are sick I don't have to fret about dealing with it in a foreign language.'

Self-Catering

Your next big decision concerns the type of holiday accommodation. Self-catering villa and caravan holidays are popular, because you don't have to worry about whether your toddler will eat the food (you can cook all the old favourites) and you have some space for playing on rainy days. You also have enough space so that you and your partner can have a semblance of a pleasant evening together once your toddler is asleep.

'Self-catering is easier with toddlers because they snack through the day and you can cater for their weird or fussy tastes.' Slur

Of course, self-catering does also mean that you still have pretty much the same chores that you have at home. One mum advises, 'Lower your standards when it comes to cooking and food if you want to relax. Plan easy, healthy dinners that don't take much preparing.'

Holiday parks are the obvious place for caravan-type holidays (and also often have campsites for tent devotees) and are usually geared up for young families, with swimming pools, kids' entertainment and lots of children running around. Some are all on-site, and others are near a beach or woodland, which one mum favours: 'I prefer smaller independent holiday parks because our idea of entertainment is playing in the woods or on the beach, and visiting places of interest.'

'Holiday parks can be great – free swimming pool, and the kids make friends and enjoy the tiny tots discos and clubs.' JiminyCricket

The quality of the sites varies hugely, so read lots of reviews or get personal recommendations before you book. You can often buy food on-site but don't expect much in the way of gourmet catering as one mum discovered: 'Would you believe it, my children went off chips after a week!'

Some holiday sites have 'kids' clubs' but you will generally be expected to stay with toddlers while they are entertained with clowns/glue/crayons – although sometimes these clubs are sufficiently diverting for you to get away with sitting in the corner drinking a coffee and reading the paper while smiling encouragingly at your child from time to time.

Camping

Some people are natural campers, loving nothing more than sitting out under the stars drinking beer while the children sleep in a cosy tent. Others find the whole thing too much like being a refugee and prefer the safety of en-suites and super-king-sized divans. Camping is an obvious holiday choice for young families, though, because it is cheap and informal and hopefully will provide your children with lots of playmates so you can sit in your collapsible chair and drink beer. On the downside, bad weather or an ill-timed vomiting bug can be more than a little irritating in the confines of a dark tent. Consequently, camping is something of a gambler's sport, but some people love it and return year after year for more outdoor adventure.

'Camping with mates ticks all the boxes so long as you remember you have to drive off-site to have a row with your husband.' Squiffy

Mumsnetters recommend doing a trial run in your back garden to see how you get on. One found this to be the perfect introduction to camping life: 'My children didn't settle, my husband was shouting, "I'm so angry I'm going to shatter into a thousand pieces," and it rained. I awoke to the sound of my daughter vomiting and it took five minutes of struggling and cursing in order to free myself from my sleeping bag.' Although by the time her posh camping equipment was delivered a couple of days later all had been forgotten: 'It's all so lovely and diddy, I want to go and try again.'

The main difference between camping pre- and post-children is the sheer amount of *stuff* that you need to take. A roof rack for the car will be an indispensable purchase, or maybe a trailer. Try to pack sensibly – put pillows and blankets at the bottom, and take packing boxes that can be re-used as baths for toddlers and storage for keeping the tent orderly.

Cooking can be a challenge. One mum suggests taking a picnic for the first night so that 'you don't have to get the cooker out before you can eat.' Another recommends 'food like tinned curry and tinned sweet and sour chicken which only needs warming up, to serve with boiled rice.' Instant porridge is an easy hot snack, especially the one where you can just add hot water. Barbecues are also popular, of course, particularly the small disposable sort. Cold dinners of baguettes and cheese can be easier than faffing about with chopped peppers of an evening, and lots of Mumsnet campers eat out as much as possible, particularly if there is a campsite diner.

'If you're heading off camping, don't rule out takeaways. We ordered a pizza on our first night and got it delivered to our pitch on the site!' Monty

One of the main enemies of the camper is wet weather. The combination of rain and toddlers is a whole new type of misery, so if the weather is at all damp dress your children from top to toe in waterproofs. If they go out first thing in the morning they should wear waterproofs, too, so when they fall over they don't get wet from the dewy grass.

Most campers seem to have a strict no-shoes-in-tent rule to prevent messy toddlers from covering the living quarters in mud and grass. Cheap doormats are recommended as a good investment.

Keeping warm is also an essential part of a pleasant camping trip. Take lots of bedding, warm pyjamas, and hot water bottles. 'Once you get cold of a night you will not get warm again,' warns one experienced camper. 'Hats and socks and fleeces should go on as soon as the sun goes down – then you can stay up warmly much later.'

'Everything will be fine as long as you have enough cake. You can live off a diet of cake, whiskey and coffee for months.' Puppydavies

Camping equipment

Things have moved on from the hazardous days of paraffin Tilley lamps. Now there is a piece of camping clobber for every eventuality. Here are some Mumsnetters' recommended camping essentials:

- a box of wine for when the kids are in bed (and corkscrew/bottle-opener)
- tent – the bigger the better
- gazebo ('They double the living space and are high enough to stand up in, with space for table and chairs.' *Skribble*)
- a picnic table with four seats that fold out ('You'll get a bad back and a wet bum on the floor.' *Sallystrawberry*)
- spare tent ('A small, cheap two-man for the kids to play in and to chuck all the toys in at night to stop the rabbits playing with them.' *Skribble*)
- something comfy to sleep on – inflatable mattresses, pillows and extra blankets ('We put one of those silver first-aid blankets on the floor of the bedrooms in the tents and then put a blanket on top. It keeps the pods really cosy.' *FeelingOld*)
- a powerful torch or lantern
- battery-operated night-lights or wind-up torches
- hot water bottle
- very warm jammies
- cooker ('Two-burner gas stoves are good.' *Sallystrawberry*)
- kettle
- brew kit ('Tea, coffee, sugar, milk, hot choc, marshmallows.' *Sallystrawberry*)
- flask (for tea or keeping milk cold/fresh)
- washing-up bowl
- first-aid kit
- citronella candles

- picnic mats ('The ones with the plastic backs.' *Sallystrawberry*)
- rigid coolbox
- storage – foldable crates or pop-up storage baskets, or those hanging storage dividers with loads of pockets
- earplugs
- clothes line and pegs
- wellies and waterproofs
- sarongs ('Take up less space than towels and dry quickly – we take one for showers, one for beach.' *Cha*)
- hats and gloves for cold evenings
- plastic bags ('Take lots of these, for those God-i-wish-i'd-brought-a-plastic-bag-to-put-this-in moments.' *Pirategirl*)
- cheapo doormat to prevent tent becoming muddy and grassy
- toys ('Swingball and blow-up balls, frisbee, skipping ropes and boules.' *Dustystar*)
- night-time toilet bucket: buckets are a much more sensible height than potties, and if you've got an old nappy bucket with a lid this will help prevent smells and will be more discreet when humping it across the campsite in the morning. ('I used our daughter's potty last year and used to fill it each morning. It was rather precarious getting it from inside to outside the tent. I had trouble getting up off it too.' *Surfermum*)
- details of nearby hotels, just in case

Cleaning a toddler while camping

Some campsites have shower blocks but toddlers are notoriously shower-phobic, so try some of these solutions instead:

- Use your sink.
- Go swimming a lot.
- Put some water in an inflatable dinghy or small paddling pool next to the tent.
- Use a large plastic packing box as a bath – you can pack food in it for the journey. ('My son thought it was fab to squeeze into a box!')

- Stand them up in a washing-up bowl and wash them down. You can either fill it from the shower block, or use water from a standpipe and add boiling water from your kettle. ('Showergel all over and *voilà* – clean kids. Much easier than traipsing to and from the showers.')

'Mine rarely get washed when we camp, much to my husband's horror. I wipe the food off their faces after they eat but pretty much leave everything else. Doesn't do them any harm and they have a good soak in the bath when they get back. That's assuming you are only camping for a few days, not weeks. They don't get smelly like adults.' Sandyballs

Wet weather strategies

Damp small children trapped in a wet tent or caravan make for one of life's grimmer miseries. Take one mum's advice: 'If it rains we don't go, or we come home early, or we retreat to a hotel. Camping should be fun – not an endurance test.' If you want to wait for the sunshine, try these suggestions for coping with rain:

- portable DVD player
- laptop computer ('We play a movie and have a family showing, snuggled up in sleeping bags.')
- playdough, toy cars, colouring books and lovely new colouring pens or crayons
- dominoes/games/puzzles
- a small plastic box of cars and a fold-up road map
- pens and paper
- books
- pubs and cafés
- indoor amusement arcades/play centres
- find an indoor pool or heated outdoor one; might as well get wet properly

- let them play in the rain ('My daughter's favourite wet-weather camping activity is to put wellies and all-in-one waterproof on and go outside. We cheer her on through the tent windows, and wait with a large towel.')

House Swaps

'Short of cash for a summer holiday? Seriously consider a house swap. You don't have to have a mansion, and more and more people are doing it.' Gameboy

House swaps are an option for an extremely cheap holiday – and there are various house-swap registers that you can join. If you can arrange a swap with a family of a similar age then 'the fiddle factor is great!' Some Mumsnetters who have house-swapped highly recommend it: 'Half of the fun for the kids is being in another house with other children's toys,' says one mother.

Hotels

Make sure you choose a hotel that's family-friendly. Give some consideration to when your child will need to eat and sleep, and find out whether the hotel can accommodate your needs.

Ask in advance whether children are welcome in the restaurant at the same time as adults (if this is what you want). Some do an earlier sitting so you can all eat together, or give families a separate room so you don't have to worry about mess and noise. Most family-friendly hotels will offer a children's tea, scheduled at a child-friendly time and often buffet-style; so you can sit and feed your little ones without them being over-tired and you being anxious about their behaviour, and they'll also have other little children to entertain them as they gobble. You can then get them to bed and, assuming the hotel also offers childcare and/ or baby-listening, have a civilised adult evening meal.

If you fancy a hotel with a pool, make sure you ask before you book whether children are welcome in the swimming pool, and if so, whether there are specified times for them.

'Hotels can be OK if you're lucky but if you end up in a Fawlty Towers model then you are doomed to spend your time ready to leap upon your child for breathing too loudly or worrying a bit of stray wallpaper.' Slur

'My husband and I have taken the kids away to smart hotels that are family-friendly and it has been fabulous,' writes one mum. 'Be careful for other guests, though. They have paid a lot of money to have a relaxing break so probably don't want your toddler running around too much. We coped with this by exhausting our son with lots of activities during the day.'

'I have delightful memories of my daughter making firm friends with our own personal butler on one particularly whizzy trip – he brought her fish fingers and a glass of milk on a silver tray with a dome and had the most wonderful grandfatherly twinkle!' Seeker

The biggest downside of hotels is that you are restricted to how you spend your evenings and a lot of parents avoid them for this reason. 'Hotel holidays are horrid with younger children,' writes one mum. 'I don't want to be stuck in a shared hotel room being quiet all evening.' On the other hand, others have found that 'sitting out on the balcony with wine while the children sleep inside is the way to go, or book a suite if your budget will stretch to it, so you can put the child/ren to sleep and order room service and watch a movie in peace.' If you would rather have a bit of proper adult time, some hotels offer childcare or babysitting services. If this is crucial to you, make sure you check on what they can offer when booking.

Some hotels are specifically geared towards the family market, and provide crèches and childcare, and there are package holiday companies that specialise in providing these services as part of the holiday deal. As one mum says, 'We would like a bit of a rest, too, so somewhere with the option of childcare is fab.'

There may be on-site kids' clubs although these tend to be for older children and may not accommodate toddlers until they are three or four. If they do take younger children, you may need to stay with them; however, if you take the paper and a cup of coffee you might get a bit of quiet time while they are making pirate hats from tissue paper.

Some family-oriented hotels have kids' clubs with movies or softplay after dinner, so you can feed them and then sit down for an adult meal at a slightly less hectic pace.

Some successful holiday ideas

'Farm cottage holidays are great. They are usually geared up to younger children, with plenty of fresh air to tire them out, animals to pet and look after, eggs to collect and other children to run riot with.' *fmf*

'We have opted for the typical family holidays in this country; we have stayed in a gorgeous cottage decked out specifically for toddlers and young children which was very relaxing. It even had a hot tub, which we used when the children had gone to bed, so felt more like a couple than parents.' *Nemoandthefishes*

'For a special occasion the whole family – aunts, uncles, grandparents, two toddlers, me and my husband – booked three cottages side by side at a posh holiday camp. It meant we all had a little privacy but there were plenty of other adults on hand to entertain our kids. And one night, we went out for a meal while doting rellies babysat.' *Fullmoonfiend*

'Camping is excellent. Dead cheap and flexible – you can cook or just eat out all week. The kids spend their time outside playing

(continued)

and making up their own games and you get to feel like a worthy parent with good, muddy, outdoorsy children.' *Slur*

'We stayed in a yurt when our son was a toddler. It was lovely – all the benefits of camping but with a proper bed on a platform. Of course we had to share the yurt with a poor-sleeping toddler which puts the dampeners on a bit: we had to have sex in the bushes outside.' *Cockles*

'Gîtes de France are a good, cheap way to holiday abroad with small children. Look for ones which have: a washing machine and a dishwasher, special "baby-friendly" status (which will be toddler-proofed), are on one floor, have a fenced garden, and garden furniture and a lawn (as opposed to weedy scrub which gets more common the further south you travel).' *Marina*

'We have had some good family city-break-type affairs in child-friendly countries – I recommend Spain and Sweden. These work well so long as you chuck any notions of a routine and stay in a city centre apartment.' *Mazzystar*

'We took our daughter to Jamaica and it worked pretty well. The resort had a little waterpark, including a lazy river, so we spent quite a lot of time in that. There was an air-conditioned crèche if we wanted to use it. The food was fine and as the restaurants opened at about 5 p.m. we even ate out with her a couple of times. On other nights, we took buffet food back to the hotel and ate on the balcony.' *Claraquitetirednow*

Skiing

Skiing with toddlers is obviously a very different experience from the skiing hols you enjoyed before children. For a start, your après-ski fun will be somewhat reduced, and by the time you've sorted out the little ones, your ski day may well be a bit shorter, but if you're a powder hound, don't panic: skiing with children is possible and can even be enjoyable – just in a different way.

Whether a skiing holiday is right for you depends a lot on your toddler's temperament.

'Take into account your own children's potential for whinging and whining: I know that mine wouldn't have made for a very happy holiday if we had taken them when they were young, because my daughter still has quite a penchant for moaning and groaning! And I think skiing holidays have quite a lot of scope for that, what with the cold, the ski-suits and the boots ... ' PestoMonster

You also need to give a lot of thought to the journey. Many resorts will have a considerable transfer time, often up windy mountain roads, so if your toddler can't bear a trip to the supermarket without throwing raisins all over the car and vomiting down himself, then you might want to bear this in mind when choosing your destination.

'I would certainly recommend using a package. There's an awful lot to sort out otherwise – including transfer, equipment hire, booking lessons, ski-passes, childcare. You'll have loads of questions about how it all works and I wouldn't try to do it yourself first time around.' Hatwoman

If both you and your partner are desperate to spend all day on the slopes, then give careful consideration to how you plan your day. You don't want to be bitterly making a snowman with your fractious toddler while watching your spouse disappear off to have fun without you. Then again, if you are in a resort where there are lots of activities for smallies and you are not too bothered by just playing in the snow, you might have a whale of a time. 'We chose a resort where there were loads of things to do if you don't ski,' writes one mum. 'I tended to go sledging most days with our son while my partner went off skiing!'

'Whatever you do, either book childcare in advance, so you can actually go out skiing, or travel with a tour operator that offers childcare packages.' Twelveyeargap

If you do want to take to the slopes, then you need to consider your childcare options. It is unlikely that you will be spending much time skiing with your toddler, so you will need someone to entertain him while you get your skiing in. 'For me the best option by far has been to take my mum or sister with me to do the childcare,' writes one mum, 'or having a rota with other family members.'

'Skiing can be a nightmare with toddlers too small to ski! If you do go, book somewhere with wall-to-wall childcare, take grandparents to babysit or be prepared to ski very little or take turns. Also be prepared to lower your expectations in case it doesn't go to plan, and pick a resort with other facilities like indoor swimming pool or mountain train rides and hire a toboggan for winter walks. Make sure your child is as well – if not better – clothed for the cold than you. There is nothing worse than a cold, wet and grizzly toddler!' LIZS

'My preference is to take a nanny with us,' writes one ski-mummy, 'so that I will know what the childcare arrangements are to be.' If you decide to take your own au pair or nanny, do agree in advance what their duties will be – hours working, days off, babysitting, and make sure that your expectations are the same as theirs. Sometimes it's best to give them a whole day off, rather than make the day too bitty by trying to do the odd hour each.

Ski activities for toddlers

Different resorts and companies will offer different provisions for toddlers. 'Our childcare service was excellent,' recalls one mum. 'Our children were taken to and from ski school, out tobogganing, for bubble car rides, to make snowmen, while we went skiing!'

'Our resort offered a "snow club" for young children in the afternoon,' writes another mum, 'which offered a mix of indoor and outdoor activities.'

Think carefully about whether you put your toddler into ski school. Just because you see two-year-old French children slaloming down the *piste*, or cousin Freddie managed a *couloir* at four, doesn't mean that your child is going to enjoy falling over in the company of (foreign) strangers.

'With our first child we were so keen to get her skiing that we paid extortionate amounts for private lessons when she was only two-and-a-half. The following year (having, of course, forgotten it all) she dropped out of ski school after a day and had to be persuaded with much bribery even to go on holiday with us the next year. With our second we didn't push it, and he's done really well. I'd say that they are more likely to be able to cope with ski school if in full-time schooling – they just have a better attention span. Of course, every child is different; if you have a kamikaze, active and keen toddler they may be ready at three or earlier, but just make sure you have a contingency childcare plan in case the ski school option doesn't pan out.' Gigi

Choose your ski school with care, and request that your child is taught as much as possible with other English-speaking children – it's just one less hurdle to jump if they can talk to each other and the teacher only has to speak one language. Always ask about class size, too, as ratios vary from school to school.

'My daughter had 15 three- and four-year-olds in her French ski school – all sobbing and falling over. The ratio was impossible and would actually have been illegal in the UK.' Biza

When it works, though, it can be magical. 'Young children will spend their first week on teensy nursery slopes and maybe the odd proper run,' writes one mum. 'Their patience and stamina is in much shorter supply than adults so they tend to have lessons that are no longer than a couple of hours, but when they finally achieve a run without falling they (and you) are so, so proud.'

Choosing your accommodation

Your main choices as far as accommodation are concerned are: hotels (pros – no washing-up or making the bed; cons – your children might not eat for a week); self-catering (pros – flexible; cons – you will have to cook and wash up); or catered chalet (pros – food is laid on for you, no babysitting worries; cons – ideally you will want to fill the chalet with familiar faces if possible). Whichever you choose, do think about your accommodation's proximity to the lifts/nursery slope/kindergarten or crèche; there's a lot to be said for being able to ski in and ski out.

'We had a great time when we booked a chalet which was in the same place as the resort kindergarten. It saved so much work. Trying to pack a bag every morning with everything you'll need (for both indoor and outdoors) and then wrapping the children up, trudging across the resort with the children, trudging back to the chalet to get your skis (and doing it twice if you forget anything) is to be avoided at all costs.' Hatwoman

Family-friendly resorts and package companies will be well-geared up with nannies and early tea-times and other activities for children. You will need to decide whether you want full-time or part-time childcare, and whether this is in the form of a nanny service or a kindergarten or crèche. You might also want to know whether the childcare service is English-speaking.

Resort-wise, America and Canada always score highly for the positive, friendly approach to children's skiing – but you have to balance this against the long, expensive journey and the jetlag. Ultimately, word of mouth is always the best source of information when choosing your resort, so do your research, ask around and read as many reviews as you can.

Ski gear for littlies

It is definitely worth investing in:

- 'Proper warm socks' *Weegle*
- 'Good quality mittens and a really warm hat' *ChippyMinton*
- 'Mittens with long cuffs overlap the jacket cuffs so you don't get exposed wrists on drag lifts and snow shooting up sleeves or into the hand when they fall or make snowballs.' *LIZS*
- 'Layers are the way to go: vest, T-shirts, long-sleeved shirts, sweatshirts, tights, then cheap ski gear.' *Weegle*
- 'Hiring gear is much more expensive than buying cheap versions, but always ask around friends and family to see if you can borrow stuff first.' *Lizp*
- 'Ebay's worth a look – and is good for selling on afterwards.' *Seeker*
- 'Try looking for skiing stuff in discount stores – the children can use their ski jackets as winter coats.' *Seeker*
- 'Children should wear helmets – you can hire these in the resort, with goggles that fit properly.' *ChippyMinton*
- 'Goggles stop their eyes from running with the cold air as well as keeping the snow off. If you go for sunglasses make sure you get ones that wrap round the back of your child's head so that they will stay on.' *Debinaustria*

Holidaying with Grandparents

If you have amenable grandparents who would like to come along and help you out with childcare, then you might want to consider holidaying with them. The pluses are that there is another lap for your toddler to wriggle around on, and someone else to chat to and play with. And if you are lucky, the grandparents might offer to babysit the odd night so you can have some time to enjoy a child-free drink or dinner.

The downsides are that you will obviously lose your privacy, and will have to sit down and have a nice cup of tea and a garibaldi when your child has her siesta, rather than running naked into the bedroom.

If you can arrange for grandparents to come along for part of the holiday, without causing too much offence, then sometimes a couple of days of their presence can be a nice break without driving you completely barmy.

Holidaying with Friends

Holidaying with friends can provide opportunities for the children to be distracted or even taken off your hands for a bit, but as one Mumsnetter points out, 'You do need friends willing to put up with your kids.'

'We have been to country houses with doting childless friends,' writes one lucky mum, 'but I must stress it is very important to ensure high levels of dotingness.'

It is much less stressful to holiday with friends who have their own children, as their expectations will be more realistic, although be warned that holidaying with another family is a very good way of testing a friendship.

'Holidaying with friends is a winner so long as they are not your bestest bestest mates (they won't be by the end). Far better to do it with more casual friends because then everyone is too polite to say anything about your parenting skills even when they've sunk a bottle of Barolo, and you can also disappear for the day without offending anyone.' Squiffy

'Diluting the toddler-madness with another family has worked for us so far,' writes one mum. 'We share the cooking and other self-catering chores, give each couple a night out on their own and then get a babysitter for one night so the grown-ups can have dinner together.'

The most crucial thing is to talk *before* you go away about each family's expectations. Suggested discussion areas include:

- Do you expect to eat mostly in or out? If eating in, who will cook and who will wash up? If eating out, what sort of budget are you planning on spending and who is looking after the children? Do you want to go as far as a rota for cooking/shopping/cleaning/babysitting?
- Do you want to have a kitty for shopping – and can you promise to remain calm when one family wants to buy (expensive) red wine and you drink only white?
- Do your children have similar routines? (i.e. Do you want the children to eat with you, or eat earlier and then go to bed?)
- What's your attitude to TV/Nintendos/Game Boys?
- Do you want to take childcare? If one family takes a nanny/au pair/granny, will they help the other family and who will pay for them?
- Do you like to veg out at the beach/pool/campsite, or do you like to go on trips, and do you mind if the other family does the opposite?

This may all sound a bit clinical and unnecessary but it's much better to work it out before you go than have your precious holiday fortnight ruined, with the result that you no longer speak to your (now ex-) friends.

If you go away with a large group it can be reasonably cheap if you are filling a large holiday home to capacity. You can benefit from having company from the other adults in the evening and, as long as you agree on a rota, cooking for the group can be inexpensive. And as one mum writes, you will also have the added marriage-enhancing bonus of 'bonding with your husband while judging your friends' poor parenting skills.'

Another Mumsnetter advises going away 'at the same time as friends – not *with* friends, you understand, but to the same resort at the same time.' This means you still have a high degree of privacy and family-time if you want it, but can get together for meals or activities so that the children can play together and leave you alone for a bit.

What to pack

You will always forget something – so if you can bear the geekiness of it then keep a holiday spreadsheet on your computer and update it each time you go on holiday. This will save you from forgetting the 'parent' part of the baby-listening monitor every time you go away. Apart from the obvious (such as two sacks of clothes for each day), here are some items that you might need on your holiday packing list:

- small medical kit – thermometer, antiseptic cream, children's paracetamol, tweezers, plasters, antihistamine, any medication
- inhaler – even if only needed once or twice a year, that once or twice is bound to be 200 miles from home
- digital camera (and batteries/charger) and/or camcorder
- tissues/loo roll
- nightwear/sleeping bag
- hairbrush/baby shampoo/baby toothpaste/toothbrush/ flannels/suncream
- waterproof coat with a hood and wellies
- gloves, hat, scarf or UV suit and/or UV tent, depending on weather expectations
- bedrail if your child uses one – also handy if your toddler sneaks into your bed in the night
- baby monitor (yes, both parts)
- night-light
- non-slip bathmat
- buggy (one that reclines, so they can nap while you are drinking your beer)
- toddler toilet seat – small fold-up ones are available
- nappies/night-time pants
- hip-seat or sling if you use one
- plastic sandwich bags – useful to sneak into the hotel dining room at breakfast so you can pinch uneaten food for snacks during the day
- plastic carrier bags
- a plastic box of toys (40 tiny toys preferable to four big ones)
- favourite cuddle-toy for night-time/comfort
- big stash of dummies
- safety pins – for pinning blankets around feeble unlined curtains to prevent early-morning wakings

Getting There

Travelling with children can be a hard slog, because long journeys bore little minds with short attention spans.

'The holiday part for me is easy; my son just "is" wherever we are. We bring a few cars and he's right at home. It's the journey that's the tricky bit.' Kitbit

If you have a long car journey, consider driving at night when the children can sleep; it can save you a lot of stress. If this is not possible, then bear in mind that while you might generally occupy your children with wholesome pursuits such as nature rambles and teaching them to knit, a long car journey is not a test of your alpha-parenting skills. The days when you and your siblings were cheerily bundled into the boot of your dad's Ford Escort and told to play I-Spy are long gone, so don't waste time wringing your hands and spotting red cars; take the easy route and buy some mobile technology.

'We have invested in a multi-function MP3/ video-player. It takes up no space in hand-luggage, the battery lasts for hours, and you can download and plug junior into his favourite movies.' Ladymuck

Portable DVD players are perfect for car journeys – you can get ones which hook over the back of the front seats, and even dual ones so that two children can view a screen each. Take a stash of their favourite DVDs and you can be good for an hour or more.

MP3 players and iPods are a good investment, too, and can either be listened to via suitable headphones (if you have reached the limit of your patience listening to Dawn French reading the exciting adventures of Kipper the Dog) or transmitted via the car radio or plugged into a set of speakers.

'Treat your child to a Magnadoodle for long journeys. They give endless possibilities for drawing and doodling and because the drawing stick is attached, they are unable to lose it.' Jona

Presents are a popular choice for breaking up long journeys. Buy several cheap toys from the pound shop and wrap them up. Then present a new gift to the child on a regular basis. This is particularly popular for journeys on planes. 'I buy a new toy specifically for long journeys,' writes one mum. 'I use the usual distractions first until my son's patience runs out, then out comes the new toy and the world seems a better place to him all of a sudden.'

'Get a TV dinner tray for the car (a tray with a cushion underneath) so that your child has something to lean on while colouring, doing puzzles, playing with cars etc.' Nella

Regular snacks are an essential part of your travelling kit. It's bad enough travelling with a bored child, but travelling with a bored and hungry child is best avoided at all costs. Small things like raisins, fruit and muesli bars are favourites.

'On long journeys I make sure my kids each have a rucksack full of their own choice of books and games and plenty of snacks and drinks. Most importantly, don't travel any longer than an hour and a half before stopping – this seems to break up the boredom.' Porkypig

Travelling by rail

There's a lot to be said for letting the train take the strain. 'On the train there's more space and interesting things to see,' points out one mum, 'and no need to be strapped in all the time.' Take a collapsible buggy and book a space next to the disabled area, so that (if no one needs to use the space assigned for wheelchair users) your toddler can sleep in his buggy on the off-chance that he falls asleep. Don't forget to take a book for yourself in case he does.

Give some thought to logistics if you need to change trains. Carrying bags, a buggy and a fractious toddler over a bridge to another platform will make you want to cry. 'Changing trains can be really difficult,' warns one experienced traveller. 'Travel light! Rucksacks are better than bags or, better still, take a toddler backpack – this leaves you the buggy to pile all the bags into and a hand free to hold on to a sibling.'

'Be reassured that a long train journey is a hundred times more fun and easier than a long car journey,' encourages one Mumsnetter. 'Just do make sure he doesn't press the Open button when you are on the loo!'

Travelling by plane

Taking a toddler on a plane can be a terrifying prospect. Every parent's worst nightmare is having their unpredictable toddler confined in a small space with 100 pairs of eyes waiting for a shout or thrown toy so that they can begin a synchronised chorus of tutting. However, Mumsnet frequent fliers have plenty of tips to make the plane less of a trauma.

First, make sure that you take your lightweight, collapsible buggy with you and ask if you can take it to the gate. This will mean that you can keep it with you until you are actually at the steps of the plane, when the cabin staff carry it on to the plane and put it in the hold for you. You then have somewhere to hang your bags and a place for your toddler to nap if there are delays or if she is tired.

A few airports have crèches equipped with toys, books and rest rooms. Check this out before you travel; there's nothing worse than suffering a three-hour delay with bored children only to find the 'children's centre' just as your flight is announced.

Under-twos can usually travel free, but this will mean that you are supposed to juggle him on your lap for the entire flight. It is generally easier to pay the (often discounted) fare, if your budget will stretch to this, so that you have an extra seat for him. If you don't, there are some techniques to ensure that you can sneakily secure yourself an extra seat, as long as your flight isn't full. Every traveller's worst nightmare is the torture of being stuck in front of a screaming, kicking toddler for a long flight. Bear this in mind and use your fellow travellers' natural repulsion to your advantage.

'Here's a trick: Get on the plane, sit down and plonk your son in the seat next to you – between you and your husband. Then wait for everyone else to get on board. If the plane is not completely full, NO ONE will want to sit in a row of three that includes a toddler. And you'll get an extra seat for him to crawl around on.' Squeaver

Lots of airlines allow families with young children to board first, which gives you an added advantage.

'If seats are not allocated in advance then get as near to the front as possible and bagsy a row of seats. Open a packet of Wotsits and spread over child's face, then let him grin at everyone – they will avoid you like the plague. Fake sick will have the same effect, but remove once everyone is seated so the flight attendants don't twig.' Scramble

Generally aisle seats are useful on larger planes because you don't have to ask anyone to move for you if you need the loo – and if the aisle is free they can have a little wander. Alternatively, a seat near the bulkhead (where there is a 'wall' in front of you) may have a bit of extra room, so your toddler could play on the floor.

'Pre-book children's meals on flights. They get served first and you'll avoid the endless wait for food. Or better still, if your toddler's at all fussy

– take your own. Some airlines have a rather strange view on what constitutes a children's meal.' Stephanie1974

As far as entertaining your toddler is concerned, if it keeps them quieter than the roar of the engines and doesn't involve irritating your fellow passengers, then let them do it.

'Re-usable stickers, the sort you get on a folding picture/scene, are great to keep in your hand luggage when travelling. Our two-year-old spent about 30 minutes arranging them on the window of the aeroplane and we also used them on the big sliding windows of our villa to "act out" numerous stories.' MotherofOne

Have a rucksack packed with tiny toys and small snacks, and produce something new on a regular basis. (And make sure you've got a spare outfit in there, too – including a spare top for you.)

Where possible, time your flight to coincide with naps, and encourage your toddler to sleep as soon as the plane takes off by giving him his dummy, milk or favourite comforter. The sheer relief, gratitude and joy of being the parent of a sleeping toddler on a flight is indescribable. If you've booked a seat for your toddler and you think your child will sleep best, or just be more comfy in a car seat, ask in advance if you can take one with you. Most long-haul airlines should be fine with this. You can secure it with the regular seatbelt.

Jetlag

Some children fit easily into a new time-zone. 'My daughter hardly seemed to suffer from jetlag when I took her to Asia,' writes one mum. 'It was me that was knocked for six.' But other children really feel it. If you want to avoid a crabby child insisting that it's time to get up and play at 3 a.m., take heed of these tips.

- Keep them hydrated with drinks and juices.
- If you think you (and they) will sleep, try to get a night flight. Jetlag is much worse when you haven't had sleep, and you won't be able to sleep unless they do.
- Attempt to fit into the new time-zone straight away, so even if you're knackered, stay up as long as possible until 'proper' bedtime.
- Keep them awake during the day. Fresh air can help; try local parks and swimming pools.
- In the new time-zone, let your toddler nap a little if they are very tired, but not too much.

'Wake them up at the proper waking-up time, and stick to your normal day and night-time routine. I kept mine going until normal bedtime (7 p.m.). The jetlag didn't last too long, a couple of days maximum. The hardest bit was waking them up and keeping them going until bedtime.'

Alipiggie

Mumsnetiquette: Airport security measures

Mumsnetters have had many things confiscated at airports during family holidays abroad, including a toy snake ('Because it might scare an old lady'), a plastic light sabre, a blunt baby's fork, child's safety scissors, a plastic sword, an oboe ('It looked like a machine gun'), nappy rash cream, eyelash curlers, an apple strudel, and a sword made from balloons. One mum had a scary moment when traces of explosives were found on her son's Game Boy ('Luckily they decided it must be a false positive!'). And pity the Mumsnetter whose wife became hysterical when a security guard tried to confiscate her referee's whistle: 'She was shouting "What the f*** do you think I am going to do with it? WHISTLE THE PILOT TO DEATH?" Later she had to explain to our daughter that she had used some very bad words and was very naughty and shouldn't have done that.'

Car Seats

If you are planning to travel by car while on holiday, and are not taking your own car and seat, then you will need to give some thought to obtaining the right car seat for your child.

- Research current car seat standards and local regulations before you go.
- If you are staying with relatives who will be ferrying you about, you might want to take your own car seat, or you could buy a suitable car or booster seat in a local supermarket. Or they might be able to borrow one for the duration of your stay.
- If you are hiring a car on holiday, always phone up the hire company before your holiday to make sure that they are supplying the right number and type of child car seats.

Keeping cool in the heat

- Avoid going out in hottest part of day – keep out of the midday sun if you can.
- Keep hydrated.
- Buy suncream and sunblock with a high SPF.
- Wear light cotton clothes as much as possible. Long loose sleeves are better than short.
- Sun tents are pop-up tents with a high SPF which are handy for shading little ones in open spaces such as beaches (although they can get stuffy).
- UV sunsuits are great for protecting young skin and covering up arms and legs.
- Sun hats with back flaps will keep the sun off your toddler's neck.
- Buy a suitable shade for the buggy – you can get ones that fit all the way over it.
- Fill a mist spray bottle with cold water to spray over everyone when it gets too hot.
- Get a sunshade for the car if you are hiring one.
- Buy a parasol and a paddling pool or inflatable boat which you can fill with water for cool splashing play in a shaded area.

- If you are hiring a car, get one with air-conditioning. If that's not possible, buy a portable fan that you can plug into the cigarette-lighter.
- Go native and encourage everyone to have a siesta after lunch in order to keep out of the midday sun. Alternatively, get out the DVD player that kept you sane on the outward journey; an hour or so of Disney should cool you all down. Ideally, your little one will have a sleep and so have extra energy to stay up late in the evening, which will save you worrying about babysitters.

Getting the Children to Bed

Whether you want to spend your evenings drinking wine and watching the sun go down or playing snakes and ladders with an ungracious loser will determine whether you are the sort of parent who wants to get their children to bed at the usual time or thinks that 'staying up late' is part of the package of a jolly family holiday.

Some holiday camps and child-friendly hotels offer evening entertainment for the children if you want to keep yours awake in the evenings. This can be fun for them but less fun for you, unless, as one Mumsnetter writes, 'you like watching hundreds of kids smeared in various foods doing the Macarena in a darkened room with flashing lights surrounded by desperate-to-impress Red Coats.'

If, on the other hand, you prefer to spend a little bit of grown-up time with your partner, then you may find yourself counting down the hours until bedtime. If your child is used to a bedtime winding-down routine, then keeping to that as much as possible should hasten the arrival of the dreamtime fairies. You might need to improvise with a packing box for a bath but with a bit of luck the fresh holiday air will have exhausted the little darlings and they will fall asleep pronto.

'If your child is used to sleeping in a dark room then a length of blackout lining and a couple of safety pins can be a very useful addition to holiday luggage – it allows you to darken a room however flimsy the curtains.' JulieG

If your child is a night-time wetter or recently toilet trained, give some thought to whether you want to risk bed-stripping on holiday. Some parents put their toddlers into pull-ups for night-time while on holiday. One mum says: 'I tell him they are Holiday Pants and he puts them on with no questions asked.'

Some Enchanted Evening: How to Make the Most of Holiday Nights

When you are holidaying with children, you don't really get much time to relax or talk to each other, other than bellowing, 'What do you mean you forgot the nappies?' Once the littlies are in bed and asleep, however, you have a chance of clawing back a little bit of 'us-time', although whispering to each other in a dark hotel room at 8 p.m. is not ideal.

A balcony might be one solution if the weather is warm – although this obviously raises safety concerns while your child is awake! At least make sure you have a table and chairs so you have somewhere to sit. Some hotels have a baby-listening service though not all parents are happy to leave their children alone in a room. Some hotels have babysitting services so enquire about this if you would like the possibility of spending a peaceful evening in the bar, but obviously, this will add to the cost.

Some parents opt to go out in the evenings with their toddler in a buggy so that he can sleep when he gets tired while you continue to nurse your beer. You then transfer them into their beds back at the hotel. This can be a good option if you're holidaying in a country where toddlers are generally out and about in the evenings. If you think your toddler will cope, you may even get a lie-in if they stay up later than usual; then again you may just get the same early start with a grumpier, sleep-deprived child.

If evenings in without worrying about childcare are your priority, self-catering wins hands-down. Enjoying a glass of wine on a porch while the sun goes down – or even in the lounge of the caravan with the rain crashing on the roof – is pretty nice. 'We specifically got accommodation last year with comfy seats in the lounge area,' writes one mum. 'My husband took his laptop and a selection of DVDs, so we'd watch a film while downing cheap sangria from the supermarket.'

A miscellany of tips for jolly holidays

'When you go on holiday, get a small rucksack for your little one to carry (or even better pull along on wheels); great for teddy, book, crayons, biscuits etc. Makes them feel very involved and important, and saves you carrying more stuff.' *Ems*

'Plait your daughter's hair into lots of small braids. It means she can go in the water without the dreaded de-tangling session afterwards. It's dead easy to wash and looks cool.' *Summac*

'Always put suncream on before going out, and especially if you're heading for the beach. Saves their tears as you try to hold down a wriggling child while massaging in an abrasive sand-and-suncream mix.' *TM2*

'If it's not too hot, wear wetsuits on the beach. Put them on before you go and wear them back. Much easier than messing about with cossies and struggling back into clothes with wet, sandy skin, and kids can stay in the water for ages without getting cold.' *Cornsilk*

(continued)

'Collect all the tourist leaflets you can. When planning a day out, a quick rummage through them gives ideas of where to go and all the details such as opening times, admission price and directions.' *MammyM*

'If you're going to a crowded place with your children, wear something colourful on top so at least they can spot you easily if they lose sight of you.' *Tigermoth*

'In crowded places write your mobile number on your child's arm in biro, so if they get lost, they just go up to another mummy, flash the number and you get a call!' *Beachyhead*

'If you are going out for a meal (or anywhere small children might find boring) always bring along some small pocket-size toys or activity books to keep them amused. Just give them the toys one at a time throughout the meal.' *Gloworm*

'I've always found a cheap bottle of bubbles very handy to take on holiday. Great for the kids to chase on the beach or grassed areas.' *Rosehip*

'Buy a small, inflatable paddling pool. They take up no space when in the packet and you can put it on your patio and keep your child safely by your side.' *Rhiannon*

'For beach holidays, invest in one of those towelling, hooded robes. Great for either staving off pneumonia when they come out of the sea/pool, covering up to keep out of the sun, or going to a café for lunch.' *bigberta*

Leaving the Kids Behind

For those lucky parents who have willing and able relatives or childcare, the luxurious dream of a child-free break is a real possibility. For a day or maybe more, you could be the lucky recipient of lie-ins, adult conversation, relaxing meals and the chance of marital intimacy without running the risk of spectators.

Particularly if you have young children, getting together for a while without the constant whining of tinies can rejuvenate your relationship and – it's a cliché but true – help you to remember what you saw in each other in the first place, before you started running a nursery. And it is always fun to see if you can find things to talk about other than the children.

'It's great for us to spend time together, for the grandparents to have time with their grandkids, and for the children to form a good relationship with their grandparents. So we all win.' Zubb

Generally, as long as you have lovely, doting relatives who will spoil your child for a few days, then you will miss them far more than they miss you. 'We cried more than the kids did when we said goodbye,' writes one mum, and another confesses, 'I did get upset at the airport when I saw families with little boys like mine!'

However, be reassured that it will not ruin your holiday entirely. 'We had a great time,' says one Mumsnetter reassuringly, 'and our daughter keeps asking when she's going to stay at her aunty's while Mummy and Daddy go in the plane again.'

'The first time I did really miss my daughter and rang loads but it was still nice to get away. Now I just ring to say good morning and again to say goodnight. The children love it because they are thoroughly spoiled for the whole weekend.'
Amynnixmum

Are We There Yet?

'A change is as good as a rest.' Well, it isn't really, but sometimes it's the nearest that you are going to bloody well get, so you may as well jump in and enjoy it. As long as your expectations are nice and low, you will have the possibility of enjoying yourself, and as long as you indulge your toddler with the occasional ice-cream, they will undoubtedly have a whale of a time.

Make sure your standards are lower than normal, too. 'Let small stuff go,' advises one mum. 'Don't piss off other holidaymakers, don't break stuff and don't injure yourselves or others. Everything else – close eyes and ignore. That's it really.'

'How to holiday: throw toddler into the car with a change of underwear and a swimsuit; no room for anything else because the boot will be full with the buggy. Drive via the Channel, crossing depends on how seasick you all get. Arrive at the most high spec mobile home you can afford. Empty car. Visit *supermarché* and stock up on ice-lollies, Nutella and things to barbecue. Negotiate with husband as to whether you do the morning or afternoon childcare shift. Swig wine with your baguette and pretend you are enjoying yourself. About four years later you will discover that you have found the perfect family holiday.' ChippyMinton

Above all, as another mum says, 'Keep telling yourself that there's no such thing as a vacation. It's just childcare in a different climate. Once you accept this you'll enjoy yourself.'

Bon voyage!

Appendix: Useful Websites for Parents of Toddlers

Working

DirectGov Work and Families (www.direct.gov. uk/en/Employment/Employees/WorkAndFamilies)
Guidance on family employment rights, including your rights when a child is born or adopted.

ChildcareLink (www.childcarelink.gov.uk)
National and local childcare information: find childcare in your area.

Ofsted (www.ofsted.gov.uk)
The official body for inspecting childcare providers such as nurseries and childminders. Provides links to reports and official publications as well as a FAQ and contact details.

Working Families (www.workingfamilies.org.uk)
Free legal and practical advice service for parents and carers. Information on family-friendly ways of working, childcare options, tax credits and benefits.

Money & Savings

Department of Work and Pensions (www.dwp.gov.uk)
Government department with information about benefits as well as information for employees.

HM Revenue & Customs (www.hmrc.gov.uk/childcare)
Information and guidance about tax and National Insurance contributions (NICs) on employer-supported childcare (childcare vouchers).

Child Tax Credits (www.taxcredits.inlandrevenue.gov.uk)
Information about Child Tax Credits, entitlements and how much you may get.

Entitledto (www.entitledto.com)
Calculator and information about the benefits and tax credits to which you may be entitled.

Child Trust Fund (www.childtrustfund.gov.uk)
Information about the Child Trust Fund (CTF) savings and investment account for children.

Health & Nutrition

NHS Direct (www.nhsdirect.nhs.uk)
A good place to start when your child is poorly. Official website for the NHS 24-hour telephone helpline, NHS Direct: information about health problems and how to keep healthy, and advice on when to see your GP. It has a useful list of common questions about children's health at www.nhsdirect.nhs.uk/questions/category/index.aspx

NHS Choices: child health 1-5 (www.nhs.uk/LiveWell/Childhealth1-5)
Information and videos about toddlers' food, allergies, recommended health checks and travel health, plus how to find local health services.

NHS24 (www.nhs24.com)
Scotland's version of NHS Direct, telephone helpline, self-help guide and local services finder.

Health and Social Care in Northern Ireland (www.hscni.net)
Gateway to health services, advice and online medical databases.

NHS Immunisation (www.immunisation.nhs.uk)
Information on disease and vaccinations, plus parents can create personalised immunisation charts for their children.

National Travel Health Network and Centre (www.nathnac.org/travel/index.htm)
Advice on dealing with insect bites, food and water hygiene, avoiding sunburn and information about specific destinations.

**National Library for Health – child health (www.cks.library.nhs.
uk/information_for_patients#-325248)**
Comprehensive list of patient information sheets about children's
health.

BBC Health (www.bbc.co.uk/health)
Current health news, A–Z conditions database and interactive
first-aid guide.

Eat Well, Be Well (www.eatwell.gov.uk)
Information about food and nutrition from the Food Standards
Agency.

**ERIC (Education and Resources for Improving Childhood
Continence)**
(www.eric.org.uk)
Advice for parents on children's bedwetting and soiling. It also
sells protection for bedding and bedwetting alarms.

Ask a Health Visitor (www.healthvisitors.com/hv/25/592)
Online facility for asking health visitors the questions you meant
to ask but forgot, plus list of FAQs already posed by other parents.

Breastfeeding

Association of Breastfeeding Mothers (www.abm.me.uk)
A charity run by mothers for mothers, committed to giving
friendly support and supplying the right information to all women
wishing to breastfeed.

Le Leche League UK (www.laleche.org.uk)
Breastfeeding support from pregnancy through to weaning.

Kellymom (www.kellymom.com)
Information and advice about all aspects of breastfeeding and
parenting.

www.mumsnet.com/Talk/breast_and_bottle_feeding
Instant online advice, encouragement and support on the liveliest
Talk boards on the net.

Parenting

Elizabeth Pantley (www.pantley.com/elizabeth)
Information about the 'No-cry series' from Elizabeth Pantley.

Gingerbread (www.gingerbread.org.uk)
The Organisation for Lone Parent Families.

www.mumsnet.com/Talk/parenting
Advice, encouragement and support from the people who know best – other parents.

One Parent Families Scotland (www.opfs.org.uk)
Advice and support for lone parents, including telephone helpline.

Parentlineplus (www.parentlineplus.org.uk)
National charity working for and with parents, provides Q&A and telephone advice line.

Understanding Childhood (www.understandingchildhood.net)
Downloadable leaflets about children's emotional health.

Cry-sis (www.cry-sis.com)
Helpline for parents with excessively crying or sleepless children.

Things to do

Day Out With The Kids (www.dayoutwiththekids.co.uk)
Ideas for family days out and child-friendly things to do, plus places around the UK for indoor play when it's cold and raining.

National Association of Toy and Leisure Libraries (www.natll.org.uk)
Information about local toy libraries.

Cbeebies – make and do (www.bbc.co.uk/cbeebies/make)
Lots of ideas for things to make with your toddler, based around animals and nature, or favourite Cbeebies characters.

BBC Parents' Music Room (www.bbc.co.uk/music/parents/yourchild/18mnths_3years)
A practical guide to give you the confidence to support your child's musical development and music education, with helpful tips on things you can do.

Shopping

Ladybird Prints (www.ladybirdprints.com)
An archive of illustrations from Ladybird books that can be bought as prints or canvases. If you want Peter and Jane smiling down at you from your nursery wall, this is the place to shop.

Wall Glamour and What Is Blik (www.wallglamour.co.uk and www.whatisblik.com)
Fab wall stickers and wall art for children's (and grown-up's) rooms.

Muddy Puddles (www.muddypuddles.com)
Clothes for making the most of rainy days (and sunny ones).

Arabella Miller (www.arabellamiller.com)
Organic clothing for littlies.

Muddy Faces (www.muddyfaces.co.uk)
Outdoor play items and den-building kits.

Cardboard Toys (www.cardboardtoys.com)
All sorts of cardboard play houses and cardboard toys – eco-friendly and great fun. If you need to buy a rocket for your baby, this is the place to shop.

Lapin and Me (www.lapinandme.co.uk)
A bit cupcake-twee but 'lots of cute stuff'.

Moo.com (www.moo.com)
Make tiny sticker books from your own photos – good currency with bribeable toddlers.

Nordic Kids (www.nordickids.co.uk)
Scandinavian cool for your child – funky cuddlies and groovy clothes.

Cotton Bunting (www.cottonbunting.co.uk)
Cheaper than Cath Kidston!

Special Needs

BIBIC (www.bibic.org.uk)
The British Institute for Brain Injured Children offers practical help
to families caring for children with conditions such as autism,
cerebral palsy, Down's syndrome, developmental delay, traumatic
and acquired brain injury – as well as specific learning difficulties
such as attention deficit hyperactivity disorder, dyslexia and
dyspraxia.

**Children's Social Services (www.everychildmatters.gov.
uk/socialcare/socialservices)**
Children's social services seek to promote the well-being of
children in need and support their families. You can also contact
your local council for more information on local services.

Contact A Family (www.cafamily.org.uk)
Contact A Family puts parents of children diagnosed with medical
conditions in touch with each via support groups and has a
medical directory of more than 350 condition entries covering
more than 900 rare disorders.

Early Support (www.earlysupport.org.uk)
Government programme for families with children under five
with additional support needs associated with disability or
emerging special educational need.

Face2Face Network (www.face2facenetwork.org.uk)
Befriending service for parents of children with special needs.

Homestart (www.home-start.org.uk)
Parent volunteers supporting families.

I CAN (www.ican.org.uk)
Works to support the development of speech, language and
communication skills in all children with a special focus on
children with a communication disability.

IPSEA (www.ipsea.org.uk)
The Independent Panel for Special Education Advice provides free independent advice for parents of children with special educational needs.

www.mumsnet.com/Talk/special_needs
A lively and supportive community of parents of children with special needs offering empathy, encouragement and practical advice.

National Autistic Society (www.nas.org.uk)
Help, support and services for families with autistic children and individuals with autism.

Parents' Centre (www.parentscentre.gov.uk)
Information and support for parents on how to help with your child's learning. Also includes Code of Practice, which gives guidance to pre-schools, state schools, LEAs and anyone else who helps to support children with special educational needs.

Portage (www.portage.org.uk)
Home-visiting educational service for pre-school children with additional support needs and their families.

Steps (www.steps-charity.org.uk)
Support for parents of children affected by a lower limb condition such as talipes or a hip condition.

Sure Start (www.surestart.gov.uk)
Government programme providing multidisciplinary services for children, partly via local children's centres. May provide local services (or signposting to services) for children and families with special needs.

Index

bedrooms
    moving toddler out of 255
    for new baby 255
    sharing 277–8
    Time Out in 11
beds
    bunkbeds 278
    co-sleeping 102–4
    keeping toddlers in their own 106–8
    moving to a big bed 115
    raising head of 164
bedtime 48–9, 94
    on holiday 311–12
    routines 94, 116–18, 265–6
    with two children 265–6
beef, iron content 55
behaviour 3–49
    aggressive behaviour 20–1
    bath phobia 39–41
    bedtime 48–9
    brushing hair 36–7
    CHAT test for autism 196–7
    cleaning teeth 37–9
    discipline 6–13
    dressing child 34–6
    giving up dummies 28–9
    inappropriate behaviour 41–6
    manners 30–4
    separation anxiety 22–5
    tantrums 13–20
    thumb-sucking 26–7
bicarbonate of soda, for chicken-pox 168
biting 21
bits
    naming 47–8
    playing with 44–6
blackcurrant squash 164, 165
blackout blinds 121, 122–3, 312
bladder, potty training 127–56
blinds, blackout 121, 122–3, 312
blisters, chicken-pox 166
blocked noses 163
boats 284
bones, broken 173–4
books
    bedtime routines 117
    reading while breastfeeding 263
    telling your child about new
        baby 255

'boot camp' approach, potty training
    140–1, 142
bowels
    potty training 127–56
    threadworms 178–80
boys, potty training 146–7
BRAT diet 169
bread, nutritional values 55, 56
breastfeeding
    new babies 263
    websites 319
breastmilk, for conjunctivitis 183
bribery
    coping with toddlers and new
        babies 267
    fussy eaters 61
    getting child to sleep 95
    potty training 143–4, 152
broken bones 173–4
brothers see siblings
brushing
    hair 36–7
    teeth 37–9
bubbles, blowing 314
buffets 79
buggies
    air travel 306
    train travel 306
bulk cooking 80
bunkbeds 278

C
Caesarean section 261
cafés, potty training and 148
caffeine 57
calamine lotion, for chicken-pox 167–8
calcium 55–6
camomile tea 164
camping holidays 286–91, 293–4
caravan holidays 285–6, 313
'care mats', potty training 148
cars
    car seats 174, 310
    car sickness 184–5
    holiday travel 304, 305
    keeping cool in 310–11
    potty training and 148
    sunshades 310
cerebral palsy 193

kitchen sink, bathing in 41
kitchens, children in 83
knickers 138

L

lactulose 151
language
    foreign holidays 284
    speech problems 193
    swearing 41–4
    telling your child about new baby
        254
laundry, sheets with vomit on 170
lavender oil 163
laxatives 151
leaflets, tourist 314
lemon, drinks for sick children 164
letters, thank you 31–2
lice 180–1
lights
    bedtime routines 117
    and early waking 121
    night-lights 111
listening, and tantrums 14
Local Education Authorities (LEAs),
       special needs children 203
lollies 164

M

Magnadoodle 305
mango and strawberry smoothie 75
manners 30–4
Manuka honey 184
massage, aromatherapy 174
maternity leave 211–12, 213, 264
mattresses, cot 115
meal-planning 81–2
mealtimes 53–4
    fussy eaters 53, 54
    table manners 33–4
meat, iron content 55
medicines
    for car sickness 185
    cold relief 163
    persuading toddler to take 165
melatonin 122
melon 75
mercury, in fish 57
milestones, special needs children
       194, 200

milk
    calcium content 55
    and loss of appetite 61
    protein content 55
    semi-skimmed milk 56
milkshakes 74
    bananaberry thickshake 75
    chocolate and banana
      milkshake 75
molluscum contagiosum 183–4
money see finances
monsters, night-time fears 111–13
'morning clocks' 121
mother and toddler groups
    special needs children 201
    stay-at-home mothers 246–7
mothers
    illness 186–8
    working 209–45
motivation, working from home 220
mouth exams 171
MP3 players, holiday travel 304
music, bedtime routines 117

N

nail paint, to stop thumb-sucking 26–7
naming bits 47–8
nannies 223, 227–8
    agencies 224, 228, 237, 240
    choosing 237–42
    duties 228
    finding 224
    pros and cons 233
    qualifications 239
    sharing 240
    skiing holidays 297, 299
    tasks 241–2
    what to look for in 239
    and working from home 220
nappies 133
    pull-ups 143, 148, 312
    see also potty training
nappy rash 154
naps
    giving up 118–19
    on planes 308
    and potty training 142
National Childbirth Trust (NCT) 247
National Childminding Association 233
National Insurance, nannies 238

www.mumsnet.com